# Microsoft® Windows®
# Administrator's Automation
# Toolkit

*Don Jones*

PUBLISHED BY
Microsoft Press
A Division of Microsoft Corporation
One Microsoft Way
Redmond, Washington 98052-6399

Library of Congress  Control Number: 2005922202
Printed and bound in the United States of America.

1 2 3 4 5 6 7 8 9   QWT   9 8 7 6 5

Distributed in Canada by H.B. Fenn and Company Ltd.
A CIP catalogue record for this book is available from the British Library.

Microsoft Press books are available through booksellers and distributors worldwide. For further information about international editions, contact your local Microsoft Corporation office or contact Microsoft Press International directly at fax (425) 936-7329. Visit our Web site at www.microsoft.com/learning/. Send comments to rkinput@microsoft.com.

Microsoft, Active Directory, ActiveX, FrontPage, JScript, Microsoft Press, MSDN, MSN, Visual Basic, Visual Studio, Win32, Windows, Windows NT, and Windows Server are either registered trademarks or trademarks of Microsoft Corporation in the United States and/or other countries. Other product and company names mentioned herein may be the trademarks of their respective owners.

The example companies, organizations, products, domain names, e-mail addresses, logos, people, places, and events depicted herein are fictitious. No association with any real company, organization, product, domain name, e-mail address, logo, person, place, or event is intended or should be inferred.

This book expresses the author's views and opinions. The information contained in this book is provided without any express, statutory, or implied warranties. Neither the authors, Microsoft Corporation, nor its resellers, or distributors will be held liable for any damages caused or alleged to be caused either directly or indirectly by this book.

**Acquisitions Editor:** Martin DelRe
**Project Editor:** Karen Szall
**Technical Editor:** Bob Hogan
**Copy Editor:** Victoria Thulman
**Production:** Elizabeth Hansford
**Indexer:** Julie Bess

Body Part No. X11-06977

*For Clyde, Ziggy, Buffy, and Tigger: Miss ya, guys.*
*Thanks for taking the trip with us.*

# Contents at a Glance

# Contents

**Part III  Disk and File Management Tasks**

**10  File, Disk, and Volume Management . . . . . . . . . . . . . . . . . . . . . . 167**

**Part IV   Security and Network Management Tasks**

**12    General Network and Server Management Tasks. . . . . . . . . . . . . . . . . . 223**

**Part V   IIS 6.0 Tasks**

# Acknowledgments

I'd like to first thank everyone who's worked so hard to make this book a reality, particularly the project editor, Karen Szall; the book's acquisitions editor and champion, Martin DelRe; the technical editor, Bob Hogan; and the copy editor, Victoria Thulman. Any mistakes you find are all mine, because they've worked really hard to spot them all and help me correct them. I'd also like to thank the Microsoft Scripting Guys, who've done so much work—largely of their own volition and during much of their own free time—to promote scripting and automation as a viable, desirable part of a Microsoft Windows administrator's job. Of course, the Windows® Script Host (WSH) team deserves kudos for making administrative scripting in general so approachable and powerful, as does everyone who works to make enabling technologies such as Windows Management Instrumentation (WMI) and Microsoft® Active Directory® Services Interface a reality. Finally, I'd like to thank the hardworking folks at SAPIEN Technologies, who produce the PrimalScript script editor. Without their product's support for the WSF format, I never would have been able to produce so many scripts that run as command-line tools so quickly and so easily. Your hard work for this often overlooked and underappreciated format is definitely appreciated by me.

# Introduction

Welcome to *Microsoft® Windows® Administrator's Automation Toolkit*. This book is designed to help you quickly automate over 100 common Windows administrative tasks. In some cases, I show you how to automate tasks using existing tools such as those included with the Windows operating system or those available for download from the Web. In many other cases, however, I provide you with tools that I designed to help you get the job done. These tools are all written in Microsoft Visual Basic® Scripting Edition (VBScript), and execute under the Windows Script Host (WSH), which is included with the Windows operating system. Just because these tools are written in VBScript doesn't mean that you need to know anything about scripting. In fact, I've purposely written the tools in a format that allows you to simply run them as command-line tools, meaning that you don't need to encounter any scripting at all. However, because the tools are written in VBScript, you have the option of opening them up in Microsoft Notepad or in another script editor and making changes to them, extending their capabilities, and so forth. In fact, I'll even give you some pointers for doing that in the first few chapters.

Administrative automation is rapidly becoming a hot topic in many organizations. Today's "do more with less" economy rewards companies—and administrators—who can become more efficient through the automation of day-to-day administration or other time-consuming tasks. Too many administrators, however, just don't have the time to learn a scripting language, making it difficult for them to boost their efficiency through automation. That's where this book comes in—it provides you ready-to-run tools for a number of automation tasks.

## Document Conventions

The next sections describe the conventions used in this book.

**Reader Alert Conventions**    Reader alerts are used throughout the book to point out useful information.

| Reader Alert | Meaning |
|---|---|
|  Tip | Provides a helpful bit of inside information about specific tasks or functions |
|  Note | Alerts you to supplementary information |
|  Caution | Contains important information about possible data loss, breaches of security, or other serious problems |
| On the CD | Identifies tools or additional information available on the CD that accompanies the book |

**Command-Line Examples**    The following style conventions are used in documenting command-line tasks throughout this guide.

| Element | Meaning |
|---|---|
| **Bold font** | Characters that you type exactly as shown, including commands and parameters. User interface elements also appear in boldface type. |
| *Italic font* | Variables for which you supply a specific value. For example, *Filename.ext* can refer to any valid file name. |
| `Monospace font` | Code samples. |
| `%SystemRoot%` | Environment variable. |

## Automation Toolkit Companion CD

The CD that accompanies this book includes all the scripts that I wrote, providing you with quick and easy access to them. Tools that are downloadable or are included with Windows aren't included on this CD; each chapter includes information about obtaining tools that are neither on this CD nor included with Windows. The CD also includes a training video, *VBScript Essentials for Windows Administrators*, that can give you a jump-start into administrative scripting if you're so inclined. If you'd like to pursue scripting beyond the topics included in the training video, I invite you to visit my

Web site, *http://www.ScriptingAnswers.com*. You'll find additional script samples, training, discussion forums for questions and answers, and more resources, all designed for Windows administrative scripting.

### Support Policy

Microsoft does not support the tools supplied on the *Microsoft Windows Administrator's Automation Toolkit* CD. Microsoft does not guarantee the performance of the tools or any bug fixes for these tools. However, Microsoft Press provides a way for customers who purchase *Windows Administrator's Automation Toolkit* to report any problems with the software and to receive feedback for such issues. To report any issues or problems, send an e-mail message to *rkinput@microsoft.com*. This e-mail address is only for issues related to *Windows Administrator's Automation Toolkit*.

Microsoft Press also provides corrections for books and companion CDs through the World Wide Web at *http://www.microsoft.com/learning/support/*. To connect directly to the Microsoft Knowledge Base and enter a query regarding a question or issue you have, go to *http://support.microsoft.com*. For issues related to the Windows family of operating systems, refer to the support information included with your product. You're also welcome to contact the author at *http://www.ScriptingAnswers.com* to ask questions or discuss problems that you might have regarding the scripts included on the CD that accompanies this book.

# System Requirements

To use the *Microsoft Windows Administrator's Automation Toolkit* companion CD-ROM, you'll need a computer equipped with the following configuration:

- Microsoft Windows Server™ 2003, Windows 2000, or Windows XP
- Pentium II (or similar) with 266-megahertz (MHz) or higher processor
- Microsoft Internet Explorer 5.5 or later
- Adobe Acrobat or Acrobat Reader
- CD or DVD drive
- Microsoft Windows Media Player 9 (or later version; required to play the *VBScript Essentials for Windows Administrators* training video included on the CD-ROM)

You will also need to have the Windows Script Host (WSH) version 5.6 or later, installed. WSH is a core component of Windows 2000 and later, so unless you've taken special steps to remove the software, it should already be installed.

# Part I
# Understanding Windows Automation

Chapter 1

# Windows Automation Essentials

The Microsoft® Windows® operating system includes a number of command-line tools that you can use to automate simple tasks such as shutting down a single remote computer, but you can use scripting to tie those tools and other technologies together. Scripting provides the means to perform any given administrative task multiple times in a consistent, easy-to-use fashion. For example, you can use scripting to shut down *multiple* remote computers, add users to Microsoft Active Directory®, and reconfigure multiple services on a computer. Automating Windows administration generally involves some kind of scripting.

## Automating Windows Administration

If you work in a company that uses both Windows and UNIX technologies, you might have had a chance to see how the UNIX administrators administer their servers. If so, you're probably grateful that you work with systems that run Windows, because in general, its graphical user interfaces, helpful tools, and other easy-to-understand features make day-to-day administration easier. However, UNIX administrators often claim an efficiency advantage because of the powerful scripting and automation tools built into UNIX. What many of them don't realize is that Windows has equally powerful tools, both in the form of command-line tools (over 60 new ones are included in Microsoft Windows Server™ 2003, for example) and in the form of Microsoft Visual Basic® Scripting Edition (generally referred to as *VBScript*), which is the native Windows Component Object Model (COM)–based scripting language.

Unfortunately, VBScript does carry a pretty hefty learning curve, and even the command-line utilities provided by the Windows operating system, which are easier to use than VBScript, can be somewhat daunting for many busy administrators who don't have time to learn them. That's where this book comes in handy. Rather than trying to teach you scripting, or even just listing all the available command-line tools, this book offers a task-oriented approach to automation. Simply look up the task you want to automate, fill in a few blanks, and you're ready to go. Even though many of these tasks are automated through the power of VBScript and COM, you won't need to know very much about either to use this book.

You will, however, need to know a few basics, such as how to run and edit the scripts (which all appear on the CD that accompanies this book) and the command-line tools. That's what this chapter will cover. In keeping with the just-get-started spirit of this book, I'll be covering this material quickly using minimal details, but I'll provide you with some references throughout in case you'd like to learn more about these technologies on your own.

**Tip**    If you're interested in teaching yourself to write VBScript, I can recommend two sources. One is *Managing Windows with VBScript and WMI* (Addison-Wesley, 2004), a book I wrote that takes a step-by-step approach to administrative scripting. Another option is Ed Wilson's *Microsoft Windows Scripting Self-Paced Learning Guide* (Microsoft Press, 2004), which is conveniently included in e-book format on the CD that accompanies this book. Once you've moved a bit beyond the basics, you can visit my Web site, *http://www.ScriptingAnswers.com*, where you'll find a variety of free resources for Windows administrators who are using scripts to automate their environments.

# VBScript and the Windows Script Host

The Windows Script Host, or WSH, is an executable file included with all versions of Windows since Microsoft Windows 98. (WSH was an optional installation for Windows 98 and was included in the base installation of Microsoft Windows Me and later versions.) Microsoft Windows NT® 4.0 can run WSH, too, because WSH was first included with the Windows NT 4.0 Option Pack. Most importantly, Microsoft offers the latest version of WSH—version 5.6 at the time this book was written—for Windows 98, Windows Me, the Windows NT 4.0 family of products, the Microsoft Windows 2000 family, Windows XP, and Windows Server 2003. You can download the latest version from *http://www.microsoft.com/scripting*, which is the scripting home page on the Microsoft Web site.

> **Tip**   Generally, the latest version of WSH is included with the most recent service pack for the Windows 2000 product family and later. However, I recommend downloading and installing WSH 5.6 regardless, unless you've checked the file properties for *%systemroot%*\System32\WScript.exe and assured yourself that you have the latest version.

WSH doesn't actually implement VBScript—WSH is capable of running scripts written in any installed Microsoft ActiveX® Script Language. VBScript is one such language, as is Microsoft JScript®, which is a Microsoft implementation of the industry-standard ECMAScript language (based on Netscape's JavaScript language). VBScript is probably the most popular of these languages.

WSH is available in two flavors, both of which are included in all WSH installations: WScript and CScript.

# WScript

WScript (manifested as WScript.exe on your computer) is the default version of WSH on newly installed Windows-based systems. Simply put, that means double-clicking a WSH-related file format (such as .js, .vbs, and .wsf) causes the script to execute in WScript. WScript is designed for a graphical environment (the "W" stands for "Windows"), so many of WSH's built-in commands generate graphical displays. For example, the built-in WScript.Echo command displays a simple dialog box with an OK button. The only downside to running a script using WScript is that some scripts output a lot of information, and having to click OK after each message can become annoying for users. For that reason, many administrators prefer to run their scripts using CScript.

> **Tip**   If WScript isn't the default script host, you can make it the default. Open a command-line window and execute `WScript //H:WScript`.

# CScript

CScript (manifested as CScript.exe on your computer) is designed to execute command-line scripts. The primary difference between CScript and WScript can be seen when running commands like WScript.Echo. When running in CScript, this command outputs text to the command line and continues without waiting; in WScript, as described earlier, the command displays a dialog box and waits for the user to click OK. As you can imagine, CScript's handling of WScript.Echo is much more appropriate when a lot of information is being produced, because you can just watch the information scroll by in the command-line window and not click any buttons. For most of the scripts in this book, I assume that you are setting CScript as the default host. If you're not, many of the scripts in this book will remind you to use CScript so that their extensive output isn't displayed in dozens of dialog boxes. Having to click dozens of OK buttons can be tiresome!

> **Tip**   If CScript isn't the default host, you can make it the default. Open a command-line window and execute CScript //H:CScript.

## WSH and Security

WSH 5.6 includes a comprehensive security system that's designed to prevent unknown scripts from running on your computers. This system uses digital certificates to identify script authors and can be configured to *not* run any scripts that aren't digitally signed by a trusted certification authority. Chapter 2, "Automation and Security," contains a complete explanation of how this security system works and how you can obtain a certificate, sign your scripts, and configure the WSH security features. I mention all this right now in case you're planning to jump right in and start using some of the scripts in this book. If you are, you'll need to check your environment's WSH security settings (which can be configured at a domain level through Software Restriction Policies set in Group Policy) before proceeding.

## WSF Scripts

Most of the scripts in this book are presented in the Windows Script Files (WSF) format. I'll discuss that format in more depth in Chapter 3, "Working with VBScript," but for now be aware that few of these scripts can be successfully executed simply by double-clicking them. In most cases, you have to run a script from a command line, providing one or more command-line switches to specify server names, operational parameters, and so forth, just as you would with any command-line utility. Be sure to read the instructions included with each task for details about running the scripts.

For example, a script named Restart.wsf might be executed by typing the following:

```
Restart.wsf /file:servers.txt /action:shutdown
```

In most cases, switches for scripts in this book are specified by starting with a forward slash, the name of the switch, a colon, and the value you're providing for the switch. These scripts are written in VBScript, so they aren't much different from a more traditional command-line utility—generally you can even use the /? switch to see a list of the script's command-line switches and an example of how to use the script.

## Reviewing, Editing, and Testing Scripts

I strongly encourage you to review any script before running it and to run a script in a test environment before running it in any production environment. Keep in mind that neither myself nor the publisher has any real idea what your environment looks like. The scripts and techniques in this book are intended to work in a typical environment, but yours might be far from typical. Therefore, carefully review and test the scripts prior to using them in any production environment.

Scripts can be readily reviewed in a simple text editor such as Microsoft Notepad. WSF files, however, have XML formatting that can make the actual scripts somewhat difficult to read. In these cases, you can consider a commercial script editor, such as SAPIEN PrimalScript (*http://www.primalscript.com*), XLnow OnScript (*http://www.onscript.com*), Adersoft VBSEdit (*http://www.vbsedit.com*), and Admin Script Editor (*http://www.adminscripteditor.com*). Most of these tools are available as trial versions so that you can try them to determine whether you like them. Free tools like the Programmer's File Editor (downloadable from *http://www.download.com*) can also be useful because they provide more script-specific formatting than Notepad.  Search for "Programmer File Editor or PFE."

Scripts should always be tested in a dedicated test or lab environment, preferably one that mimics your production environment to the greatest degree practical. For example, I use Microsoft Virtual PC to build virtual domain controllers and member servers that are configured similarly to my production servers. This allows me to test scripts on the virtual servers before deploying the scripts to production. You can even use Virtual PC features to undo the results of a test, instantly reverting the virtual environment to its pretesting state so that the environment is ready for another test.

## Command-Line Tools

You can accomplish many of the automation tasks in this book not with scripts but with the many command-line tools included with Windows Server 2003, with the Support Tools supplied on the Windows Server 2003 CD, or with tools downloadable from the Microsoft Web site. Third-party tools aren't used in this book because guaranteeing their long-term availability is difficult, but you should definitely spend some time exploring the Web to locate other useful command-line tools.

Whenever a tool isn't available as part of a basic Windows Server 2003 installation, I provide information about where you can obtain the tool. I've focused entirely on freely available tools, so even though you might have to download the tool, you won't have to pay any extra for it—either your use of the tool is included in your Windows Server 2003 license or the tool is freely available to anyone. Please note, however, that tools not included with the Windows operating system might be unsupported. If the tools don't work as described in your environment, you won't be able to contact Microsoft Product Support Services (PSS), myself, or the publisher of this book for assistance. Rest assured that everything worked when I tested it, but because of variations in your environment, a particular tool or technique might not work for you in the way described. I do invite you to visit my Web site, *http://www.ScriptingAnswers.com*, where you can post a message in the Forums and receive help from other site users about getting the tool to work in your environment.

# Summary

In this chapter, you were introduced to the world of scripting and automation so that you can begin using the various scripts included in this book. You should now understand the differences between WScript.exe and CScript.exe, as well as know where to find the various command-line tools used throughout this book.

If you'd like to modify any of the scripts included in the CD that accompanies this book, be sure to check out Chapter 3, "Working with VBScript," in which I explain the WSF format and the standards used in producing these scripts. However, before you do anything else, I strongly recommend that you read the next chapter, which will deal with the all-important issue of security as it relates to scripting and automation.

Chapter 2
# Automation and Security

Unfortunately, the same beneficial technologies that make scripting and automation possible can also be used to create malicious software. Many viruses, for example, have been written in Microsoft Visual Basic® Script (VBScript), even though VBScript is also an excellent tool for automation. Configuring your environment to allow beneficial administrative scripts while protecting your environment against malicious scripts is a crucial skill you must master before proceeding.

# Windows Script Host Security

For most of its history, the Windows Script Host (WSH) hasn't offered much in the way of security. In the latest release (as of the writing of this book), however, WSH adds some powerful security options designed to make scripting safer and more secure.

## What Not to Do

I've run across three basic methods that various administrators have cobbled together to "protect" their environments from malicious scripts. None of these methods, however, are foolproof, and they might offer a dangerous false sense of security.

### Deleting WScript.exe and CScript.exe

Deleting WScript.exe and CScript.exe physically removes the WSH executables. Unfortunately, doing so completely disables administrative scripting using VBScript, which means that most of the scripts in this book won't run. Additionally, both WScript.exe and CScript.exe are monitored by Windows File Protection (WFP), so it's possible for Windows® to replace the files if they're deleted. Further, these files are part of the core Windows operating system (and have been since Windows 2000), so they show up in some hotfixes, in all service packs, and so forth, presenting a number of opportunities for the files to be replaced, even if you delete them. As a result, you might *think* you've deleted the files, but the files are likely to come back at some point, leaving you just as vulnerable as you were before you deleted them.

### Disassociating File Name Extensions

WSH is associated with several file name extensions, including .vbs, .js, .wsf, .wsh, and .wsc. By removing these file name extension associations from the registry, you can prevent Windows from automatically launching WSH when a user double-clicks a file that has one of these extensions.

However, it's a fairly trivial task for an attacker to execute scripts anyway. WScript.exe and CScript.exe accept the name of any text file, regardless of its name or extension, and attempt to execute the file if it contains something recognizable as a script. Attackers need only to create a batch file, Program Information File (PIF), or other file that launches WScript.exe or CScript.exe and passes the name of a complete script. Even though the .vbs file name might no longer be associated with WSH, a VBScript file can still be executed. Essentially, changing the file name extension associations offers no protection whatsoever; it's merely a speed bump in an attacker's way.

### Changing NTFS Permissions

I've seen a few enterprising administrators use security templates to reconfigure all their computers so that the NTFS file permissions on WScript.exe and CScript.exe don't allow anyone to execute the files. This approach does, of course, stop scripting altogether, severely limiting your options for administrative scripting. Also, you're messing around with the file permissions on core Windows operating system files, which is usually a recipe for eventual disaster. It's also quite possible for a service pack to reset the permissions on these files, leaving you unprotected.

## Understanding Trust

The key to scripting security is to allow *your* scripts (or other beneficial scripts) to execute while preventing other people's scripts from running. In other words, you want to allow *trusted* scripts to run but prevent *untrusted* scripts from running. That's a simple enough concept, but you need some means of helping WSH distinguish between the scripts you trust and the ones you don't. For example, could you tell WSH that scripts coming from a certain intranet file server are trusted but others aren't? Bad idea—malicious scripts could be too easily copied to your "trusted" location, fooling

WSH. Also, the scripts in your "trusted" location could be modified, which should in theory render them untrusted until you have a chance to review them and decide they can be trusted again.

Digital certificates provide a way of identifying trusted scripts. How? You start by identifying a *trusted root certification authority*. This is an internal or external organization that you believe does a good job of ensuring the identity of individuals and organizations to whom they issue digital certificates. In other words, if a certification authority (CA) issues a certificate to Microsoft, you need to trust that the CA did a good job of confirming Microsoft's corporate identity before issuing that certificate.

This certificate works kind of like a driver's license. You might not realize it, but everyone in the United States pretty much accepts all the departments of motor vehicles as trusted CAs of sorts. When the photo on a person's driver's license matches his face, you accept his identity as stated on the license. The license in this sense acts as a certificate, and the issuer of that license is the CA. Passports serve a very similar function on an international level. We all trust that the authorities issuing these documents have done a good job of confirming the document holder's actual identity and that the information on the document is accurate and trustworthy. If one state's department of motor vehicles started issuing licenses to anyone who asked for them without requiring any proof of identity, we'd all eventually stop trusting that state's department as a CA and stop accepting the licenses it issued.

So who do you trust? On your computer, go to Control Panel and open Internet Options. Select the Content tab and click the Publishers button. Then, select the Trusted Root Certification Authorities tab. You *trust* each CA listed, meaning you firmly believe that each of them does a good job of validating the identities of their certificate recipients. Wait a minute–what did you say? You *don't* trust all of those CAs? In reality, you probably have no idea what procedures most of those CAs use to validate certificate recipients' identities, and for that reason you should consider modifying the list to remove the CAs you don't explicitly trust or know about. Do some research, if necessary, to discover what procedures those CAs use, and leave the ones whose procedures you feel are trustworthy and thorough. Remove the others.

> **Tip**    In a domain-based environment, you can use Group Policy to centrally configure the trusted CA list on domain client computers running Windows 2000 Professional or Windows XP Professional, as well as server computers running Windows 2000 or Windows Server™ 2003.

Why are these CAs so important? Because among other tasks, they issue code-signing certificates, which are used to digitally sign program code such as scripts. WSH 5.6 (which is a free download from *http://www.microsoft.com/scripting*) can be configured to run only those scripts that are digitally signed using a certificate issued from a trusted CA. Sound confusing? It's not. A trusted CA—that's one on the list in Internet Options—issues a code-signing certificate. That certificate is used to sign a script, which WSH will regard as trusted and which WSH will run normally. WSH can be configured to not run untrusted scripts, which are all scripts that are unsigned and that were signed using a certificate issued by an untrusted CA.

Signing provides two important assurances. First, it tells you the identity of the script's author (assuming the issuing CA did a good job of verifying that identity prior to issuing the script). If a script turns out to be malicious, you have a good shot at tracking down the author. Second, a signature assures you that the script wasn't changed since it was signed. If it was changed, the signature will be invalid; this ensures that the script is exactly as the author intended it.

## Digitally Signing a Script

Signing a script is easy. First, you need to obtain a code-signing certificate. You can usually obtain one from a commercial CA for about $300 per year (rates vary among CAs), or from an internal CA if your organization has one. Keep in mind that the CA who issues your certificate must be a trusted CA on all computers where you expect your script to execute. Once you obtain the certificate, you must install it. The installation process copies the script into the special, protected certificate store on your computer.

Then, you write a very short script to do the actual signing. Assuming your certificate has a name of "IT Department" and that you want to sign the script C:\MyScript.vbs, you'd use the following code:

```
Set oSigner = WScript.CreateObject("Scripting.Signer")
oSigner.SignFile "C:\MyScript.vbs", "IT Department"
```

It's really that easy. A signature block is written into C:\MyScript.vbs, and the script is signed. From that point, you can't edit the script unless you plan to sign it again later; the signature itself includes a sort of fingerprint for the script, and if the script changes, the signature becomes invalid.

**On the CD**    All scripts included on the CD that accompanies this book were signed using a digital certificate issued by Microsoft. All computers running Windows will, by default, trust the issuer of this certificate and allow these scripts to run even when WSH is configured to not run untrusted scripts. However, if you modified the list of trusted root certification authorities, your computer (or computers) might not trust the scripts included on the CD that accompanies this book. In that case, you will need to either reconfigure your computer to trust the Microsoft certification authority, or re-sign the scripts using a certificate that your computer has been configured to trust.

I should point out that some professional script editors include built-in script signing capabilities. SAPIEN PrimalScript (*http://www.sapien.com*), for example, allows you to specify a certificate and have all scripts automatically signed using that certificate each time the script is saved. This convenient feature can make utilizing the WSH trust policy more practical, because your scripts will always be properly signed (and therefore trusted). Many script editors—SAPIEN PrimalScript as well as XLnow OnScript (*http://www.onscript.com*)—include features that integrate with WSH trust policy, allowing you to configure the trust policy on your script development computer by using a graphical user interface.

## Configuring the Windows Script Host Trust Policy

By default, WSH 5.6 treats all signed and unsigned scripts identically, executing them without question. This preserves backward-compatibility with prior versions of WSH, which did not include certificate-based security features. However, WSH 5.6 can be configured to behave differently by using registry keys. There are a number of registry keys that you'll want to examine:

- **HKEY_LOCAL_MACHINE\SOFTWARE\Microsoft\Windows Script Host \Settings\UseWINSAFER**   Set this *REG_SZ* value to 0 (zero) if you aren't using Windows XP or Windows Server 2003 Software Restriction Policies (SRP). SRP is another more flexible way of controlling which software is allowed to run on your computers, and by default WSH defers to SRP rather than using its own trust policy settings. The default setting for this value is 1, which effectively disables the WSH trust policy on computers running Windows XP and Windows Server 2003.

- **HKEY_LOCAL_MACHINE\SOFTWARE\Microsoft\Windows Script Host \Settings\TrustPolicy**   Set this *REG_DWORD* value to 0 (zero) to invoke the default behavior of running any script, trusted or not. Set the value to 1 to run trusted scripts and to prompt the user for untrusted scripts. I don't recommend setting the value to 1, because most users will select simply to run the script, defeating the security feature. Set the value to 2 to always run trusted scripts, and never run untrusted scripts. Note that this value does not exist by default, meaning you might have to create it to set it.

- **HKEY_LOCAL_MACHINE\SOFTWARE\Microsoft\Windows Script Host \Settings\SilentTerminate**   Set this *REG_SZ* value to 1 to suppress the error message normally displayed when WSH refuses to run an untrusted script. The default, 0 (zero), will display a short dialog box informing the user that untrusted scripts can't be executed. This feature kicks in only when WSH refuses to run an untrusted script because of the *TrustPolicy* setting described in the preceding bullet.

- **HKEY_CURRENT_USER\SOFTWARE\Microsoft\Windows Script Host\Settings \TrustPolicy**   This per-user setting has the same effect as the computerwide *TrustPolicy* value under HKEY_LOCAL_MACHINE, described earlier. However, the per-user setting will normally override the computerwide policy, allowing you to configure the WSH trust policy on a user-by-user basis, if desired. If this value isn't present on your computer (it might not be, by default), you'll need to manually create it to set it.

- **HKEY_LOCAL_MACHINE\SOFTWARE\Microsoft\Windows Script Host \Settings\IgnoreUserSettings**   Set this *REG_DWORD* value to 1 to always obey the computerwide *TrustPolicy* value, even when a conflicting per-user value exists. The default setting is 0 (zero), allowing the HKEY_CURRENT_USER setting to have precedence. This value might not exist by default, so you might have to create it to set it.

Of course, manually configuring all your computers to the desired registry settings can be time-consuming. You could implement logon scripts written in VBScript (which will run even when unsigned, thanks to the default WSH trust policy setting of zero) that sets the desired registry values accordingly. For example:

```
'create a shell object
Set oShell = CreateObject("WScript.Shell")

'write the registry key
oShell.RegWrite "\HKCU\SOFTWARE\Microsoft\" & _
 "Windows Script Host\Settings\TrustPolicy", 2, "REG_SZ"
```

This code snippet sets the per-user *TrustPolicy* value to 2. Keep in mind that on computers running Windows XP and Windows Server 2003, the per-user setting (and the per-machine setting, for that matter) will not have any effect as long as the *UseWIN-SAFER* value is set to its default of 1. Alternatively, you can push this registry setting out via Group Policy. I created a Group Policy administrative template (an .adm file) that you can import into a Group Policy object (GPO) to configure all WSH-related registry settings. You can download this template from the Downloads section of *http://www.ScriptingAnswers.com*. A copy is also included on the CD that accompanies this book.

# The Windows Script Host Trust Policy in Action

When WSH executes a script using either CScript.exe or WScript.exe, it first checks to see whether the script is signed. If it isn't signed, the script is untrusted. If it is signed, WSH checks to see whether the signing certificate was issued by a CA listed on the trusted root publishers list in Internet Options. If the certificate was issued by a trusted CA, the script is trusted; otherwise, the script is untrusted.

At that point, the registry settings kick in. If *UseWINSAFER* is set to 1 on computers running Windows XP or Windows Server 2003, WSH stops checking because SRP has precedence. If *UseWINSAFER* is set to 0 on all computers running versions of Windows other than Windows XP and Windows Server 2003, WSH continues checking. (Keep in mind that WSH runs on everything from Windows 95 to later versions, although SRP is present only on Windows XP and Windows Server 2003.) If the *IgnoreUserSettings* value is 0 (zero), WSH checks the *TrustPolicy* value under HKEY_CURRENT_USER. If the value is missing or set to zero, untrusted scripts are executed. If the value is set to 1, the user is prompted before an untrusted script is run. If the value is set to 2, untrusted scripts are not run. Trusted scripts always run, of course. If *IgnoreUserSettings* is set to 1, the *TrustPolicy* value under HKEY_LOCAL_MACHINE is used instead. In any event, WSH will display an error message whenever it refuses to execute an untrusted script, provided the *SilentTerminate* value is set to 1 and not 0 (zero).

So here's my recommendation: set the *TrustPolicy* to 2 at both the HKEY_LOCAL_MACHINE and the HKEY_CURRENT_USER levels (just to be safe). If you're not using SRP, set *UseWINSAFER* to 0 and set *IgnoreUserSettings* to 1. Obtain a code-signing certificate from a trusted CA, and sign all your scripts. Your scripts— and scripts from other trusted sources—will execute, but other scripts won't, helping to protect your environment.

---

### Antivirus Software and Script Blocking

Most antivirus scanners include some form of a script blocking feature. They often implement this feature by modifying the registry so that the antivirus software is called rather than certain WSH components. This allows the antivirus software to block the script, prompt the user for an action, and so forth.

If you've implemented the WSH trust policy features as outlined, these antivirus script blocking features become more of an annoyance than a real protection. Consider disabling that particular feature of the antivirus software, unless the software can mimic the WSH trust policy functionality of running trusted scripts without prompting the user. That will give you an extra layer of protection, which is always a good idea. However, an antivirus solution that forces users to approve even signed, trusted scripts is simply an annoyance.

---

# Remote Scripting and Security

Whenever you write a script that will reach out and touch other computers, you're performing *remote scripting*. Obviously, some security measures come into play, because Windows isn't going to let just anyone modify a computer's configuration, restart the computer, or perform any of the other tasks you can accomplish with remote scripting. In the next few sections, I'll help you understand how remote scripting and security work together, and how you can configure your computers to most effectively respond to your remote scripts while maintaining an acceptable level of security against potentially malicious scripts.

## Basic Scripts

Generally speaking, all scripts that you run will execute with whatever permissions your user account has. If your script is connecting to a remote file share and trying to delete a file, your user account must have the necessary permissions on the remote computer to delete the file. For basic operations like file and folder manipulation and registry manipulation, WSH doesn't provide any means of passing an alternate set of credentials. However, that doesn't mean you can't execute scripts under alternate credentials.

For example, you might log on to your client computer using a nonadministrative account. (Doing so is always a good idea and is in keeping with the Principle of Least Privilege. By using a nonadministrative account, you limit the amount of damage something like a virus can cause.) However, you might need to run a script that modifies files on a remote file server and that requires domain administrator permissions to do so. WSH doesn't allow you to provide an alternate user name and password, but you *can* execute your script using the Windows built-in Runas command, which does allow you to specify alternate credentials. If your script was named C:\MyScript.vbs, you'd simply execute the following:

```
Runas WScript.exe c:\MyScript.vbs /user:AdminUser@domain.com
```

You could specify CScript.exe instead of WScript.exe, of course. By specifying the alternate user—AdminUser, from the targeted domain—Runas will prompt you for that user's password and execute WSH under that user's credentials. WSH, in turn, will load MyScript.vbs and execute it under AdminUser's credentials. For more information about the Runas command, consult the Windows documentation.

## Windows Management Instrumentation Scripts

Many of the scripts in this book utilize Windows Management Instrumentation, or WMI, to accomplish their tasks. WMI uses a straightforward security model, usually (but not always) impersonating the credentials of the user who runs the script. Older versions of WMI can, in some circumstances, default to not using impersonation; newer versions (like that included with Windows Server 2003) will always use impersonation by default. In other words, the WMI service, running on the remote computer, utilizes *your* user credentials to carry out the script's tasks. Alternately, scripts can provide WMI with the credentials of another user. Many of the scripts in this book include parameters that you can use to specify alternate credentials, and these are passed to WMI.

The credentials WMI uses must have some specialized permissions on the remote computer. Local administrators usually have the necessary permissions (they do by default, at least), but if you provide nonadministrator credentials, some extra configuration of the remote computers might be required. Specifically, you'll need to modify the Distributed Component Object Model (DCOM) permissions so that the user credentials used by WMI have the DCOM Remote Launch privilege. (Refer to *http:// msdn.microsoft.com/library/default.asp?url=/library/en-us/wmisdk/wmi/ connecting_through_windows_firewall.asp* for details.)

Additionally, WMI by default provides full access only to administrators. Nonadministrator accounts have restricted access to the information in WMI, and some scripts might not work correctly as a result. You can, however, modify WMI's permissions to allow access to nonadministrative users. (Refer to *http://msdn.microsoft.com/library /default.asp?url=/library/en-us/wmisdk/wmi/locating_the_wmi_control.asp* for information about locating the WMI Control, which is used to configure WMI, and refer to *http://msdn.microsoft.com/library/default.asp?url=/library/en-us/wmisdk /wmi/setting_namespace_security.asp* for information about setting WMI namespace security.)

> **Tip**    Rather than spend hours reconfiguring your remote computers, I recommend you use a user account that has administrative privileges on the remote computers. A user account that is a member of the Domain Admins group, for example, is perfect. Although you might not use this user account to run the scripts, you can provide the account's credentials to the script so that WMI will work properly without complex reconfiguration of the remote computer.

## Firewalls

Remember that many versions of Windows, including Windows XP and Windows Server 2003, include built-in firewall software. On Windows XP Service Pack 2 and later, and on Windows Server 2003 Service Pack 1 and later, that firewall software is enabled by default. Other computers might have third-party firewall software enabled. In any case, where a firewall is enabled, you might not be able to establish the type of connection necessary to run scripts on remote computers, because those computers' firewalls might block the necessary TCP/IP ports. WMI scripts, for example, require specific TCP ports to connect to remote computers; scripts that utilize Active Directory Services Interface (ADSI) use different ports to connect to remote computers. Whenever a script generates an error indicating that it cannot connect to a remote computer, always start your troubleshooting process by checking that remote computer's firewall software. You can temporarily disable the remote computer's firewall and see whether your script starts to work; if it does, you know that the firewall was blocking the script's access to the remote computer. In that case, you'll need to reconfigure the firewall to permit the necessary traffic.

**Caution**   Do not reconfigure firewall software without first checking your organization's policies regarding firewall configuration. You might need to obtain permission before modifying the firewall, and you should document any changes you make.

Typically, server computers always allow traffic related to services that they offer, such as Active Directory®, and file and print sharing. Client computers often have more restrictive firewall settings and might not allow any incoming traffic. Scripts that use the *File-SystemObject (FSO)* object to manipulate files and folders on remote computers need the Windows Firewall's File and Print Sharing exception enabled (on Windows XP Professional with Service Pack 2 or later, and on Windows Server 2003 with Service Pack 1). Scripts that connect to WMI on remote computers need a special exception added to the Windows Firewall (again, on Windows XP Professional with Service Pack 2 or later, and on Windows Server 2003 with Service Pack 1). This is a one-time process and requires you to run two command-line utilities on the computer running the script:

```
netsh firewall add portopening
    protocol=tcp port=135 name=DCOM
netsh firewall add allowedprogram
    program=%windir%\system32\wbem\unsecapp.exe
    name=UNSECAPP
```

You also have to configure the remote computers to allow the incoming WMI traffic:

```
netsh firewall set service RemoteAdmin
```

**Note**   The preceding steps assume that the computers' Windows Firewall software is not being centrally controlled through Group Policy. If Group Policy is being used to configure Windows Firewall, you must apply these changes within Group Policy instead. Consult the documentation for your version of Windows to determine the proper Group Policy configuration.

Other firewall software will require different steps to allow TCP port 135; consult the software's documentation for instructions.

# Summary

Although scripting can be an excellent way to automate Windows administrative tasks, scripting can also be used to create malicious software. And because scripting has been used maliciously so often in the past, many managers and administrators are wary of allowing any kind of scripting in their environments. However, Windows Script Host 5.6 was specifically designed with new script-related security features, allowing you to ensure, if desired, that only the scripts you create can execute in your environment. The key lies in digital signatures, which form the basis for a chain of trust that allows WSH to distinguish between trusted and untrusted scripts.

Chapter 3

# Working with VBScript

Although you can automate many of the tasks in this book by using simple command-line tools, you can automate others by utilizing VBScript files. As you're aware, VBScript offers a powerful, flexible, and relatively easy-to-understand scripting language that can harness many of the features built into the Windows® operating system. Another advantage of VBScript is that its scripts are contained in simple text files. This makes scripts in general easier for you to modify and this book's scripts in particular a starting point for any number of other automation scripts.

## The File Format

Most of the scripts in this book are provided in a file format known as WSF. You might be familiar with the simpler VBS file format, which simply places VBScript code into a text file. The WSF format is only a little more complex, and it offers some helpful features. For example, the WSF format allows a script to define its command-line input arguments, enabling the Windows Script Host (WSH) to automatically generate command-line syntax help, much like any command-line tool. Therefore, WSF makes this book's scripts completely accessible as standard command-line tools, so you don't have to have any VBScript experience at all. If, however, you *do* have some VBScript experience, understanding the WSF file format will help you better understand these scripts and allow you to modify them.

# A Sample WSF File

The following code sample is a complete WSF file used to update the password that a specified service uses to log on. The script performs this reconfiguration on a list of computers contained in a normal text file. Spend a moment reviewing this script before I walk through each of its sections so that you can see what the WSF format is all about.

**Note**   Don't worry that some of the lines of code seem to wrap from line to line at unusual points. You're not meant to type this script in yourself; like all other scripts in this book, you'll find the complete script included on the CD that accompanies this book.

**Sample WSF File to Update Service Logon Passwords**

```
<?xml version="1.0" ?>
<package>
    <comment>
    PrimalCode wizard generated file.
    </comment>
    <job id="Updsvc" prompt="no">
        <?job error="false" debug="false" ?>
        <runtime>
            <description>
Updates services accounts, running on computers listed in a text file, to use a
new logon password.
            </description>
            <named helpstring="Filename from which to read computer names"
name="file" required="true" type="string"/>
            <named helpstring="Service name to change"
name="service" required="true" type="string"/>
            <named helpstring="New password service should use to log on"
name="password" required="true" type="string"/>
            <usage>
Example:

 Updsvc /file:c:\computers.txt /service:Messenger /password:m$r%3d7@

Does not change the service's logon ACCOUNT, just the password.
            </usage>
        </runtime>
        <script id="Updsvc" language="VBScript">
<![CDATA[
'=======================================================================
'
' Updsvc
'
' AUTHOR: Don Jones
' DATE  : 7/31/2004
'
```

```
' COMMENT:
'
'========================================================================

'make sure the correct number of arguments was passed;
'if not, display the usage of this command and quit
If WScript.Arguments.Count < 3 Then
    WScript.Arguments.ShowUsage
    WScript.Quit
End If

'pull specified arguments into string variables
Dim sFile, sService, sPassword
sFile = WScript.Arguments.Named("file")
sService = WScript.Arguments.Named("service")
sPassword = WScript.Arguments.Named("password")

'declare variables and filesystemobject
Dim oFSO, oTS, sClient, oWMIService, oService
Set oFSO = CreateObject("Scripting.FileSystemObject")

'ensure the input file exists
If oFSO.FileExists(sFile) Then

    'open the input file
    Set oTS = oFSO.OpenTextFile(sFile)

    'read through the input file until the end
    Do Until oTS.AtEndOfStream

        'retrieve the next computer name
        sClient = oTS.ReadLine

        'connect to the remote WMI service
        On Error Resume Next
        Set oWMIService = GetObject("winmgmts:" _
          & "{impersonationLevel=impersonate}!\\" & _
          sClient & "\root\cimv2")

        If Err = 0 Then
            'connected - retrieve specified service instance
            Set oService = oWMIService.ExecQuery _
            ("Select * from Win32_Service WHERE Name" & _
              " = '" & sService & "'")

            If Err = 0 Then
                'retrieved - change password for the service
                errReturn = oService.Change( , , , , , , _
                , sPassword)

                If errReturn = 0 Then
                    'change successful
                    WScript.Echo sClient " changed."
```

```
                    Else
                        'change not successful
                        WScript.Echo sClient " not changed."
                    End If

                Else
                    'no matching instances of Win32_Service found
                    WScript.Echo sClient & ": Error retrieving service"
                End If

            Else
                'couldn't connect to remote WMI service
                WScript.Echo sClient & ": Error connecting"
            End If

        'loop up for next computer in file
        Loop

        'close text file
        oTS.Close

Else
  'input file does not exist
  WScript.Echo "Input file does not exist"
End If
]]>
        </script>
    </job>
</package>
```

Notice that except for some elements like *<script>* and *</job>*, the preceding listing looks pretty much like a standard VBScript listing. Because WSF files use an XML-based formatting system, however, there are a few important elements to call to your attention.

## Breaking Down the Sample WSF File

WSF files all begin with a section of XML-formatted information that defines the contents of the script, the script's command-line arguments, and so forth. First in the file is a line defining the WSF format version being used, which is always 1.0, and next is an XML tag that defines the beginning of the WSF package:

```
<?xml version="1.0" ?>
<package>
```

Next is a *<comment>* section, which allows you to include a description of the entire WSF file. This is an optional section, and some scripts don't include it. Notice in the preceding listing that my WSF file contains a comment indicating it was generated by a wizard within the script editor I use:

```
<comment>
PrimalCode wizard generated file.
</comment>
```

The next two lines define the *job*, or the script, contained within the WSF file. Although WSF files can actually contain multiple jobs (you use a command-line argument to specify which job you want to run), this capability isn't used in this book. I find it easier to utilize scripts when only one job is contained within the file. The job definition lines perform two important tasks: enabling or disabling both error message display and debugging capabilities.

```
<job id="Updsvc" prompt="no">
    <?job error="false" debug="false" ?>
```

As you can see from the preceding lines, this script will not display error messages and will not allow a debugger (such as the Windows Script Debugger) to be launched should an error occur. Many of the scripts in this book will specify these options, making these scripts cleaner looking and cleaner running command-line tools. Feel free to change the "false" values to "true" if you'd like to enable error messages or debugging.

> **Tip**   If you plan to debug scripts, you need a debugger. Microsoft provides a basic free debugger, the Windows Script Debugger, at *http://www.microsoft.com/scripting*. Microsoft Visual Studio® can also be used to debug scripts, although I don't find it to be well-suited to that task because it's such a big, complex tool. Some script editors, such as SAPIEN PrimalScript (*http://www.primalscript.com*) and XLnow OnScript (*http://www.onscript.com*) include built-in debuggers of their own.

The last major XML section in the WSF file is the *<runtime>* section:

```
<runtime>
    <description>
Updates services accounts, running on computers listed in a text file, to use a new
logon password.
    </description>
    <named helpstring="Filename from which to read computer names"
name="file" required="true" type="string"/>
    <named helpstring="Service name to change"
name="service" required="true" type="string"/>
    <named helpstring="New password service should use to log on"
name="password" required="true" type="string"/>
    <usage>
```

```
Example:

 Updsvc /file:c:\computers.txt /service:Messenger /password:m$r%3d7@

Does not change the service's logon ACCOUNT, just the password.
        </usage>
     </runtime>
```

Most of the subsections under *<runtime>* are optional, but I include them in this book's scripts for completeness. First is the *<description>* section, which provides a text description of the script. Last—permit me to skip ahead a bit—is the *<usage>* section, which provides an example of how the script should be used.

In between are the various arguments the script accepts. This script defines three command-line arguments. Here's one of them:

```
        <named helpstring="Service name to change"
name="service" required="true" type="string"/>
```

Each *<named>* element defines a single named argument. This argument is named "*service*" and it is required, rather than optional, meaning the argument must be specified when the script is executed. This argument also includes a *helpstring*, which is just a brief description of what the argument is used for. Finally, the argument has a "*string*" type, which means it's intended to accept some text value such as the name of a service.

Arguments are specified at the command line by typing a forward slash (/), the name of the argument, a colon, and the value that the argument will be given in the script:

```
CScript.exe Updsvc.wsf /file:c:\computers.txt /service:Messenger /password:m$r%3d7@
```

The last bit of XML in the beginning of the WSF file defines the place where the VBScript code itself is located:

```
<script id="Updsvc" language="VBScript">
<![CDATA[
```

What follows is a normal VBScript, which could have been created in Microsoft Notepad or any other text editor. (The entire WSF file can be edited just fine in Notepad.)

```
'=============================================================================
'
' Updsvc
'
' AUTHOR: Don Jones
' DATE  : 7/31/2004
'
' COMMENT:
'
'=============================================================================
```

```vbscript
'make sure the correct number of arguments was passed;
'if not, display the usage of this command and quit
If WScript.Arguments.Count < 3 Then
   WScript.Arguments.ShowUsage
   WScript.Quit
End If

'pull specified arguments into string variables
Dim sFile, sService, sPassword
sFile = WScript.Arguments.Named("file")
sService = WScript.Arguments.Named("service")
sPassword = WScript.Arguments.Named("password")

'declare variables and filesystemobject
Dim oFSO, oTS, sClient, oWMIService, oService
Set oFSO = CreateObject("Scripting.FileSystemObject")

'ensure the input file exists
If oFSO.FileExists(sFile) Then

   'open the input file
   Set oTS = oFSO.OpenTextFile(sFile)

   'read through the input file until the end
   Do Until oTS.AtEndOfStream

        'retrieve the next computer name
        sClient = oTS.ReadLine

        'connect to the remote WMI service
        On Error Resume Next
        Set oWMIService = GetObject("winmgmts:" _
          & "{impersonationLevel=impersonate}!\\" & _
          sClient & "\root\cimv2")

        If Err = 0 Then
            'connected - retrieve specified service instance
            Set oService = oWMIService.ExecQuery _
             ("Select * from Win32_Service WHERE Name" & _
              " = '" & sService & "'")

          If Err = 0 Then
            'retrieved - change password for the service
                errReturn = oService.Change( , , , , , , _
                , sPassword)

                If errReturn = 0 Then
                    'change successful
                    WScript.Echo sClient " changed."
                Else
                    'change not successful
                    WScript.Echo sClient " not changed."
                End If
```

```
                    Else
                         'no matching instances of Win32_Service found
                         WScript.Echo sClient & ": Error retrieving service"
                    End If

              Else
                    'couldn't connect to remote WMI service
                    WScript.Echo sClient & ": Error connecting"
              End If

        'loop up for next computer in file
        Loop

        'close text file
        oTS.Close

Else
 'input file does not exist
 WScript.Echo "Input file does not exist"
End If+
```

Most importantly, the file finishes by closing the <script>, <job>, and <package> XML tags:

```
]]>
        </script>
    </job>
</package>
```

And that's it: you've got a WSF file. If you want to make changes to the script without changing any of the WSF-specific elements (such as the description and named arguments), you edit the portion of the file containing the script. You could also copy and paste everything between <![CDATA[ and ]]> into another file, which would give you only the script without all the WSF elements. Doing that can make the script easier to edit, but you have to be careful because the script doesn't predefine the named arguments, and any script relying on the named arguments won't prompt you for them automatically if they are missing. However, you can still run the script the same way, regardless of whether it's a .wsf or a .vbs file, because all VBScript files can accept named arguments:

```
CScript.exe Updsvc.vbs /file:c:\computers.txt /service:Messenger /password:m$r%3d7@
```

# Running WSF Files

WSF files—at least the ones I provide with this book—are intended to be run from the command line, typically using the CScript.exe version of WSH. You can run any WSF file by typing CScript.exe on a command line and then specifying the name of the WSF file:

```
CScript.exe MyFile.wsf
```

Even better, though, is that you can leave out CScript entirely and run the WSF file by itself on the command line:

```
MyFile.wsf
```

I do recommend that you make CScript your default script host by running `CScript.exe //H:CScript` one time. You can change back to the graphical WScript by running `CScript.exe //H:WScript` if you like.

You can get syntax help for the WSF files that are included in the book by running the .wsf with the */?* command-line argument:

```
MyFile.wsf /?
```

Other WSF authors might or might not include the appropriate information within the WSF to generate the help display. As I previously mentioned, you specify command-line arguments by typing a forward slash, the argument name, a colon, and then the value you want passed to the script for that argument:

```
MyFile.wsf /argument1:value1 /argument2:value2
```

Of course, I'll provide a complete reference to the arguments required by each WSF script in this book within the appropriate task descriptions.

# Windows Script Components

A few of the scripts in this book use Windows Script Components, or WSCs. These are basically Component Object Model (COM) objects written in VBScript—which is more than you need to know about them to use them! The scripts that do utilize WSCs will call your attention to that fact, and the WSCs themselves are, like the scripts, included on the CD that accompanies this book. However, WSCs do require that you perform one step to work properly—you have to *register* them. Registration adds information about the WSC to the Windows registry so that the script using the WSC can find it and load it into memory.

Registering a WSC is simple. First, copy the .wsc file to a location on your computer's local hard drive. (I don't recommend running them directly from the CD.) Next, right-click the WSC file and select Register from the shortcut menu. A message is displayed indicating that registration was successful, and you're finished. You need to do this only once per computer, but you have to do it on each computer where the WSC will be used (that is, on every computer you plan to run the script that utilizes the WSC). If you ever decide you don't need the WSC anymore, you can right-click it and select Unregister to remove the WSC's information from the registry.

WSCs use an XML-based format that's similar to the one used by WSF files. However, you don't need to open or edit any of the WSCs provided in this book to get the maximum enjoyment and utility out of them. Because the WSCs provided are used by several scripts, I don't recommend editing the WSCs at all. Doing so might render one or more dependent scripts unusable. If you want to experiment with the WSCs, make a copy and play with that, preferably on a different computer (because two WSCs with the same internal name will cause conflicts on your computer).

# Editing VBScript Files

One of the best aspects of VBScript is that you don't need any special tools to work with it. You don't need Visual Studio®, and you don't need a special editor of any kind—Notepad, included with Windows, will work just fine for simple editing. You do need to be careful when using Notepad, however, because it can append a .txt file name extension to your script. When using Notepad to save your script, always include the script's file name within double quotes to prevent Notepad from adding to the file name.

This is not to say, however, that Notepad is the best you can do for script editing. It has a number of shortcomings as a script editor for longer, more complicated scripts. For example, it doesn't do any color coding of your script to help distinguish comments, variables, statements, and so forth. It also doesn't provide any help with the VBScript syntax, and it won't do anything to help make the WSF format more comprehensible and easier to work with. Finally, Notepad makes it a bit tougher to locate script errors because it doesn't display line numbers, which is a key requirement for working with longer scripts. WSH displays script errors with a notation of the specific lines on which the errors occurred.

There are third-party script editors designed specifically for VBScript editing. Here's a selection of the more popular ones:

- **Programmer's File Editor (PFE)** (*http://www.download.com*)   This is a free editor that displays line numbers, but it isn't specifically designed for VBScript editing. Search for "Programmer File Editor" or "PFE" on the Web site.

- **Adersoft VBSEdit** (*http://www.vbsedit.com*)   This is an entry-level editor that provides syntax color-coding, pop-up assistance for VBScript statements, and other nice features.

- **SAPIEN PrimalScript** (*http://www.primalscript.com*)   This is a higher-end editor that includes integrated debugging support as well as special features to make working with WSF files easier and more straightforward.

- **XLnow OnScript** (*http://www.onscript.com*)   This is a full-featured editor that includes integrated debugging support, syntax completion, and other advanced features.

- **Admin Script Editor (ASE)** (*http://www.adminscripteditor.com*)   This is a relative newcomer that provides high-end features like pop-up syntax assistance and syntax color-coding.

Some of these editors are free but most are commercial tools, so you have to buy them. Some are inexpensive—VBSEdit, for example, costs about $30—whereas others are more full-featured and cost a good deal more. All, however, offer free trial versions on their Web sites, so you can download them and try them out for a number of days to find the editor that best meets your needs. Once you register and log in, you'll also find reviews of many of these script editors on my Web site, *http://www.ScriptingAnswers.com*, that might help you make a decision.

You don't need any of these tools to effectively use the scripts in this book. All the scripts provided are designed to be self-contained, and any required customization is handled by using command-line arguments. You don't need to have an editor or even open any of these scripts in Notepad to use them. However, if you decide you want to modify these scripts in any way—many of them can be changed to perform different yet similar tasks—a good editor is a nice tool to have.

# Summary

The WSF file format is one of those love-it-or-hate-it things. You either think it's great because of the extra features it provides, or you hate it because it makes scripting more complex, and plenty of people find scripting complex enough to start with. In my mind, the best aspect of the WSF format is that it allows an experienced scripter to create traditional command-line tools easily and make those scripts accessible to administrators who aren't experienced with scripting. The main reason I chose to use WSF was so that you don't have to crack the files open and do anything with them if you don't want to. They are also more self-documenting in terms of the arguments they require. WSF files are still easily editable, once you understand what you're looking at.

The structure of WSCs wasn't addressed because this book isn't about learning scripting. What you do need to know about WSCs is that a few of the scripts in this book will utilize them, so you need to register the WSCs to make them available to those scripts. When a script uses a WSC, it will remind you that the WSC needs to be registered before the script can function.

> **Note**   There are a number of resources for learning more about WSCs, including the MSDN® Library Web site at *http://msdn.microsoft.com/scripting*. Look under "Web Development" in the table of contents to locate the "Scripting" section.

Chapter 4

# Security Best Practices

Security is perhaps one of the most important concerns when it comes to scripting and automation. Although many administrators adopt a casual approach to security, you'll gain more respect from your managers and peers by adopting a very cautious approach to scripting and automation. This advice applies to the scripts included with this book, by the way—don't assume anything about them! They should all be tested before you use them in any production environment, because your production environment might be very different from the environment in which the scripts were written. By focusing on security as a part of every task you perform, you reduce the risk of deliberate and accidental damage to your environment.

## Principle of Least Privilege (or Access)

The Principle of Least Privilege (PoLP), sometimes referred to as the Principle of Least Access (PoLA), simply says this: perform every task with a user account that has exactly the permissions needed to accomplish that task, and no more. It's rarely possible to achieve PoLP, but you should try your best. For example, when you log on to your computer in the morning, use a user account that has only the permissions required to perform basic, nonadministrative tasks like checking e-mail. You certainly shouldn't log on by using an administrative user account. By logging on with a less privileged account, you can minimize the damage caused by any viruses or accidental actions you perform. When you do need to perform tasks requiring additional permissions, you can do so by specifying alternate credentials. And, even then, specify alternate credentials that have just enough permissions for the particular task.

Plenty of environments give their administrators a "normal" user account in addition to an administrative account, which is a good step on the road to PoLP. But why not also have a Server Operator account, an Account Operator account, and other accounts whose permissions fall between a normal user and a full administrator? Not every administrative task requires a local administrator or a domain administrator, and you should strive to use an account whose entire permission set closely matches the permissions required by the task at hand.

For example, suppose you normally log on by using a low-privilege user account, and specify a domain administrator account for your administrative tasks. Domain administrators are, by default, local administrators on all domain member computers, which is quite a lot of privilege. Were you to run a script that caused a problem, that problem could extend to every member in the domain. However, suppose that script required only the permissions associated with the Account Operators group. A problem in this case would be more limited in scope, because that group doesn't have local Administrator permissions on every computer in the domain.

# Using Alternate Credentials

So how do you actually implement PoLP? Microsoft Windows® 2000 and later versions provide a Runas command, allowing you to execute applications and command-line tools using a different user account. Runas is pretty straightforward:

```
Runas /user:username application
```

Simply specify the user account (use the user@domain or domain\user format for specifying user names from an alternate domain, if necessary) and the application to run; you'll be prompted for the user's password (or other type of credentials; Runas works with smart cards, for example), and the application will execute under that user account's credentials and permissions.

You can also right-click applications in Windows Explorer and select Run As from the shortcut menu. Doing so will prompt you, via a dialog box, for the alternate user's name and password.

# Security: Do This

Security can be straightforward, and it doesn't have to be a major burden on the way you do your job. Here are some best practices for making scripting and automation more secure (and more securable) in any environment:

- **Never log on to a computer by using an administrative user account.**   Log on with an account that has permission to do everyday tasks, such as check e-mail, and use alternate credentials—by using tools such as the Runas command—to perform tasks requiring additional permissions.

- **Digitally sign your scripts, and configure the Windows Script Host (WSH) to run only trusted scripts.**   This is described in Chapter 2, "Automation and Security."

- **Store scripts on an NTFS volume and use NTFS permissions to secure the files so that only authorized individuals can access your scripts.**   Doing so will help prevent accidental damage that might be caused by a user running some script (or other automation tool) that he shouldn't.

- **When running scripts, use a user account with the least possible permissions necessary to get the job done.**   Are you just adding user accounts to the domain? You don't need to be an enterprise administrator to accomplish that; a member of the built-in Account Operators group would work just as well as and would have significantly fewer unnecessary permissions.

- **Design your scripts to be run by members of a specific user group, either a built-in group like Server Operators or a custom group you create.**   Document the group name in the script itself by using comment lines so that future administrators will know what permissions are needed to run the script.

- **Test your scripts in a nonproduction environment.**   I like to use Microsoft Virtual PC for this purpose: I can have several virtual machines that resemble the domain controllers and other computers in my production environment. They provide safe places to run scripts for testing purposes, and resetting the virtual machines to their starting point is easy when testing is finished, or when additional tests need to be run.

# Security: Don't Do This

There are a few things you should never do when it comes to scripting and security. Follow these simple rules and your scripting environment will be much safer and more secure:

- **Never, ever, ever put user passwords of any kind into a script.**   If a script needs to use an account's password, have the script prompt for that password or accept the password as a command-line argument.

- **Avoid changing default permissions in critical areas like the registry and Windows Management Instrumentation (WMI).**   Some administrators like to manage client computers through the use of logon scripts, which often require users to have administrative permissions of some kind. Bad idea. Instead, run a script on *your* computer that remotely reconfigures client computers using *your* administrative credentials.

- **Don't use the Script Encoder (see the sidebar in this chapter, "Passwords in Scripts").**   The Script Encoder was primarily designed for Web environments utilizing VBScript and Microsoft Active Server Pages (ASP). Administrative scripts and automation tools should be protected by NTFS permissions, which prevent users from opening the scripts to begin with. There should be no need for the Encoder.

- **Don't run scripts without reviewing them unless they come from a trusted source.**   Scripts from the Internet can be useful, but you never know when a bug or piece of malicious code might cause irreparable damage to your environment. Know what you're running before you run it.

## Passwords in Scripts

I get a lot of questions about including passwords in scripts. My universal answer is don't do it. This advice applies to VBScript files as well as batch files and other scripts. Many administrators find Microsoft's Script Encoder (from *http://www.microsoft.com/scripting*) and think they've found a way to safely include passwords within scripts, because the encoder will let them "encrypt" the script and protect the password. Not so—the Encoder is *not* an encryption tool in the security sense of the word *encryption*. It's designed only to hide your script's source code from casual observation. An easy-to-use Script Decoder can be found at *http://www.aspheute.com/english/20011123.asp*. I point this out to emphasize that the Script Encoder should never be used to protect sensitive information, particularly information as sensitive as user account passwords.

Another question I get asked is whether you can script the Runas command so that Runas can be launched programmatically with alternate credentials. This is possible but not easy, and you shouldn't do it. Scripting the Runas command would necessarily involve hardcoding user passwords into a script, which is the very action you want to avoid at all costs. Microsoft deliberately made the Runas command not scriptable in that fashion because scripted passwords are trouble. In short, never type a password into script code. (Scripts might prompt for passwords, and storing the passwords in variables is fine.) The corollary of this would be never type a password into any file that can be saved to disk.

# Summary

Scripting can be a tremendously useful, beneficial tool, whether you're talking about VBScript or more traditional command-line tools. Unfortunately, scripting—and nearly any other computer-based technology—can be used to create significant damage, whether intentionally or accidentally. Security precautions are designed to prevent accidental damage as much as they are designed to prevent deliberate damage caused by an attacker or malicious user.

Scripting—VBScript in particular—earns a bad reputation from a security perspective because too many administrators treat the technology too casually. Rather than taking appropriate precautions, they treat their environments as a toy, causing their managers and other company personnel to become distrustful of scripting (and other automation techniques) after an accidental disaster or two. Don't take the easy way out and treat scripting and automation lightly. Instead, use sensible security precautions and the best practices I've outlined here to make scripting and automation a formal, respected part of your environment.

# Part II
# Computer Management Tasks

Chapter 5

# Client Management

Client management includes tasks such as managing System Restore points and client time zone settings. Automating these tasks enables you to more easily perform them and often requires scripts that can run on multiple computers. Note that many of the tasks in this chapter apply only to computers running Microsoft® Windows® XP, particularly those tasks dealing with System Restore, which is available only in Windows XP. Other tasks, such as setting the time zone on one or more computers, can be performed on a wider variety of Windows versions. Tasks automated in this chapter include:

- Set a System Restore point

- Restore to a System Restore point

- Enable or disable System Restore

- List System Restore points

- Set a computer's domain

- Change a computer name

- List a computer's time zone

# Set a System Restore Point

 **On the CD**   The sample script can be found on the CD that accompanies this book at \Chap5\SetRestorePoint\SetRestorePoint.wsf.

| Operating System | Supported? | Prerequisites |
|---|---|---|
| Microsoft Windows 2000 family | No | ■  WSH 5.6 or later |
| Windows XP Professional | Yes | ■  WMI |
| Microsoft Windows Server™ 2003 family | No | ■  Administrative permission on targeted computers |
|  |  | ■  Network connectivity to each remote computer |

## Description

This task sets a new System Restore point on one or more computers. Automation is provided by a Microsoft Visual Basic® Script (VBScript), which is contained in a WSF file and can be used as a command-line tool. The script offers a number of options for specifying the computers to be targeted, including specifying a single computer, specifying a Microsoft Active Directory® organizational unit (OU) containing computer names, and specifying a text file containing computer names. The newly created System Restore point will be given the name "Scripted Restore" within the System Restore user interface. It is a good idea to perform this task before major network-wide changes (such as modifications to a new application or a new logon script) are rolled out to ensure that each computer has a safe restore point to roll back to.

## Performing This Task Manually

To manually set a System Restore point on a computer running Windows XP Professional, follow these steps:

1.  On the Start menu, navigate to All Programs, Accessories, System Tools, and then select the System Restore tab.

2.  On the Welcome To System Restore page, select Create A Restore Point and click Next.

3.  On the Create A Restore Point page, enter a description for the restore point and click Create.

4.  Click Close.

As you can see, creating a System Restore point manually is not difficult. However, doing so on multiple computers can be very time-consuming without an automated script.

## Example

There are three basic ways to use this tool. First, you can target a single remote computer named ClientA by using the following code:

```
SetRestorePoint.wsf /computer:ClientA
```

Second, you can target a list of computers from a text file. The text file is expected to contain one computer name per line, with no other information in the file. Assuming the file is named C:\Computers.txt, you would use this syntax:

```
SetRestorePoint.wsf /list:C:\Computers.txt
```

Third, you can target an entire organizational unit of computer accounts. If your domain contains an OU named West, you would use the following syntax:

```
SetRestorePoint.wsf /container:west
```

Note that the *container* argument will work only against the default domain of the computer running the script. In other words, the OU specified must exist within the same domain that the computer running the script belongs to. If the specified OU has nested OUs, you can include their computer accounts as well by specifying one additional argument:

```
SetRestorePoint.wsf /container:west /recurse
```

Additional arguments provide more functionality to the command, as the following section explains.

## Syntax

This script can be executed as a command-line utility. Set CScript.exe to be your default script processor, as described in Chapter 3, "Working with VBScript."

| | |
|---|---|
| `/list:path`<br>`/computer:name`<br>`/container:name` | One and only one of these is required by the script. Use */list* to target a list of computers contained within a text file; use */computer* to target a single computer; use */container* to target an organizational unit within Active Directory. |
| `/recurse` | When used with */container*, also targets computers contained within nested OUs. |

| /ping | Verifies the connectivity to all targeted computers prior to attempting a connection. Using this argument will reduce the timeout wait when one or more computers cannot be reached on the network. |
| /log:path | Logs unreachable computer names to the specified file. This file can then be used later, along with the *list* argument, to retry these computers. |
| /verbose | Causes the script to display more detailed, step-by-step status messages. |

You can run this script with the */?* parameter to display the command's syntax.

## Under the Hood

This script uses the *FileSystemObject* to read computer names when the */list* argument is specified and uses Active Directory Services Interface (ADSI) to retrieve computer names when the */container* argument is specified. The script contains a subroutine named *WorkWithOU* that calls itself recursively (that is, it calls itself over and over) to process nested OUs when the */recurse* argument is specified. The real work of the script is performed by a relatively small section of VBScript code:

```
Dim oWMIService, oSysRestore, ErrResult
On Error Resume Next
Verbose " Attempting to set System Restore point on " & sName
Set oWMIService = GetObject("winmgmts:{impersonationLevel=impersonate}!\\" & sName &
"\root\default")
If Err <> 0 Then
 WScript.Echo " *** Error connecting to " & sName
 WScript.Echo "      " & Err.Description
 LogBadConnect(sName)
Else
 Set oSysRestore = oWMIService.Get("SystemRestore")
 If Err <> 0 Then
  WScript.Echo " *** Couldn't get System Restore services from " & sName
  WScript.Echo "      " & Err.Description
 Else
  ErrResult = oSysRestore.CreateRestorePoint("Scripted Restore", 10, 100)
  Verbose " " & sName & ": " & ErrResult
 End If
End If
```

The current computer name is contained in the variable *sName*. Note that the script connects to the computer's *\root\default* namespace in Microsoft Windows Management Instrumentation (WMI) and then retrieves the *SystemRestore* class from that namespace. The *SystemRestore* class provides a method named *CreateRestorePoint* that does the work of creating the new System Restore point.

# Troubleshooting

You have the opportunity to run into two main problems when using this script: first, a remote computer won't be available; or second, you won't have permission to create a System Restore point. In either case, you'll see an error message that alerts you to the problem for that computer. Make sure you have the appropriate permissions and that the computer is reachable via the network from the computer running this script. Unreachable computers can optionally be logged to a text file for a later attempt, and you can speed up the script by specifying the */ping* argument.

# To Learn More

- To learn more about how VBScript and WMI work together, read Chapter 6 in *Microsoft Windows 2000 Scripting Guide* (Microsoft Press, 2003).

- Examine the *SystemRestore* class reference in the Microsoft WMI documentation to see how the *CreateRestorePoint()* method can be used to create other restore points.

- Other System Restore script examples can be found in the Microsoft TechNet Script Center at *http://www.microsoft.com/technet/scriptcenter/scripts/desktop /restore/default.mspx*.

# Restore to a System Restore Point

> **On the CD**   The sample script can be found on the CD that accompanies this book at \Chap5\SetRestorePoint\RollbackRestorePoint.wsf.

| Operating System | Supported? | Prerequisites |
|---|---|---|
| Windows 2000 family | No | ■ WSH 5.6 or later |
| Windows XP Professional | Yes | ■ WMI |
| Windows Server 2003 family | No | ■ Administrative permission on targeted computers |
| | | ■ Network connectivity to each remote computer |

## Description

This task will restore a computer to a previously created System Restore point. Automation is provided by VBScript code, which is contained in a WSF file that can be used as a command-line tool. The script allows only a single computer to be targeted, because the process of specifying a restore point is not likely to be accurate for more than one computer at a time. This script can be used to roll back a restore point on a remote computer to which you might not have ready access, especially in situations in which that computer's user isn't familiar with the System Restore process.

## Performing This Task Manually

To perform the task manually on a computer running Windows XP Professional, follow these steps:

1. On the Start menu, navigate to All Programs, Accessories, System Tools, and then select System Restore.

2. On the Welcome To System Restore page, select Restore My Computer To An Earlier Time, and click Next.

3. On the Select A Restore Point page, select the restore point by using the calendar and list box, and click Next.

4. On the Confirm Restore Point Selection page, click Next to initiate the restore.

5. Follow any additional instructions to restart the computer after the rollback is complete.

Although rolling back to a System Restore point manually is not difficult, doing so on a remote computer without the end-user's assistance can be complicated, generally requiring a Remote Assistance or other remote control session to be initiated. The process of selecting the correct restore point can be complex and intimidating for end-users. If you as the administrator already know the restore point you need, you can use a script to perform this selection much more quickly.

# Example

This script can target only a single computer and uses the following syntax:

```
RollbackRestorePoint.wsf /computer:ClientA /point:20
```

This will connect to ClientA and roll back to restore point 20; use the List System Restore Point script in this chapter to obtain the correct restore point number.

Additional arguments provide more functionality to the command; see the following section.

# Syntax

This script can be executed as a command-line utility. Set CScript.exe to be your default script processor, as described in Chapter 3.

| | |
|---|---|
| `/computer:name` | Required. Specifies the computer name to target. |
| `/point:restorepoint` | Required. Specifies the restore point index number to roll back to. |
| `/ping` | Verifies the connectivity to the targeted computer prior to attempting a connection. Using this argument will reduce the timeout wait when the computer cannot be reached on the network. |
| `/verbose` | Causes the script to display more detailed, step-by-step status messages. |

You can run this script with the /? parameter to display the command's syntax.

# Under the Hood

This script uses Windows Management Instrumentation (WMI) to perform its primary functions, as shown here:

```
Dim oWMIService, oSysRestore, ErrResult
On Error Resume Next
Verbose " Attempting to roll back System Restore point on " & sName
Set oWMIService = GetObject("winmgmts:{impersonationLevel=impersonate}!\\" & sName &
"\root\default")
If Err <> 0 Then
 WScript.Echo " *** Error connecting to " & sName
 WScript.Echo "      " & Err.Description
 LogBadConnect(sName)
```

```
Else
 Set oSysRestore = oWMIService.Get("SystemRestore")
 If Err <> 0 Then
  WScript.Echo " *** Couldn't get System Restore services from " & sName
  WScript.Echo "       " & Err.Description
 Else
  ErrResult = oSysRestore.Restore(WScript.Arguments.Named("point"))
  Verbose " " & sName & ": " & ErrResult
 End If
End If
```

The current computer name is contained in the variable *sName*. Note that the script connects to the computer's \*root*\*default* namespace in Windows Management Instrumentation (WMI) and then retrieves the *SystemRestore* class from that namespace. The *SystemRestore* class provides a method named *Restore*, which does the work of rolling back to the specified System Restore point. You will need to use the List System Restore Point script to see a list of available restore points on the remote computer.

## Troubleshooting

You have the potential to run into three problems when using this script. First, the remote computer won't be available. Second, you won't have permission to roll back to a System Restore point. In either case, you'll see an error message that alerts you to the problem. Make sure you have the appropriate permissions (generally, Administrator permissions are required) and that the computer is reachable via the network from the computer running this script.

A third possible problem is specifying a System Restore point number that doesn't exist. In that case, you'll see an appropriate error message, and nothing will happen.

It's also possible to specify the *wrong* System Restore point. In that case, the targeted computer will be rolled back to the specified point regardless—the script does not provide an "are you sure?" prompt or any other chance to undo what you've done. Be very careful when using this script and verify the restore point number you provide.

## To Learn More

- To learn more about how VBScript and WMI work together, read Chapter 6 in *Microsoft Windows 2000 Scripting Guide* (Microsoft Press, 2003).

- Examine the *SystemRestore* class reference in the Microsoft WMI documentation to see how the *CreateRestorePoint()* method can be used to create other restore points.

- Other System Restore script examples can be found in the Microsoft TechNet Script Center at *http://www.microsoft.com/technet/scriptcenter/scripts/desktop/ restore/default.mspx*.

# Enable or Disable System Restore

> **On the CD** The sample script can be found on the CD that accompanies this book at \Chap5\SetSysRestoreStatus\SetSystemRestoreStatus.wsf.

| Operating System | Supported? | Prerequisites |
|---|---|---|
| Windows 2000 family | No | ■ WSH 5.6 or later |
| Windows XP Professional | Yes | ■ WMI |
| Windows Server 2003 family | No | ■ Administrative permission on targeted computers |
| | | ■ Network connectivity to each remote computer |

## Description

This task will enable or disable the System Restore feature on one or more computers running Windows XP. Automation is provided by a VBScript that is contained in a WSF file that is to be used as a command-line tool. The script offers a number of options for specifying the computers to be targeted, including specifying a single computer, specifying an Active Directory organizational unit (OU) containing computer names, or specifying a text file containing computer names.

System Restore consumes a configurable amount of disk space, and it does present an opportunity for users to misconfigure their computers by performing System Restore rollbacks when not necessary or by specifying an incorrect restore point during a rollback. There is also a remote possibility for System Restore to present a virus vector. If a virus is captured as part of a System Restore point, rolling back to that point will reintroduce the virus. For these and other reasons, some organizations elect to disable System Restore on their client computers running Windows XP.

## Performing This Task Manually

To perform the task manually on a computer running Windows XP Professional, follow these steps:

1. Right-click My Computer and select Properties.

2. In the System Properties dialog box, select the System Restore tab.

3. Select or clear the Turn Off System Restore check box to disable or enable System Restore, respectively.

4. Click OK.

As you can see, although configuring System Restore manually is not difficult, doing so on multiple computers can be very time-consuming without some kind of automated script.

# Example

There are three basic ways to use this tool. To use it to target a single remote computer named ClientA and enable System Restore, you would use this code:

```
SetSystemRestoreStatus.wsf /computer:ClientA /status:enable
```

You can also target a list of computers from a text file. The text file is expected to contain one computer name per line and no other information. Assuming the file is named C:\Computers.txt, you would use this syntax to disable System Restore on the computers listed in the file:

```
SetRestorePoint.wsf /list:C:\Computers.txt /status:disable
```

Finally, you can target an entire organizational unit of computer accounts. If your domain contains an OU named West, you would use the following syntax to enable System Restore:

```
SetRestorePoint.wsf /container:west /status:enable
```

Note that the *container* argument will work only against the default domain of the computer running the script. In other words, the OU specified must exist within the same domain that the computer running the script belongs to. If the specified OU has nested OUs, you can include their computer accounts as well by specifying one additional argument:

```
SetRestorePoint.wsf /container:west /recurse /status:enable
```

Additional arguments provide more functionality to the command, as shown in the following section.

# Syntax

This script can be executed as a command-line utility. Set CScript.exe to be your default script processor, as described in Chapter 3.

| | |
|---|---|
| /list:path<br>/computer:name<br>/container:name | One and only one of these is required by the script. Use */list* to target a list of computers contained within a text file. Use */computer* to target a single computer. Use */container* to target an organizational unit within Active Directory. |
| /status:en-<br>able\|disable | Required. Specify either *enable* or *disable* to enable or disable System Restore services on all the targeted computers. |

| | |
|---|---|
| /recurse | When used with /container, also targets computers contained within nested OUs. |
| /ping | Verifies the connectivity to all targeted computers prior to attempting a connection. Using this argument will reduce the timeout wait when one or more computers cannot be reached on the network. |
| /log:path | Logs unreachable computer names to the specified file. This file can then be used later, along with the /list argument, to retry these computers. |
| /verbose | Causes the script to display more detailed, step-by-step status messages. |

You can run this script with the /? parameter to display the command's syntax.

## Under the Hood

This script uses the *FileSystemObject* to read computer names when the /list argument is specified and uses Active Directory Services Interface (ADSI) to retrieve computer names when the /container argument is specified. The script contains a subroutine named *WorkWithOU* that calls itself recursively (that is, it calls itself over and over) to process nested OUs when the /recurse argument is specified. The real work of the script is performed by a relatively small section of VBScript code:

```
Select Case LCase(WScript.Arguments.Named("status"))
 Case "enable"
  ErrResult = oSysRestore.Enable("")
  Verbose "  Enable " & sName & ": " & ErrResult
 Case "disable"
  ErrResult = oSysRestore.Disable("")
  Verbose "  Disable " & sName & ": " & ErrResult
 Case Else
  Verbose "  Unknown status " & WScript.Arguments.Named("status")
End Select
```

By the time this script is reached, the variable *oSysRestore* has been set to represent the System Restore Windows Management Instrumentation (WMI) class on the current remote computer. This class provides methods to enable or disable System Restore; the value provided for the /status argument determines the method called. Note that a provision is included for an unknown value (not *enable* or *disable*) being passed to the /status argument.

# Troubleshooting

You have the potential to run into two main problems when using this script. First, a remote computer won't be available. Second, you won't have permission to configure System Restore. In either case, you'll see an error message that alerts you to the problem for that computer. Make sure you have the appropriate permissions and that the computer is reachable via the network from the computer running this script. Unreachable computers can optionally be logged to a text file for a later attempt, and you can speed up the script by specifying the */ping* argument. Generally speaking, you'll need local Administrator permissions on each targeted computer to successfully run the script.

# To Learn More

- To learn more about how VBScript and WMI work together, read Chapter 6 in *Microsoft Windows 2000 Scripting Guide* (Microsoft Press, 2003).

- Examine the *SystemRestore* class reference in the Microsoft WMI documentation to see how the *CreateRestorePoint()* method can be used to create other restore points.

- Other System Restore script examples can be found in the Microsoft TechNet Script Center at *http://www.microsoft.com/technet/scriptcenter/scripts/desktop/restore/default.mspx*.

# List System Restore Points

> **On the CD**   The sample script can be found on the CD that accompanies this book at \Chap5\ListRestorePoints\ListRestorePoints.wsf.

| Operating System | Supported? | Prerequisites |
|---|---|---|
| Windows 2000 family | No | ■  WSH 5.6 or later |
| Windows XP Professional | Yes | ■  WMI |
| Windows Server 2003 family | No | ■  Administrative permission on targeted computers |
| | | ■  Network connectivity to each remote computer |

## Description

This task will list all System Restore points on a single remote computer. Automation is provided by VBScript code, which is contained in a WSF file that can be used as a command-line tool. The script allows only a single computer to be targeted, because the process of specifying a restore point is not likely to be accurate on more than one computer at a time. Prior to using a different script to roll back to a System Restore point, this script can be used to obtain the ID number for the desired restore point.

## Performing This Task Manually

The Windows operating system does not provide a built-in, graphical means of listing all available System Restore points. You can browse the available System Restore points by using this procedure:

1. On the Start menu, navigate to All Programs, Accessories, System Tools, and select System Restore.

2. On the Welcome To System Restore page, select Restore My Computer To An Earlier Time, and click Next.

3. On the Select A Restore Point page, browse the available restore points by using the calendar and list box.

4. Click Cancel to cancel the System Restore process.

This procedure can be time-consuming when you're trying to quickly locate a particular restore point.

# Example

This script can target only a single computer and uses the following syntax:

```
ListRestorePoints.wsf /computer:ClientA
```

This code will connect to ClientA and list all restore points. Adding the */verbose* argument will also list the type of each restore point, such as an application installation restore point and a device driver installation restore point.

Additional arguments provide more functionality to the command, as explained in the following section.

# Syntax

This script can be executed as a command-line utility. You should set CScript.exe to be your default script processor, as described in Chapter 3.

| | |
|---|---|
| `/computer:name` | Required. Specifies the computer name to target. |
| `/ping` | Verifies the connectivity to the targeted computer prior to attempting a connection. Using this argument will reduce the timeout wait when the computer cannot be reached on the network. |
| `/verbose` | Causes the script to display more detailed, step-by-step status messages. Also displays the restore point type for each restore point listed. |

You can run this script with the */?* parameter to display the command's syntax.

# Under the Hood

This script uses Windows Management Instrumentation (WMI) to perform its primary functions, as shown here:

```
Set cPoints = QueryWMI(sName,"root\default","Select * From SystemRestore","","")
If Not IsObject(cPoints) Then
 WScript.Echo " *** Error retrieving System Restore points from " & sName
Else
 For Each oPoint In cPoints
  WScript.Echo oPoint.SequenceNumber & ": " & oPoint.Description
  Select Case oPoint.RestorePointType
   Case 0
    Verbose "  (application installation)"
   Case 1
    Verbose "  (application removal)"
   Case 6
    Verbose "  (restore)"
   Case 7
    Verbose "  (automatic checkpoint)"
```

```
      Case 10
       Verbose " (device driver installation)"
      Case 11
       Verbose " (first run)"
      Case 12
       Verbose " (modify settings)"
      Case 13
       Verbose " (cancelled operation)"
      Case 14
       Verbose " (backup recovery)"
      Case Else
       Verbose " (other)"
     End Select
    Next
   End If
```

The current computer name is contained in the variable *sName*. The script uses a function named *QueryWMI* to retrieve the list of System Restore points, and then lists them. A *Select...Case* construct contains all possible values for the restore point type; the *Verbose* subroutine displays the corresponding output only if the script's */verbose* argument is specified. Not displaying the restore point type provides for a more compact listing of available restore points.

## Troubleshooting

You have the potential to run into two problems when using this script. First, the remote computer won't be available. Second, you won't have permission to roll back to a System Restore point. In either case, you'll see an error message that alerts you to the problem. Make sure you have the appropriate permissions (generally, Administrator permissions are required) and that the computer is reachable via the network from the computer running this script.

## To Learn More

- To learn more about how VBScript and WMI work together, read Chapter 6 in *Microsoft Windows 2000 Scripting Guide* (Microsoft Press, 2003).

- Examine the *SystemRestore* class reference in Microsoft's WMI documentation to see how the *CreateRestorePoint()* method can be used to create other restore points.

- Other System Restore script examples can be found in the Microsoft TechNet Script Center at *http://www.microsoft.com/technet/scriptcenter/scripts/desktop/restore/default.mspx*.

# Set a Computer's Domain

No script is provided for this task. You will need the Netdom.exe command-line utility, available as part of the Support Tools for various versions of Windows. The Support Tools are available on the Windows installation CD.

| Operating System | Supported? | Prerequisites |
|---|---|---|
| Windows 2000 family | Yes | ■ Administrative permission on targeted computer |
| Windows XP Professional | Yes | |
| Windows Server 2003 family | Yes | ■ Network connectivity to the remote computer |

## Description

This task will change the workgroup or domain that a computer belongs to. To change a computer's domain membership, you must first join the computer to a workgroup (thus removing it from its domain), and then join it to the new domain.

## Performing This Task Manually

Windows provides a straightforward interface for changing a computer's domain or workgroup. Follow these steps:

1. Right-click My Computer and select Properties.

2. In the System Properties dialog box, select the Computer Name tab.

3. Click Change.

4. Specify the computer's new name, or change its domain or workgroup membership.

5. Click OK twice.

You will need to restart the computer for your changes to take effect. Though easy enough to perform, this task can be cumbersome when you need to perform it on a remote computer.

## Example

To join computer ClientA to the Company domain and restart the computer after 30 seconds, use this code:

```
Netdom join ClientA /domain:Company /reboot:30
```

**Note**   The precise syntax of the Netdom.exe utility differs from version to version. Be sure to check the Support Tools documentation accompanying your version of Windows for specifics. Also note that the syntax shown is for v2.0 of the Netdom.exe utility; earlier versions use a completely different syntax and can also join computers to workgroups.

## Syntax

This utility runs from the command line. You can create a batch file to run this command on multiple computers in sequence, but you will generally need to use it on only one or two computers at once.

| | |
|---|---|
| `/domain:name` | Required. Specifies the domain to join. |
| `/ou:path` | Optional. Specifies the OU in which to create the computer account. If left out, the computer will be created in the default container. |
| `/UserD:name /PasswordD:*` | Optional. Specifies an alternate account to be used to connect to the domain. Specify */PasswordD:\** to be prompted for a password. |
| `/UserO:name /PasswordO:*` | Optional. Specifies an alternate account for connecting to the targeted computer. Specify */PasswordO:\** to be prompted for a password. |
| `/reboot:seconds` | Optional. Specifies the number of seconds to wait before restarting the computer automatically. If omitted, the default is 20 seconds. |

You can run this script with the */?* parameter to display the command's syntax.

## Under the Hood

This task uses the Support Tools Netdom.exe utility. This utility performs two main tasks. First, it contacts a domain controller to perform the necessary changes in Active Directory to add or remove domain members. Note that this utility cannot be used to add or remove domain controllers in the domain; use Dcpromo.exe for that task.

Second, Netdom.exe can contact the targeted computer and modify its local configuration to reflect its new domain or workgroup membership. For both tasks—the domain and local computer configurations—you need to have appropriate permissions. For the domain, you will generally need to be a domain administrator; for the local computer, you will need to be recognized as a local administrator.

# Troubleshooting

The most likely cause for problems is having the targeted computer recognize you as a local administrator. If you run Netdom.exe using domain administrator credentials, the domain will recognize you, as will all domain members, meaning that you will not have a problem *removing* a computer from the domain. However, computers that are not members of the domain will obviously not recognize a domain administrator as a local administrator, meaning you will have to independently establish local administrator credentials when *adding* a computer to a domain (or changing workgroups). One way to do so is to execute the following:

```
Net use \\clienta\ipc$ /user:Administrator
```

Doing so will establish a connection from your computer to ClientA (assuming that's the computer you're targeting with Netdom.exe) and allow you to provide a password for the local Administrator account. You can, of course, specify any account with the appropriate permissions; you don't need to use the built-in Administrator account as I've done in this example. You can also use the Netdom.exe utility's */UserO* switch to specify alternate credentials.

## To Learn More

- To read more about the Netdom.exe utility, consult the documentation included with the Support Tools. You can also read *http://support.microsoft.com/kb/266651/EN-US/* for more details.

# Change a Computer Name

 **On the CD**   The sample script can be found on the CD that accompanies this book at \Chap5\ChangeComputerName\ChangeComputerName.wsf.

| Operating System | Supported? | Prerequisites |
|---|---|---|
| Windows 2000 family | No | ■ WSH 5.6 or later |
| Windows XP Professional | Yes | ■ WMI |
| Windows Server 2003 family | Yes | ■ Administrative permission on targeted computers |
|  |  | ■ Network connectivity to each remote computer |

## Description

This task will change the computer name of a remote computer. You must specify a valid new computer name, or the script will return an error indicating that the change could not be made. If you specify the /*ping* argument, the script will check to make sure the new computer name is not currently in use by another computer on the network (assuming that any computer already using the name is reachable by pinging its name).

## Performing This Task Manually

Windows does not provide a built-in, graphical means of listing all available System Restore points. You can browse the available System Restore points using this procedure:

1. Right-click My Computer and select Properties.
2. In the System Properties dialog box, select the Computer Name tab.
3. Click Change.
4. Specify the computer's new name.
5. Click OK twice.

Walking a user through this process can be difficult, and many users might not have permissions to change their computers' names. Using the script allows you to effect a name change remotely from a command line.

# Example

This script can target only a single computer and uses the following syntax:

```
ChangeComputerName.wsf /computer:ClientA /name:ClientB
```

This will connect to ClientA and rename it to ClientB. Additional arguments provide more functionality to the command; see the following section.

# Syntax

This script can be executed as a command-line utility. You should set CScript.exe to be your default script processor, as described in Chapter 3.

| | |
|---|---|
| `/computer:oldname` | Required. Specifies the computer name to target. |
| `/ping` | Verifies the connectivity to the targeted computer prior to attempting a connection. Using this argument will reduce the timeout wait when the computer cannot be reached on the network. Also checks to see that the new computer name is not currently in use by attempting to ping the new name. |
| `/verbose` | Causes the script to display more detailed, step-by-step status messages. Also displays the restore point type for each restore point listed. |
| `/name:newname` | Required. Specifies the new name for the targeted computer. |

You can run this script with the /? parameter to display the command's syntax.

# Under the Hood

This script uses Windows Management Instrumentation (WMI) to perform its primary functions, as shown here:

```
ErrResults = oComputer.Rename(WScript.Arguments.Named("name"),Null,Null)
If ErrResults <> 0 Then
 WScript.Echo " *** Error renaming: " & ErrResults
Else
 Verbose "Rename successful. Restart of remote computer is necessary."
End If
```

The current computer name is contained in the variable *sName*, whereas the argument /name contains the new computer name. The *Win32_ComputerSystem* class is represented in *oComputer*, and its *Rename()* method performs the actual work of renaming the computer.

# Troubleshooting

Security permissions can cause problems when running this script. You must be a member of the computer's local Administrators group for this script to function; the script might not work in all circumstances when run remotely on computers that are members of a domain. In those cases, you might need to modify the script to include a password and user name in the *Rename()* method:

```
ErrResults = oComputer.Rename(WScript.Arguments.Named("name"), _
  "passwprd","user@domain.com")
```

The *Rename()* method cannot be used in all cases to rename computers that are members of a domain.

# To Learn More

■ Read more about the *Win32_ComputerSystem* class at *http:// msdn.microsoft.com/library/default.asp?url=/library/en-us/wmisdk/wmi/ win32_computersystem.asp.*

■ Read more about the *Rename()* method at *http://msdn.microsoft.com/library/ default.asp?url=/library/en-us/wmisdk/wmi/ rename_method_in_class_win32_computersystem.asp.*

# List a Computer's Time Zone

> **On the CD**   The sample script can be found on the CD that accompanies this book at \Chap5\ListTimeZone\ListTimeZone.wsf.

| Operating System | Supported? | Prerequisites |
|---|---|---|
| Windows 2000 family | Yes | ■ WSH 5.6 or later |
| Windows XP Professional | Yes | ■ WMI |
| Windows Server 2003 family | Yes | ■ Administrative permission on targeted computers |
| | | ■ Network connectivity to each remote computer |

## Description

This task will list the time zone bias on one or more remote computers. The *bias* is the difference between Universal Time Coordinate (UTC, also referred to as Greenwich Mean Time, or GMT) and the computer's current local time. For example, the West Coast of the United States uses the bias -8:00 to represent eight hours earlier than UTC.

Time zone adjustment is an important configuration step because many Windows operations, especially the Kerberos authentication protocol, are time-sensitive. Ensuring proper time zone configuration will ensure proper local time display on local computers. However, manually ensuring that all computers are properly set can be time-consuming. Although using a script to *change* the time zone setting is technically difficult, using a script to *audit* the setting is relatively straightforward, allowing you to quickly identify incorrectly configured computers that need manual correction.

## Performing This Task Manually

To perform the task manually on a computer running Windows XP Professional, follow these steps:

1. Double-click the clock display in the System Notification area of the Taskbar, or double-click Date And Time from Control Panel.

2. In the Date And Time Properties dialog box, select the Time Zone tab.

3. Review the time zone setting.

4. Click OK.

As you can see, this task becomes a bit time-consuming to perform manually beyond a couple of computers. Using a script to locate incorrectly configured computers is much more efficient.

## Example

There are three basic ways to use this tool. To target only a single remote computer named ClientA, you would use this code:

```
ListTimeZone.wsf /computer:ClientA
```

You can also target a list of computers from a text file. The text file is expected to contain one computer name per line, with no other information in the file. Assuming the file is named C:\Computers.txt, you would use this syntax:

```
ListTimeZone.wsf /list:C:\Computers.txt
```

Finally, you can target an entire organizational unit of computer accounts. If your domain contains an OU named West, you would use the following syntax:

```
ListTimeZone.wsf /container:west
```

Note that the */container* argument will work only against the default domain of the computer running the script. In other words, the OU specified must exist within the same domain that the computer running the script belongs to. If the specified OU has nested OUs, you can include their computer accounts as well by specifying one additional argument:

```
ListTimeZone.wsf /container:west /recurse
```

Additional arguments provide more functionality to the command; see the following section.

## Syntax

This script can be executed as a command-line utility. Set CScript.exe to be your default script processor, as described in Chapter 3.

| | |
|---|---|
| /list:path<br>/computer:name<br>/container:name | One and only one of these is required by the script. Use */list* to target a list of computers contained within a text file. Use */computer* to target a single computer. Use */container* to target an organizational unit within Active Directory. |
| /recurse | When used with */container*, also targets computers contained within nested OUs. |

| | |
|---|---|
| /ping | Verifies the connectivity to all targeted computers prior to attempting a connection. Using this argument will reduce the timeout wait when one or more computers cannot be reached on the network. |
| /log:path | Logs unreachable computer names to the specified file. This file can then be used later, along with the */list* argument, to retry these computers. |
| /verbose | Causes the script to display more detailed, step-by-step status messages. Omitting this argument will result in a more compact, readable display of time zone settings on the targeted computers. |

You can run this script with the */?* parameter to display the command's syntax.

## Under the Hood

This script uses the *FileSystemObject* to read computer names when the */list* argument is specified and uses Active Directory Services Interface (ADSI) to retrieve computer names when the */container* argument is specified. The script contains a subroutine named *WorkWithOU* that calls itself recursively (that is, it calls itself over and over) to process nested OUs when the */recurse* argument is specified. The real work of the script is performed by a relatively small section of VBScript code:

```
Dim oObject, cObjects
On Error Resume Next
Verbose " Attempting to retrieve time zone from " & sName
Set cObjects = QueryWMI(sName,"\root\cimv2","Select * from Win32_TimeZone","","")
If Not IsObject(cObjects) Then
 WScript.Echo " *** Error connecting to WMI on " & sName
 LogBadConnect(sName)
Else
 For Each oObject In cObjects
  WScript.Echo sName & ": " & oObject.Bias
 Next
End If
```

The current computer name is contained in the variable *sName*. The script uses a function named *QueryWMI()* to retrieve the *Win32_TimeZone* class and displays its *Bias* property as script output.

Notice that the bias reported by the script is listed in minutes, not in hours; you can divide the reported bias by 60 to determine the number of hours between the computer's configured time zone and UTC.

# Troubleshooting

Permissions and connectivity are the primary problems you're likely to encounter with this script. Ensure that the account running the script has administrative permissions on targeted computers and that network connectivity is available to all targeted computers. (Specify the */ping* argument to allow the script to more easily handle unreachable computers.)

# To Learn More

- Learn more about the *Win32_TimeZone* class at *http://msdn.microsoft.com/ library/default.asp?url=/library/en-us/wmisdk/wmi/win32_timezone.asp.*

- Read more about time issues and how they can affect the Windows operations at *http://labmice.techtarget.com/windows2000/timesynch.htm.*

## Chapter 6
# Server Management

Server management is obviously a broad category. For this chapter, I provide information specific to the Shadow Copy functionality of Microsoft® Windows Server™ 2003. Tasks automated in this chapter include:

- Enabling Volume Shadow Copy on a specified volume on one or more servers

- Inventorying Shadow Copy information on one or more servers

# Enable Shadow Copy

> **On the CD**   The sample script can be found on the CD that accompanies this book at \Chap6\MakeShadowCopy\MakeShadowCopy.wsf.

| Operating System | Supported? | Prerequisites |
|---|---|---|
| Microsoft Windows® 2000 family | No | ■  Windows Script Host (WSH) 5.6 or later |
| Windows XP Professional | No | ■  Microsoft Windows Management Instrumentation (WMI) |
| Windows Server 2003 family | Yes | ■  Administrative permission on targeted computers |
| | | ■  Network connectivity to each remote computer |

## Description

The Windows Server 2003 Shadow Copy functionality is enabled on a per-volume basis (although Shadow Copies are made only of files residing in shared folders within that volume). This task creates a single Shadow Copy for a specified volume on one or more servers. Using Shadow Copies is recommended because it allows a user to retrieve an older version of a file on her own—she doesn't have to contact your organization's help desk and request that a backup tape be used to restore a previous version of a file.

## Performing This Task Manually

Creating a Shadow Copy for a specific volume isn't difficult, but it becomes time-consuming when you must perform this task on multiple computers. To manually enable Shadow Copy, follow these steps:

1. Right-click the desired volume in My Computer, and select Properties from the shortcut menu.

2. Select the Shadow Copies tab. You can manage the Shadow Copy feature on *all* volumes, no matter which volume you right-clicked.

3. Select the desired volume from the list. The list indicates how many shared folders are available on the volume.

4. Click Enable to enable the Shadow Copies feature.

5. Read the information presented in the Enable Shadow Copies dialog box, and then click Yes.

After Shadow Copies is enabled, you can create a new Shadow Copy by clicking the Create Now button in the volume's Properties dialog box.

# Example

You can use this tool in three ways. First, you can target a single remote computer named ServerA and create a Shadow Copy for the C:\ volume:

```
MakeShadowCopy.wsf /computer:ServerA /volume:C:\
```

Second, you can target a list of computers from a text file. The text file is expected to contain one computer name per line, with no other information in the file. Assuming the file is named C:\Computers.txt, you would use this syntax to create a Shadow Copy on the E volume of each server:

```
MakeShadowCopy.wsf /list:C:\Computers.txt /volume:E:\
```

Third, you can target an entire organizational unit (OU) of computer accounts. If your domain contains an OU named West, you would use the following syntax:

```
MakeShadowCopy.wsf /container:west /volume:E:\
```

Note that the /container argument will work only against the default domain of the computer running the script. In other words, the OU specified must exist within the same domain that the computer running the script belongs to. If the specified OU has nested OUs, you can include their computer accounts as well by specifying one additional argument:

```
MakeShadowCopy.wsf /container:west /recurse /volume:E:\
```

Additional arguments provide extra functionality to the command, as described in the following section titled "Syntax."

# Syntax

This script can be executed as a command-line utility. Set CScript.exe to be your default script processor, as described in Chapter 3, "Working with VBScript."

| | |
|---|---|
| /list:path<br><br>/computer:name<br><br>/container:name | One and only one of these is required by the script. Use /list to target a list of computers contained within a text file. Use /computer to target a single computer. Use /container to target an organizational unit within Active Directory®. |
| /volume:Letter:\ | Specifies the volume on which to create a Shadow Copy. The volume name should be specified as a drive letter, followed by a colon and a backslash. |

| | |
|---|---|
| /recurse | When used with *container*, also targets computers contained within nested OUs. |
| /ping | Verifies the connectivity to all targeted computers prior to attempting a connection. Using this argument will reduce the timeout wait when one or more computers cannot be reached on the network. |
| /log:path | Logs unreachable computer names to the specified file. This file can then be used later, along with the *list* argument, to retry these computers. This argument works only when used in conjunction with the *ping* argument. |
| /verbose | Causes the script to display more detailed, step-by-step status messages. |

You can run this script with the */?* parameter to display the command's syntax.

## Under the Hood

This script uses the *FileSystemObject* to read computer names when the */list* argument is specified and uses Active Directory Services Interface (ADSI) to retrieve computer names when the */container* argument is specified. The script contains a subroutine named *WorkWithOU*, which calls itself recursively (that is, it calls itself over and over) to process nested OUs when the */recurse* argument is specified. The real work of the script is performed by a relatively small section of VBScript code:

```
Dim oStorage, errResult, oWMIService
On Error Resume Next
Verbose " Attempting to set Shadow Copy on " & sName
Set oWMIService = GetObject("winmgmts:{impersonationLevel=impersonate}!\\" & sName &
"\root\cimv2")
If Err <> 0 Then
 WScript.Echo " *** Error connecting to " & sName
 WScript.Echo "      " & Err.Description
 LogBadConnect(sName)
 Else
 Set oStorage = oWMIService.Get("Win32_ShadowCopy")
 If Err <> 0 Then
  WScript.Echo " *** Couldn't get Shadow Copy services from " & sName
  WScript.Echo "      " & Err.Description
 Else
  ErrResult = oStorage.Create(WScript.Arguments.Named("volume"),"ClientAccessible")
  Verbose "  " & sName & ": " & errResult
 End If
End If
```

The current computer name is contained in the variable *sName*. Note that the script connects to the computer's *\root\cimv2* namespace in Microsoft Windows Management Instrumentation (WMI) and then retrieves the *Win32_ShadowCopy* class from that namespace. This class provides a method named *Create()* that accepts the volume name and a parameter; the parameter indicates that the created Shadow Copy should be accessible to clients. In Windows Server 2003, only *"ClientAccessible"* is used for the second parameter.

If you use this tool with the */verbose* argument, you'll see an error code number for each targeted server. A 0 (zero) means that the command completed successfully; anything else means it didn't. The following list provides some of the common error codes:

- **1** Access denied
- **2** Volume not found
- **4** Shadow Copies not supported (generally for removable or FAT volumes)
- **9** Maximum number of shadow copies reached

Other numbers indicate general failures on the part of the Shadow Copy provider within Windows itself.

## Troubleshooting

This script has the potential for three major types of errors. First, a remote computer won't be available. Second, you won't have permission to enable Shadow Copies. In either case, you'll see an error message that alerts you to the problem for that computer. Make sure you have the appropriate permissions and that the computer is reachable via the network from the computer running this script. Unreachable computers can optionally be logged to a text file for a later attempt, and you can speed up the script by specifying the */ping* argument.

Third, it's possible that an error will occur during the Shadow Copy enabling. In that case, an error code will be reported by the script, as just described.

## To Learn More

- To learn more about the Shadow Copies feature, consult the Help and Support Center within Windows Server 2003.
- You can also read more about Shadow Copies at *http://www.microsoft.com /windowsserver2003/techinfo/overview/scr.mspx*.
- Other script samples dealing with Shadow Copy can be found in the TechNet Script Center at *http://www.microsoft.com/technet/scriptcenter/scripts/shadow /default.mspx*.

# Inventory Shadow Copy

> **On the CD**   The sample script can be found on the CD that accompanies this book at \Chap6\ShadowCopyInventory\ShadowCopyInventory.wsf.

| Operating System | Supported? | Prerequisites |
|---|---|---|
| Windows 2000 family | No | ■ WSH 5.6 or later |
| Windows XP Professional | No | ■ WMI |
| Windows Server 2003 family | Yes | ■ Administrative permission on targeted computers |
| | | ■ Network connectivity to each remote computer |

## Description

This tool lists all Shadow Copy information for the specified server or servers. For each Shadow Copy on a server, the tool specifically lists the following items:

- **Volume name**   The volume on which the Shadow Copy exists.
- **State**   The Shadow Copy's current status. The script will display the status as a text string. Not all volumes provide state information; a blank will be displayed when this is the case.
- **Exposed name**   The file system name of the Shadow Copy when it is exposed to clients.
- **Count**   The number of shadow copies in the Shadow Copy set.

## Performing This Task Manually

Windows doesn't provide a detailed user interface that exposes the Volume Name, State, Exposed Name, and Count. You can use the Shadow Copies user interface (reachable by right-clicking a volume, selecting Properties, and selecting the Shadow Copies tab) to view available shadow copies on a given server and a given volume, but the status information is not available.

## Example

You can use this tool in three basic ways. First, you can target a single remote computer named ServerA:

```
ShadowCopyInventory.wsf /computer:ServerA
```

Second, you can target a list of computers from a text file. The text file is expected to contain one computer name per line, with no other information in the file. Assuming the file is named C:\Computers.txt, you would use this syntax:

```
ShadowCopyInventory.wsf /list:C:\Computers.txt
```

Third, you can target an entire organizational unit of computer accounts. If your domain contains an OU named West, you would use the following syntax:

```
ShadowCopyInventory.wsf /container:west
```

Note that the *container* argument will work only against the default domain of the computer running the script. In other words, the OU specified must exist within the same domain that the computer running the script belongs to. If the specified OU has nested OUs, you can include their computer accounts as well by specifying one additional argument:

```
ShadowCopyInventory.wsf /container:west /recurse
```

Additional arguments provide extra functionality to the command. See the following section titled "Syntax."

## Syntax

This script can be executed as a command-line utility. Set CScript.exe to be your default script processor, as described in Chapter 3.

| | |
|---|---|
| `/list:path`<br>`/computer:name`<br>`/container:name` | One and only one of these is required by the script. Use *list* to target a list of computers contained within a text file. Use *computer* to target a single computer. Use *container* to target an organizational unit within Active Directory. |
| `/recurse` | When used with *container*, also targets computers contained within nested OUs. |
| `/ping` | Verifies the connectivity to all targeted computers prior to attempting a connection. Using this argument will reduce the timeout wait when one or more computers cannot be reached on the network. |
| `/log:path` | Logs unreachable computer names to the specified file. This file can then be used later, along with the *list* argument, to retry these computers. This argument works only when used in conjunction with the *ping* argument. |
| `/verbose` | Causes the script to display more detailed, step-by-step status messages. |

You can run this script with the */?* parameter to display the command's syntax.

# Under the Hood

This script uses the *FileSystemObject* to read computer names when the */list* argument is specified and uses Active Directory Services Interface (ADSI) to retrieve computer names when the */container* argument is specified. The script contains a subroutine named *WorkWithOU*, which calls itself recursively (that is, it calls itself over and over) to process nested OUs when the */recurse* argument is specified. The real work of the script is performed by a relatively small section of VBScript code:

```
Dim oWMIService, cCopies, oCopy, sState
Verbose " Connecting to WMI on " & sName
Set cCopies = QueryWMI(sName,"root\cimv2","Select * From Win32_ShadowCopy","","")
If Not IsObject(cCopies)
 WScript.Echo " *** Could not retrieve shadow copies from " & sName
Else
 WScript.Echo ""
 WScript.Echo "Shadow copies on " & sName
 WScript.Echo "Volume,State,Name,Count"
 For Each oCopy In cCopies
  Select Case oCopy.State
   Case 0
    sState = "Unknown"
   Case 1
    sState = "Preparing"
   Case 2
    sState = "ProcessingPrepare"
   Case 3
    sState = "Prepared"
   Case 4
    sState = "ProcessingPrecommit"
   Case 5
    sState = "Precommitted"
   Case 6
    sState = "ProcessingCommit"
   Case 7
    sState = "Committed"
   Case 8
    sState = "ProcessingPostCommit"
   Case 9
    sState = "Created"
   Case 10
    sState = "Aborted"
   Case 11
    sState = "Deleted"
   Case 12
    sState = "Count"
   Case Else
    sState = "****"
  End Select
  WScript.Echo oCopy.VolumeName & "," & sState & "," & oCopy.ExposedName & ","
& oCopy.Count
 Next
End If
```

The current computer name is contained in the variable *sName*. Note that the script connects to the computer's *\root\cimv2* namespace in Windows Management Instrumentation (WMI) and then retrieves the *Win32_ShadowCopy* class from that namespace. Next, the script lists specific properties of that class for each instance retrieved. You can modify this script, if desired, to list other properties of each Shadow Copy.

Also note that this script will output most of its information (assuming you are not using the */verbose* argument) in a comma-delimited format. This allows you to run the script and capture its output to a text file, if you want, for use within a report. You can open the resulting file in an application such as Microsoft Excel to view the report in a columnar format. Use standard command-line redirection to capture the script's output to a text file.

## Troubleshooting

This script has the potential for two major types of errors. First, a remote computer won't be available. Second, you won't have permission to enable Shadow Copies. In either case, you'll see an error message that alerts you to the problem for that computer. Make sure you have the appropriate permissions and that the computer is reachable via the network from the computer running this script. Unreachable computers can optionally be logged to a text file for a later attempt, and you can speed up the script by specifying the */ping* argument.

## To Learn More

- To learn more about the Shadow Copies feature, consult the Help and Support Center within Windows Server 2003.

- You can also read more about Shadow Copies at *http://www.microsoft.com /windowsserver2003/techinfo/overview/scr.mspx*.

- Other script samples dealing with Shadow Copy can be found in the TechNet Script Center at *http://www.microsoft.com/technet/scriptcenter/scripts/shadow /default.mspx*.

Chapter 7

# Inventorying and Reporting

This chapter presents a set of automation tasks that don't actually *do* anything to the targeted system, but rather simply retrieve information for you, which helps you better understand what your current environment looks like, how it's configured, and so forth. Many of these tasks can't be easily performed manually, because Microsoft® Windows® doesn't include much in the way of cross-server reporting capabilities. Additionally, most of the scripts provided for this chapter provide the capability to output their information to comma-delimited files, which you can then open in an application such as Microsoft Excel. This output feature allows you to view information in a columnar format, or more easily export the information to a database or other reporting system.

Most of the scripts in this chapter work very similarly by querying a set of Microsoft Windows Management Instrumentation (WMI) instances and writing their properties to the screen or to the designated output file. You should therefore be able to review and modify these scripts, if desired, to provide reporting functionality not specifically listed in this chapter. Tasks automated in this chapter include:

- Listing installed hotfixes
- Listing event log entries
- Listing installed hardware
- Listing Internet Explorer configuration information
- Listing network adapter configuration information
- Listing installed service packs
- Listing scheduled tasks
- Listing installed software

# List Installed Hotfixes

> **On the CD**   The sample script can be found on the CD that accompanies this book at \Chap7\Listhotfixes\ListHotfixes.wsf.

| Operating System | Supported? | Prerequisites |
|---|---|---|
| Microsoft Windows 2000 family | Yes | ■ WSH 5.6 or later |
| | | ■ WMI |
| Microsoft Windows XP Professional | Yes | ■ Administrative permission on targeted computers |
| Microsoft Windows Server™ 2003 family | Yes | ■ Network connectivity to each remote computer |

## Description

Freely available tools like the Microsoft Baseline Security Analyzer (MBSA) can easily list the various updates or hotfixes that *aren't* installed on your computers, but some auditing activities require a report of those updates that *are* installed, along with the date they were installed. MBSA's graphical user interface (and even its command-line version) doesn't provide this information in a format that lends itself to use within an audit report; however, the script provided in this chapter, ListHotfixes.wsf, does.

## Performing This Task Manually

There is no manual way to obtain a complete list of installed hotfixes. Most but not all hotfixes are listed in the computer's Add Or Remove Programs Control Panel application. You can also obtain a list of installed hotfixes from a variety of third-party tools and tools provided by Microsoft®, but the Windows® operating system doesn't provide a ready means for obtaining such a list.

## Example

As with many of the tools in this book, you can use this one in three different ways. First, you can use it to target a single remote computer named ServerA, for example:

```
ListHotfixes.wsf /computer:ServerA
```

Second, you can target a list of computers from a text file. The text file is expected to contain one computer name per line and no other information. Assuming the file is named C:\Computers.txt, you would use this syntax:

```
ListHotfixes.wsf /list:C:\Computers.txt
```

Third, you can target an entire organizational unit of computer accounts. If your domain contains an OU named West, you would use the following syntax:

```
ListHotfixes.wsf /container:west
```

Note that the */container* argument will work against only the default domain of the computer running the script. In other words, the OU specified must exist within the same domain that the computer running the script belongs to. If the specified OU has nested OUs, you can include their computer accounts as well by specifying one additional argument:

```
ListHotfixes.wsf /container:west /recurse
```

Additional arguments provide extra functionality to the command; see the following section titled "Syntax." Specifically, the following will write the tool's output to a comma-delimited file named C:\MyOutput.csv:

```
ListHotfixes.wsf /container:west /recurse /output:C:\MyOutput.csv
```

## Syntax

This script can be executed as a command-line utility. Set CScript.exe to be your default script processor, as described in Chapter 3, "Working with VBScript."

| | |
|---|---|
| `/list:path`<br>`/computer:name`<br>`/container:name` | One and only one of these is required by the script. Use */list* to target a list of computers contained within a text file. Use */computer* to target a single computer. Use */container* to target an organizational unit within Microsoft Active Directory®. |
| `/output:path` | Specifies the file to which the tool's output should be written. The file specified will be overwritten if it already exists. |
| `/recurse` | When used with */container*, also targets computers contained within nested OUs. |
| `/ping` | Verifies the connectivity to all targeted computers prior to attempting a connection. Using this argument will reduce the timeout wait when one or more computers cannot be reached on the network. |
| `/log:path` | Logs unreachable computer names to the specified file. This file can then be used later, along with the */list* argument, to retry these computers. Requires that you specify the */ping* argument. |
| `/verbose` | Causes the script to display more detailed, step-by-step status messages. |

You can run this script with the */?* parameter to display the command's syntax.

# Under the Hood

This script relies on Windows Management Instrumentation (WMI) to perform the bulk of its work. The workhorse section of this script is shown here:

```
Dim cFixes, oFix, sOutput
Verbose " Connecting to WMI on " & sName
If WScript.Arguments.Named.Exists("output") Then

LogFile(WScript.Arguments.Named("output"),"computer,hotfix,installdate,installedby",
True)
Else
    WScript.Echo "Computer, hotfix ID, install date, installed by"
End If
Set cFixes = QueryWMI(sName,"root\cimv2","Select * From Win32_QuickFixEngineering","
",""")
If Not IsObject(cFixes) Then
    WScript.Echo " *** Couldn't connect to WMI on " & sName
Else
    For Each oFix In cFixes
        sOutput = sName & "," & oFix.HotFixID & "," & oFix.InstallDate & ","
& oFix.InstalledBy
        If WScript.Arguments.Named.Exists("output") Then
            LogFile(WScript.Arguments.Named("output"),sOutput,False)
        Else
            WScript.Echo sOutput
        End If
    Next
```

The current computer name is contained in the variable *sName*. Note that the script connects to the computer's \*root*\*cimv2* namespace in Microsoft Windows Management Instrumentation (WMI), and then retrieves the *Win32_QuickFixEngineering* instances from that namespace. This query returns a list of all installed hotfixes; the script then looks at each one and outputs its relevant information, using properties of the class.

# Troubleshooting

As with most scripts, connecting to the remote computer (or computers) and having the permissions necessary to list hotfixes (generally, local Administrator permissions) leaves open the potential for errors. This script will catch most errors and display an appropriate message, moving on to the next targeted computer if possible.

Because this script has the option to output to a file using the */output* argument, it's also possible that you'll receive an error if you specify that the file be created in a location where you don't have the necessary file system permissions, or if you specify a file name that already exists and you don't have permission to delete and re-create that file. In both cases, the script will attempt to continue, but you'll receive errors each time the log file access is attempted. To break the script's execution, press Ctrl+C in the command-line window.

## To Learn More

- You can download individual hotfixes from the Windows Update Catalog, or use the Windows Update Web site (*http://windowsupdate.microsoft.com*) to automatically apply needed updates to a particular computer.

- The TechNet Script Center includes other script samples that demonstrate how to work with hotfixes and service packs: *http://www.microsoft.com/technet /scriptcenter/scripts/srvpacks/default.mspx*.

# List Event Log Entries

 **On the CD**  The sample script can be found on the CD that accompanies this book at \Chap7\ListEvents\ListEvents.wsf.

| Operating System | Supported? | Prerequisites |
|---|---|---|
| Windows 2000 family | Yes | ■ WSH 5.6 or later |
| Windows XP Professional | Yes | ■ WMI |
| Windows Server 2003 family | Yes | ■ Administrative permission on targeted computers |
| | | ■ Network connectivity to each remote computer |

## Description

Quickly listing event logs—and having the ability to archive them, if desired—is a core administrative task in Windows. A number of third-party companies produce tools to assist with this task; Microsoft released Microsoft Operations Manager (MOM) in part to help better manage event logs. This script provides the simplest possible event log management functionality, gathering all events from a designated log on one or more computers and either displaying those events on the screen or logging them to a text file you specify.

## Performing This Task Manually

The Windows Event Viewer provides the means to review events on remote computers. However, the Windows operating system does not provide a built-in way to gather events from multiple computers into a single display or report. As I've mentioned, MOM and a number of third-party utilities from companies such as Winternals Software and NetIQ provide high-end event log management.

To view a remote computer's event log using Windows Event Viewer, follow these steps:

1. Right-click My Computer and select Manage from the context menu.

2. Right-click Computer Management (Local) and select Connect To Another Computer.

3. Enter the desired computer name, or browse for the computer.

4. Expand the System Tools node.

5.  Select the Event Viewer folder.

6.  To export an event log to a file, right-click the event log and select Save Log File As.

This process is obviously cumbersome when you want to pull and archive events from a number of computers.

# Example

As with many of the tools in this book, you can use this one in three different ways. First, you can use it to target a single remote computer named ServerA, for example:

```
ListEvents.wsf /computer:ServerA /evtlog:Application
```

Note that the *log* argument is used to specify the log you want to pull. Valid entries include *Application*, *Security*, and *System*; servers might have additional logs available for DNS, Active Directory, and so forth.

Second, you can target a list of computers from a text file. The text file is expected to contain one computer name per line and no other information. Assuming the file is named C:\Computers.txt, you would use this syntax:

```
ListEvents.wsf /list:C:\Computers.txt /evtlog:Security
```

Third, you can target an entire organizational unit (OU) of computer accounts. If your domain contains an OU named West, you would use the following syntax:

```
ListEvents.wsf /container:west /evtlog:System
```

Note that the *container* argument will work against only the default domain of the computer running the script. In other words, the OU specified must exist within the same domain that the computer running the script belongs to. If the specified OU has nested OUs, you can include their computer accounts as well by specifying one additional argument:

```
ListEvents.wsf /container:west /recurse /log:Application
```

Additional arguments provide more functionality to the command. See the following section titled "Syntax." Specifically, the following will write the tool's output to a comma-delimited file named C:\MyOutput.csv:

```
ListEvents.wsf /container:west /recurse /output:C:\MyOutput.csv /evtlog:System
```

# Syntax

This script can be executed as a command-line utility. You should set CScript.exe to be your default script processor, as described in Chapter 3.

| | |
|---|---|
| `/list:path`<br>`/computer:name`<br>`/container:name` | One and only one of these is required by the script. Use /list to target a list of computers contained within a text file. Use /computer to target a single computer. Use /container to target an organizational unit within Active Directory. |
| `/output:path` | Specifies the file to which the tool's output should be written. The file specified will be overwritten if it already exists. |
| `/evtlog:logname` | Required. Specifies the log to pull. Valid entries for *logname* include *System*, *Application*, and *Security*, although others might also be available depending on the services a particular computer is running. |
| `/recurse` | When used with /container, also targets computers contained within nested OUs. |
| `/ping` | Verifies the connectivity to all targeted computers prior to attempting a connection. Using this argument will reduce the timeout wait when one or more computers cannot be reached on the network. |
| `/log:path` | Logs unreachable computer names to the specified file. This file can then be used later, along with the /list argument, to retry these computers. Requires that you specify the /ping argument. |
| `/verbose` | Causes the script to display more detailed, step-by-step status messages. |

You can run this script with the */?* parameter to display the command's syntax.

# Under the Hood

This script relies on Microsoft Windows Management Instrumentation (WMI) to perform the bulk of its work. The workhorse section of this script is shown here:

```
Dim cEvents, oEvent, sOutput
Verbose " Connecting to WMI on " & sName
Set cEvents = QueryWMI(sName,"root\cimv2","Select * From Win32_NTLogEvent WHERE
LogFile = ' " & wscript.arguments.named("evtlog") & "'","","")
If Not IsObject(cEvents) Then
    WScript.Echo " *** Couldn't connect to WMI or get events on " & sName
Else
    For Each oEvent In cEvents
        sOutput = sName & "," & oEvent.Category & "," & oEvent.eventcode & ","
```

```
& oEvent.message & "," & oEvent.sourcename & "," & oEvent.timewritten & ","
& oEvent.type
        If WScript.Arguments.Named.Exists("output") Then
            LogFile WScript.Arguments.Named("output"),sOutput,False
        Else
            WScript.Echo sOutput
        End If
    Next
End If
```

The current computer name is contained in the variable *sName*. Note that the script connects to the computer's \*root*\*cimv2* namespace in Windows Management Instrumentation, and then retrieves the *Win32_NTLogEvent* instances from that namespace. Each instance of *Win32_NTLogEvent* represents a single event entry; notice that the query limits the instances returned to those that have a *LogFile* property equal to the log specified in the /*log* argument. Thus, the query returns all events for the specified log.

## Troubleshooting

As with most scripts, connecting to the remote computer or computers and having the permissions necessary to list events (generally, local Administrator permissions) leaves open the potential for errors. This script will catch most errors and display an appropriate message. It then moves on to the next targeted computer if possible.

Because this script has the option to output to a file by using the /*output* argument, you might receive an error when you specify that the file be created in a location where you don't have the necessary file system permissions, or when you specify a file name that already exists and you don't have permission to delete and re-create that file. In both cases, the script will attempt to continue, but you'll receive errors each time the log file access is attempted. To break the script's execution, press Ctrl+C in the command-line window.

## To Learn More

- Read more about Windows Event Viewer in the Windows Help and Support Center.

- The TechNet Script Center includes other script samples that demonstrate how to work with event logs: *http://www.microsoft.com/technet/scriptcenter/scripts /logs/eventlog/default.mspx*.

# List Installed Hardware

**On the CD**    The sample script can be found on the CD that accompanies this book at \Chap7\ListHardware\ListHardware.wsf.

| Operating System | Supported? | Prerequisites |
|---|---|---|
| Windows 2000 family | Yes | ■ WSH 5.6 or later |
| Windows XP Professional | Yes | ■ WMI |
| Windows Server 2003 family | Yes | ■ Administrative permission on targeted computers |
| | | ■ Network connectivity to each remote computer |

## Description

This script lists all Plug and Play hardware installed on one or more computers. This is useful for discovering which computers contain a particular piece of hardware, for example. Simply log the script's output to a log file (using the */output* argument) and then use a text editor like Microsoft Notepad or Microsoft Word to search for the specific piece of hardware you're interested in. The search will identify each computer containing that hardware.

## Performing This Task Manually

Reviewing installed hardware is difficult using Windows system's graphical user interface. Device Manager (accessible by right-clicking My Computer and then selecting Manage) displays all installed hardware devices but doesn't provide any means for producing a report. Windows provides no built-in means for displaying all hardware that is installed on multiple computers all at once.

Systems management software, such as Microsoft Systems Management Server (SMS), typically includes hardware inventory capabilities. These capabilities usually install an inventory agent on each managed computer, allowing the agent to inventory hardware and forward the results to a central database for reporting.

## Example

You can use this script in three different ways. First, you can use it to target a single remote computer named ServerA, for example:

```
ListHardware.wsf /computer:ServerA
```

Second, you can target a list of computers from a text file. The text file is expected to contain one computer name per line and no other information. Assuming the file is named C:\Computers.txt, you would use this syntax:

```
ListHardware.wsf /list:C:\Computers.txt
```

Third, you can target an entire organizational unit of computer accounts. If your domain contains an OU named West, you would use the following syntax:

```
ListHardware.wsf /container:west
```

Note that the *container* argument will work against only the default domain of the computer running the script. In other words, the OU specified must exist within the same domain that the computer running the script belongs to. If the specified OU has nested OUs, you can include their computer accounts as well by specifying one additional argument:

```
ListHardware.wsf /container:west /recurse
```

Additional arguments provide more functionality to the command. (See the following section titled "Syntax." Specifically, the following will write the tool's output to a comma-delimited file named C:\MyOutput.csv:

```
ListHotfixes.wsf /container:west /recurse /output:C:\MyOutput.csv
```

## Syntax

This script can be executed as a command-line utility. Set CScript.exe to be your default script processor, as described in Chapter 3.

| | |
|---|---|
| `/list:path`<br>`/computer:name`<br>`/container:name` | One and only one of these is required by the script. Use */list* to target a list of computers contained within a text file. Use */computer* to target a single computer. Use */container* to target an organizational unit within Active Directory. |
| `/output:path` | Specifies the file to which the tool's output should be written. The file specified will be overwritten if it already exists. |
| `/recurse` | When used with */container*, also targets computers contained within sub-OUs. |
| `/ping` | Verifies the connectivity to all targeted computers prior to attempting a connection. Using this argument will reduce the timeout wait when one or more computers cannot be reached on the network. |

| /log:path | Logs unreachable computer names to the specified file. This file can then be used later, along with the */list* argument, to retry these computers. Requires that you specify the */ping* argument. |
|---|---|
| /verbose | Causes the script to display more detailed, step-by-step status messages. |

You can run this script with the */?* parameter to display the command's syntax.

# Under the Hood

Windows Management Instrumentation (WMI) is used to query the installed hardware:

```
Dim cItems, oItem, sOutput
Verbose " Connecting to WMI on " & sName
Set cItems = QueryWMI(sName,"root\cimv2","Select * From Win32_PnPEntity","","")
If Not IsObject(cItems) Then
    WScript.Echo " *** Couldn't connect to WMI on " & sName
Else
    For Each oItem In cItems
        sOutput = sName & "," & oItem.description & "," & oItem.deviceid & ","
& oItem.name & "," & oItem.service
        If WScript.Arguments.Named.Exists("output") Then
            LogFile WScript.Arguments.Named("output"),sOutput,False
        Else
            WScript.Echo sOutput
        End If
    Next
End If
```

The current computer name is contained in the variable *sName*. Note that the script connects to the computer's *\root\cimv2* namespace in Windows Management Instrumentation (WMI), and then retrieves the *Win32_PnPEntity* instances from that namespace. Each instance of this class represents a single Plug and Play *entity*, or device. The properties of the entity–*DeviceID*, *Name*, and *Service*–are included in the script's output. You could modify this script to query a different class, such as *Win32_POTSModem*, which represents installed modems. If you modify the class, be sure to check the class in the WMI documentation to see what properties are available. For *Win32_POTSModem*, for example, the properties *DeviceID*, *DriverDate*, and *DeviceType* might contain relevant information.

# Troubleshooting

As with most scripts, connecting to the remote computer or computers and having the permissions necessary to list installed hardware opens up the potential for errors. This script will catch most errors and display an appropriate message, and then move on to the next targeted computer if possible.

Because this script has the option to output to a file using the */output* argument, you might receive an error when you specify that the file be created in a location where you don't have the necessary file system permissions, or when you specify a file name that already exists and you don't have permission to delete and re-create that file. In both cases, the script will attempt to continue, but you'll receive errors each time the log file access is attempted. To break the script's execution, press Ctrl+C in the command-line window.

## To Learn More

- The TechNet Script Center includes other script samples that demonstrate how to work with hardware: *http://www.microsoft.com/technet/scriptcenter/scripts /hardware/default.mspx*.

# List Internet Explorer Configuration

**On the CD**   The sample script can be found on the CD that accompanies this book at \Chap7\ListIEConfig\ListIEConfig.wsf.

| Operating System | Supported? | Prerequisites |
|---|---|---|
| Windows 2000 family | Yes | ■ WSH 5.6 or later |
| Windows XP Professional | Yes | ■ WMI |
| Windows Server 2003 family | Yes | ■ Administrative permission on targeted computers |
|  |  | ■ Network connectivity to each remote computer |

## Description

This script connects to multiple computers and uses WMI to obtain their Internet Explorer configurations. Like other scripts in this chapter, this script offers an */output* argument to write the script's output to a text file; however, this script creates a formatted report rather than a comma-separated value (CSV) file, because Internet Explorer's configuration is more complex than can be easily represented in a single CSV file.

## Performing This Task Manually

There is no manual way to retrieve all this Internet Explorer configuration information in one place. Much of this configuration information can be obtained from the Internet Options Control Panel application. However, some information, such as the installed version of Internet Explorer and the product ID, can be obtained by opening Internet Explorer and selecting About from the Help menu. In any event, there is no built-in means for retrieving this information from multiple computers at once.

## Example

This script can be used in three different ways. First, you can use it to target a single remote computer named ServerA, for example:

```
ListIEConfig.wsf /computer:ServerA
```

Second, you can target a list of computers from a text file. The text file is expected to contain one computer name per line and no other information. Assuming the file is named C:\Computers.txt, you would use this syntax:

```
ListIEConfig.wsf /list:C:\Computers.txt
```

Third, you can target an entire organizational unit of computer accounts. If your domain contains an OU named West, you would use the following syntax:

```
ListIEConfig.wsf /container:west
```

Note that the *container* argument will work against only the default domain of the computer running the script. In other words, the OU specified must exist within the same domain that the computer running the script belongs to. If the specified OU has nested OUs, you can include their computer accounts as well by specifying one additional argument:

```
ListIEConfig.wsf /container:west /recurse
```

Additional arguments provide more functionality to the command; see the following section titled "Syntax." Specifically, the following will write the tool's output to a text file named C:\MyOutput.txt.

```
ListHotfixes.wsf /container:west /recurse /output:C:\MyOutput.txt
```

# Syntax

This script can be executed as a command-line utility. Set CScript.exe to be your default script processor, as described in Chapter 3.

| | |
|---|---|
| `/list:path`<br>`/computer:name`<br>`/container:name` | One and only one of these is required by the script. Use */list* to target a list of computers contained within a text file. Use */computer* to target a single computer. Use */container* to target an organizational unit within Active Directory. |
| `/output:path` | Specifies the file to which the tool's output should be written. The file specified will be overwritten if it already exists. |
| `/recurse` | When used with */container*, also targets computers contained within nested OUs. |
| `/ping` | Verifies the connectivity to all targeted computers prior to attempting a connection. Using this argument will reduce the timeout wait when one or more computers cannot be reached on the network. |
| `/log:path` | Logs unreachable computer names to the specified file. This file can then be used later, along with the */list* argument, to retry these computers. Requires that you specify the */ping* argument. |
| `/verbose` | Causes the script to display more detailed, step-by-step status messages. |

You can run this script with the */?* parameter to display the command's syntax.

## Under the Hood

This script uses WMI to retrieve Internet Explorer information. It begins by querying various classes from WMI's *root\cimv2\Applications\MicrosoftIE* namespace:

```
Set cCache = QueryWMI(sName,"root\cimv2\Applications\MicrosoftIE","Select * From
MicrosoftIE_Cache","","")
Set cCOM = QueryWMI(sName,"root\cimv2\Applications\MicrosoftIE","Select * From
MicrosoftIE_Object","","")
Set cConnection = QueryWMI(sName,"root\cimv2\Applications\MicrosoftIE","Select *
From MicrosoftIE_ConnectionSettings","","")
Set cFileVersion = QueryWMI(sName,"root\cimv2\Applications\MicrosoftIE","Select *
From MicrosoftIE_FileVersion","","")
Set cLAN = QueryWMI(sName,"root\cimv2\Applications\MicrosoftIE","Select * From
MicrosoftIE_LANSettings","","")
Set cZones = QueryWMI(sName,"root\cimv2\Applications\MicrosoftIE","Select * From
MicrosoftIE_Security","","")
Set cSummary = QueryWMI(sName,"root\cimv2\Applications\MicrosoftIE","Select * From
MicrosoftIE_Summary","","")
```

The current computer name is contained in the variable *sName*; the QueryWMI function is built into the script and does the work of connecting to the remote computer's WMI service and retrieving the query results. For each class, the script writes the key class properties:

```
sOutput = sOutput & "  COM Settings" & vbCrLf
For Each oItem In cCOM
   sOutput = sOutput & "    Code base: " & oItem.CodeBase
   sOutput = sOutput & "    Program file: " & oItem.ProgramFile
   sOutput = sOutput & "    Status: " & oItem.Status
Next
```

The *sOutput* variable contains all the script's output. After the script, ListIEConfig.wsf, completely populates *sOutput* with all the desired configuration information, *sOutput* is written to the screen or, if the */output* argument is specified, to a text file.

## Troubleshooting

As with most scripts, connecting to the remote computer or computers and having the permissions necessary to retrieve the configuration information leaves open the potential for errors. This script will catch most errors and display an appropriate message, and then move on to the next targeted computer if possible.

Because this script has the option to output to a file by using the */output* argument, you might receive an error if you specify that the file be created in a location where you don't have the necessary file system permissions, or if you specify a file name that already exists and you don't have permission to delete and re-create that file. In both cases, the script will attempt to continue, but you'll receive errors each time the log file access is attempted. To break the script's execution, press Ctrl+C in the command-line window.

## To Learn More

- The TechNet Script Center includes other script samples that demonstrate how to work with the Internet Explorer configuration: *http://www.microsoft.com /technet/scriptcenter/scripts/desktop/ie/default.mspx.*

# List Network Adapter Configuration

> **On the CD**    The sample script can be found on the CD that accompanies this book at \Chap7\ListNICConfig\ListNICConfig.wsf.

| Operating System | Supported? | Prerequisites |
|---|---|---|
| Windows 2000 family | Yes | ■ WSH 5.6 or later |
| Windows XP Professional | Yes | ■ WMI |
| Windows Server 2003 family | Yes | ■ Administrative permission on targeted computers |
| | | ■ Network connectivity to each remote computer |

## Description

This task retrieves key network adapter configuration information—such IP address, DHCP status, DNS domain and host name—from one or more computers and displays that information on the screen. By using the *output* argument, the script can generate this information to a file instead. This task is useful for quickly learning which computers on your network have particular IP addresses, inventorying Media Access Control (MAC) addresses, and so on.

## Performing This Task Manually

Some of the information retrieved by this script might already be accessible on your network through a dynamic name resolution service such as Dynamic DNS or WINS (Windows Internet Name Service), both of which store computer name-to-IP address mappings. These services might also store the MAC address of each computer. However, using these services to create a report might be difficult or impossible depending upon the server software's capabilities.

You can retrieve all this information for a single computer by running the Windows *Ipconfig* command on that computer followed by the */all* argument:

```
Ipconfig /all
```

However, using this approach to obtain information from multiple computers can be time-consuming.

# Example

As with many of the tools in this book, you can use this one in three different ways. First, you can use it to target a single remote computer named ServerA, for example:

```
ListNICConfig.wsf /computer:ServerA
```

Second, you can target a list of computers from a text file. The text file is expected to contain one computer name per line and no other information. Assuming the file is named C:\Computers.txt, you would use this syntax:

```
ListNICConfig.wsf /list:C:\Computers.txt
```

Third, you can target an entire organizational unit of computer accounts. If your domain contains an OU named West, you would use the following syntax:

```
ListNICConfig.wsf /container:west
```

Note that the *container* argument will work against only the default domain of the computer running the script. In other words, the OU specified must exist within the same domain that the computer running the script belongs to. If the specified OU has nested OUs, you can include their computer accounts as well by specifying one additional argument:

```
ListNICConfig.wsf /container:west /recurse
```

Additional arguments provide more functionality to the command; see following section titled "Syntax." Specifically, the following will write the tool's output to a comma-delimited file named C:\MyOutput.csv:

```
ListNICConfig.wsf /container:west /recurse /output:C:\MyOutput.csv
```

# Syntax

This script can be executed as a command-line utility. Set CScript.exe to be your default script processor, as described in Chapter 3.

| | |
|---|---|
| /list:path<br>/computer:name<br>/container:name | One and only one of these is required by the script. Use */list* to target a list of computers contained within a text file. Use */computer* to target a single computer. Use */container* to target an organizational unit within Active Directory. |
| /output:path | Specifies the file to which the tool's output should be written. The file specified will be overwritten if it already exists. |
| /recurse | When used with */container*, also targets computers contained within nested OUs. |

| /ping | Verifies the connectivity to all targeted computers prior to attempting a connection. Using this argument will reduce the timeout wait when one or more computers cannot be reached on the network. |
| /log:path | Logs unreachable computer names to the specified file. This file can then be used later, along with the /list argument, to retry these computers. Requires that you specify the /ping argument. |
| /verbose | Causes the script to display more detailed, step-by-step status messages. |

You can run this script with the /? parameter to display the command's syntax.

# Under the Hood

This script relies on Windows Management Instrumentation (WMI) to perform the bulk of its work. The workhorse section of this script is shown here:

```
Dim cNICs, oNIC, sOutput
Set cNICs = QueryWMI(sName,"root\cimv2","Select * From Win32_NetworkAdapterConfigura
tion","","")
If Not IsObject(cNICs) Then
    WScript.Echo " *** Couldn't connect to WMI on " & sName
Else
    For Each oNIC In cNICs
        sOutput = sName & "," & oNIC.DefaultIPGateway & "," & oNIC.DHCPEnabled & ","
& oNIC.DNSDomain & "," & oNIC.DNSHostName & "," & oNIC.IPAddress & ","
& oNIC.MACAddress
        If WScript.Arguments.Named.Exists("output") Then
            LogFile WScript.Arguments.Named("output"),sOutput,False
        Else
            WScript.Echo sOutput
        End If
    Next
End If
```

The current computer name is contained in the variable *sName*. Note that the script connects to the computer's \*root*\*cimv2* namespace in Windows Management Instrumentation (WMI) and then retrieves the *Win32_NetworkAdapterConfiguration* instances from that namespace. This query returns a list of all installed adapters and their configurations. The script then simply looks at each one and outputs its relevant information, using properties of the class.

Note that a computer can have multiple adapters, and that each adapter can have multiple configurations. This script supports these scenarios and will list each unique adapter configuration combination independently. You could also modify the script to list other properties of interest; refer to the WMI documentation on the *Win32_NetworkAdapterConfiguration* class for more details about available properties.

# Troubleshooting

As with most scripts, connecting to the remote computer (or computers) and having the permissions necessary to list network adapter configurations (generally, local Administrator permissions) leaves open the potential for errors. This script will catch most errors and display an appropriate message, and then move on to the next targeted computer if possible.

Because this script has the option to output to a file by using the */output* argument, you might receive an error if you specify that the file be created in a location where you don't have the necessary file system permissions, or if you specify a file name that already exists and you don't have permission to delete and re-create that file. In both cases, the script will attempt to continue, but you'll receive errors each time the log file access is attempted. To break the script's execution, press Ctrl+C in the command-line window.

# To Learn More

- To learn more about the Windows Ipconfig utility, consult the Windows Help and Support Center.

- The TechNet Script Center includes other script samples that demonstrate how to work with network configuration: *http://www.microsoft.com/technet /scriptcenter/scripts/network/client/default.msx*.

# List Installed Service Pack

**On the CD**   The sample script can be found on the CD that accompanies this book at \Chap7\ListServicePack\ListServicePack.wsf.

| Operating System | Supported? | Prerequisites |
|---|---|---|
| Windows 2000 family | Yes | ■ WSH 5.6 or later |
| Windows XP Professional | Yes | ■ WMI |
| Windows Server 2003 family | Yes | ■ Administrative permission on targeted computers |
| | | ■ Network connectivity to each remote computer |

## Description

This script creates a report—either on the screen or in a text file—that lists each targeted computer's name, the version of Windows it is running, and the version of the latest service pack. Windows versions take the form of *major.minor.build*, with Windows XP (for example) returning 5.1.2600. Service packs generally have only a major number but are expressed as *major.minor*, such as 2.0 for Service Pack 2.

This script is useful for quickly checking your computers to determine what Windows operating system and service pack they are running. This script does *not* check to see whether the installed service pack is intact; it's possible, for example, for a computer to have Service Pack 2 installed but to have specific files overwritten with older versions of those files, which effectively removes a portion of the service pack.

## Performing This Task Manually

You can check the installed service pack on a single computer by right-clicking My Computer and selecting Properties from the shortcut menu. Retrieving this information from multiple computers generally requires the use of a tool, such as Microsoft Systems Management Server and Microsoft Baseline Security Analyzer. This script provides basic functionality for retrieving the current service pack version.

## Example

As with many of the tools in this book, you can use this one in three different ways. First, you can use it to target a single remote computer named ServerA, for example:

```
ListServicePack.wsf /computer:ServerA
```

Second, you can target a list of computers from a text file. The text file is expected to contain one computer name per line and no other information. Assuming the file is named C:\Computers.txt, you would use this syntax:

```
ListServicePack.wsf /list:C:\Computers.txt
```

Finally, you can target an entire organizational unit of computer accounts. If your domain contains an OU named West, you would use the following syntax:

```
ListServicePack.wsf /container:west
```

Note that the *container* argument will work against only the default domain of the computer running the script. In other words, the OU specified must exist within the same domain that the computer running the script belongs to. If the specified OU has nested OUs, you can include their computer accounts as well by specifying one additional argument:

```
ListServicePack.wsf /container:west /recurse
```

Additional arguments provide more functionality to the command; see the following section titled "Syntax." Specifically, the following will write the tool's output to a comma-delimited file named C:\MyOutput.csv:

```
ListServicePack.wsf /container:west /recurse /output:C:\MyOutput.csv
```

# Syntax

This script can be executed as a command-line utility. Set CScript.exe to be your default script processor, as described in Chapter 3.

| | |
|---|---|
| `/list:path`<br>`/computer:name`<br>`/container:name` | One and only one of these is required by the script. Use */list* to target a list of computers contained within a text file. Use */computer* to target a single computer. Use */container* to target an organizational unit within Active Directory. |
| `/output:path` | Specifies the file to which the tool's output should be written. The file specified will be overwritten if it already exists. |
| `/recurse` | When used with */container*, also targets computers contained within nested OUs. |
| `/ping` | Verifies the connectivity to all targeted computers prior to attempting a connection. Using this argument will reduce the timeout wait when one or more computers cannot be reached on the network. |

| /log:path | Logs unreachable computer names to the specified file. This file can then be used later, along with the /list argument, to retry these computers. Requires that you specify the /ping argument. |
| /verbose | Causes the script to display more detailed, step-by-step status messages. |

You can run this script with the /? parameter to display the command's syntax.

## Under the Hood

This script relies on Windows Management Instrumentation (WMI) to perform the bulk of its work. The workhorse section of this script is shown here:

```
Dim cFixes, oFix, sOutput
Verbose " Connecting to WMI on " & sName
Set cFixes = QueryWMI(sName,"root\cimv2","Select * From Win32_OperatingSystem",
"","")
If Not IsObject(cFixes) Then
    WScript.Echo " *** Couldn't connect to WMI on " & sName
Else
    For Each oFix In cFixes
        sOutput = sName & "," & oFix.Version & "," & oFix.ServicePackMajorVersion &
"." & oFix.ServicePackMinorVersion
        If WScript.Arguments.Named.Exists("output") Then
            LogFile WScript.Arguments.Named("output"),sOutput,False
        Else
            WScript.Echo sOutput
        End If
    Next
End If
```

The current computer name is contained in the variable *sName*. Note that the script connects to the computer's *\root\cimv2* namespace in Windows Management Instrumentation (WMI), and then retrieves the *Win32_OperatingSystem* instances from that namespace. Although WMI supports the concept of multiple operating systems, in practice, only one instance will be returned by this query. You could modify the script to also report other operating system properties, such as the page file size and operating system manufacturer.

## Troubleshooting

As with most scripts, connecting to the remote computer or computers and having the permissions necessary to list service pack information (generally, local Administrator permissions) leaves open the potential for errors. This script will catch most errors and display an appropriate message, and then move on to the next targeted computer if possible.

Because this script has the option to output to a file by using the */output* argument, you might receive an error if you specify that the file be created in a location where you don't have the necessary file system permissions, or if you specify a file name that already exists and you don't have permission to delete and re-create that file. In both cases, the script will attempt to continue, but you'll receive errors each time the log file access is attempted. To break the script's execution, press Ctrl+C in the command-line window.

## To Learn More

- You can download the Microsoft Baseline Security Analyzer from *http://www.microsoft.com/mbsa*.

- The TechNet Script Center includes other script samples that demonstrate how to work with hotfixes and service packs: *http://www.microsoft.com/technet/scriptcenter/scripts/srvpacks/default.mspx*.

# List Scheduled Tasks

> **On the CD**    The sample script can be found on the CD that accompanies this book at \Chap7\ListTasks\ListTasks.wsf.

| Operating System | Supported? | Prerequisites |
|---|---|---|
| Windows 2000 family | Yes | ■ WSH 5.6 or later |
| Windows XP Professional | Yes | ■ WMI |
| Windows Server 2003 family | Yes | ■ Administrative permission on targeted computers |
| | | ■ Network connectivity to each remote computer |

## Description

This task creates a report of scheduled tasks on one or more computers, providing a way to quickly inventory all scheduled task operations on multiple computers. The output of this script includes information about the schedules of these tasks, as well as the basic command line used to execute the tasks. Regularly running this script can be a valuable part of change management efforts because it creates a consistent, complete inventory of scheduled tasks across your enterprise.

## Performing This Task Manually

There is no built-in way to obtain a complete list of scheduled tasks on multiple computers. Windows Server 2003 includes a command-line utility named Schtasks, which replaces the older At.exe command included with prior versions of Windows. Both Schtasks and At.exe list the scheduled tasks on a single computer, but Schtasks does not contain the functionality to view tasks scheduled on multiple remote computers.

## Example

You can use this script in three different ways. First, you can use it to target a single remote computer named ServerA, for example:

```
ListTasks.wsf /computer:ServerA
```

You can also target a list of computers from a text file. The text file is expected to contain one computer name per line and no other information. Assuming the file is named C:\Computers.txt, you would use this syntax:

```
ListTasks.wsf /list:C:\Computers.txt
```

Finally, you can target an entire organizational unit of computer accounts. If your domain contains an OU named West, you would use the following syntax:

```
ListTasks.wsf /container:west
```

Note that the *container* argument will work against only the default domain of the computer running the script. In other words, the OU specified must exist within the same domain that the computer running the script belongs to. If the specified OU has nested OUs, you can include their computer accounts as well by specifying one additional argument:

```
ListTasks.wsf /container:west /recurse
```

Additional arguments provide more functionality to the command; see the following section titled "Syntax." Specifically, the following will write the tool's output to a comma-delimited file named C:\MyOutput.csv:

```
ListTasks.wsf /container:west /recurse /output:C:\MyOutput.csv
```

# Syntax

This script can be executed as a command-line utility. Set CScript.exe to be your default script processor, as described in Chapter 3.

| | |
|---|---|
| /list:path<br>/computer:name<br>/container:name | One and only one of these is required by the script. Use */list* to target a list of computers contained within a text file. Use */computer* to target a single computer. Use */container* to target an organizational unit within Active Directory. |
| /output:path | Specifies the file to which the tool's output should be written. The file specified will be overwritten if it already exists. |
| /recurse | When used with */container*, also targets computers contained within nested OUs. |
| /ping | Verifies the connectivity to all targeted computers prior to attempting a connection. Using this argument will reduce the timeout wait when one or more computers cannot be reached on the network. |
| /log:path | Logs unreachable computer names to the specified file. This file can then be used later, along with the */list* argument, to retry these computers. Requires that you specify the */ping* argument. |
| /verbose | Causes the script to display more detailed, step-by-step status messages. |

You can run this script with the */?* parameter to display the command's syntax.

## Under the Hood

This script relies on Windows Management Instrumentation (WMI) to perform the bulk of its work. The primary section of this script is shown here:

```
Dim cJobs, oJob, sOutput
Verbose " Connecting to WMI on " & sName
Set cJobs = QueryWMI(sName,"root\cimv2","Select * From Win32_ScheduledJob","","")
If Not IsObject(cJobs) Then
    WScript.Echo " *** Couldn't connect to WMI on " & sName
Else
    For Each oJob In cJobs
        sOutput = sName & "," & oJob.Caption & "," & oJob.command & ","
& oJob.daysofmonth & "," & oJob.daysofweek & "," & oJob.jobstatus & "," & oJob.name &
"," & oJob.owner & "," & oJob.runrepeatedly & "," & oJob.starttime & ","
& oJob.untiltime
        If WScript.Arguments.Named.Exists("output") Then
            LogFile(WScript.Arguments.Named("output"),sOutput,False)
        Else
            WScript.Echo sOutput
        End If
    Next
End If
```

The current computer name is contained in the variable *sName*. The script connects to the computer's \*root*\*cimv2* namespace in Windows Management Instrumentation (WMI), and then retrieves the *Win32_ScheduledJob* instances from that namespace. This query returns a list of all scheduled tasks. The script then looks at each tasks and outputs the relevant information for each by using properties of the class. Some of the scheduled task properties, such as *DaysOfMonth* and *DaysOfWeek*, can be difficult to interpret, so I recommend viewing those tasks for which you know the schedule (or can look the schedule up in the graphical user interface) to compare the results of this script. Doing so will help you become more familiar with how this information is output by the operating system.

Also note that this script might return the message "***Couldn't connect to WMI" when a targeted computer has no scheduled tasks. This is normal and expected, because no instances of the *Win32_ScheduledJob* class are returned to the script.

## Troubleshooting

As with most scripts, connecting to the remote computer or computers and having the permissions necessary to list scheduled tasks (generally, local Administrator permissions, to view all tasks regardless of owner) leaves open the potential for errors. This script will catch most errors and display an appropriate message, and then move on to the next targeted computer if possible.

Because this script has the option to output to a file by using the */output* argument, you might receive an error if you specify that the file be created in a location where you don't have the necessary file system permissions, or if you specify a file name that already exists and you don't have permission to delete and re-create that file. In both cases, the script will attempt to continue, but you'll receive errors each time the log file access is attempted. To break the script's execution, press Ctrl+C in the command-line window.

## To Learn More

- To learn more about the At.exe or Schtasks commands, consult the Windows Help and Support Center.

- The TechNet Script Center includes other script samples that demonstrate how to work with scheduled tasks: *http://www.microsoft.com/technet/scriptcenter /scripts/os/tasks/default.mspx*.

# List Installed Software

> **On the CD**   The sample script can be found on the CD that accompanies this book at \Chap7\ListSoftware\ListSoftware.wsf.

| Operating System | Supported? | Prerequisites |
|---|---|---|
| Windows 2000 family | No | ■ WSH 5.6 or later |
| Windows XP Professional | Yes | ■ WMI |
| Windows Server 2003 family | Yes | ■ Administrative permission on targeted computers |
| | | ■ Network connectivity to each remote computer |

## Description

This task utilizes WMI and the Windows Installer service to retrieve a list of installed applications on one or more computers, and to display that information on the screen or in a report. This task is useful for discovering which computers have particular software installed, or for auditing the software packages installed on a set of computers.

## Performing This Task Manually

Opening the Add Or Remove Programs Control Panel application allows you to view the applications installed on a single computer; however, there is no built-in way to perform this task against remote computers. Software solutions like Microsoft Systems Management Server (SMS) can inventory and report on installed applications. In fact, tools like SMS can create a more comprehensive report than this script can. This script relies on Windows Installer to report installed software. Software not installed via the Windows Installer service will not be reported by this script, but might be detected by solutions like SMS. However, most newer software is installed by Windows Installer and will be correctly reported by this script.

## Example

As with many of the tools in this book, you can use this one in three different ways. First, you can use it to target a single remote computer named ServerA, for example:

```
ListSoftware.wsf /computer:ServerA
```

Second, you can target a list of computers from a text file. The text file is expected to contain one computer name per line and no other information. Assuming the file is named C:\Computers.txt, you would use this syntax:

```
ListSoftware.wsf /list:C:\Computers.txt
```

Third, you can target an entire organizational unit of computer accounts. If your domain contains an OU named West, you would use the following syntax:

```
ListSoftware.wsf /container:west
```

Note that the *container* argument will work against only the default domain of the computer running the script. In other words, the OU specified must exist within the same domain that the computer running the script belongs to. If the specified OU has nested OUs, you can include their computer accounts as well by specifying one additional argument:

```
ListSoftware.wsf /container:west /recurse
```

Additional arguments provide more functionality to the command; see the following section titled "Syntax." Specifically, the following will write the tool's output to a comma-delimited file named C:\MyOutput.csv:

```
ListSoftware.wsf /container:west /recurse /output:C:\MyOutput.csv
```

# Syntax

This script can be executed as a command-line utility. Set CScript.exe to be your default script processor, as described in Chapter 3.

| | |
|---|---|
| `/list:path`<br>`/computer:name`<br>`/container:name` | One and only one of these is required by the script. Use */list* to target a list of computers contained within a text file. Use */computer* to target a single computer. Use */container* to target an organizational unit within Active Directory. |
| `/output:path` | Specifies the file to which the tool's output should be written. The file specified will be overwritten if it already exists. |
| `/recurse` | When used with */container*, also targets computers contained within nested OUs. |
| `/ping` | Verifies the connectivity to all targeted computers prior to attempting a connection. Using this argument will reduce the timeout wait when one or more computers cannot be reached on the network. |
| `/log:path` | Logs unreachable computer names to the specified file. This file can then be used later, along with the */list* argument, to retry these computers. Requires that you specify the */ping* argument. |
| `/verbose` | Causes the script to display more detailed, step-by-step status messages. |

You can run this script with the */?* parameter to display the command's syntax.

# Under the Hood

This script relies on Windows Management Instrumentation (WMI) to perform the bulk of its work. The primary section of this script is shown here:

```
Dim cApps, oApp, sOutput
Verbose " Connecting to WMI on " & sName
Set cApps = QueryWMI(sName,"root\cimv2","Select * From Win32_Product","","")
If Not IsObject(cApps) Then
    WScript.Echo " *** Couldn't connect to WMI on " & sName
Else
    For Each oApp In cApps
        sOutput = sName & "," & oApp.Description & "," & oApp.InstallDate2 & ","
& oApp.Version
        If WScript.Arguments.Named.Exists("output") Then
            LogFile(WScript.Arguments.Named("output"),sOutput,False)
        Else
            WScript.Echo sOutput
        End If
    Next
End If
```

The current computer name is contained in the variable *sName*. Note that the script connects to the computer's *\root\cimv2* namespace in Windows Management Instrumentation (WMI), and then retrieves the *Win32_Product* instances from that namespace. This query returns a list of all installed software. The script then looks at each item and outputs its relevant information by using properties of the class.

# Troubleshooting

As with most scripts, connecting to the remote computer or computers and having the permissions necessary to list installed software (generally, local Administrator permissions) leaves open the potential for errors. This script will catch most errors and display an appropriate message, moving on to the next targeted computer if possible.

Because this script has the option to output to a file by using the */output* argument, you might receive an error if you specify that the file be created in a location where you don't have the necessary file system permissions, or if you specify a file name that already exists and you don't have permission to delete and re-create that file. In both cases, the script will attempt to continue, but you'll receive errors each time the log file access is attempted. To break the script's execution, press Ctrl+C in the command-line window.

## To Learn More

- You can use the Msiexec command-line utility to install and manage applications from the command line. To learn more about this utility, consult the Windows Help and Support Center.

- The TechNet Script Center includes other script samples that demonstrate how to work with applications: *http://www.microsoft.com/technet/scriptcenter/scripts/apps/user/default.mspx*.

# Chapter 8
# Registry Management

When thinking about automation, many administrators don't consider automating their registry management tasks. This is surprising, because the Microsoft® Windows® operating system has relatively few built-in tools for automating registry management. Whether you need to inventory registry keys or set them on multiple computers, registry management is often a time-consuming and manual process.

Tasks automated in this chapter include:

- Creating registry keys and values on multiple computers
- Checking registry permissions on multiple computers
- Setting registry values on multiple computers
- Inventorying registry values on multiple computers

# Create a Registry Key or Value

> **On the CD**   The sample script can be found on the CD that accompanies this book at \Chap8\CreateRegKey\CreateRegKey.wsf and \Chap8\CreateRegKey\ CreateRegValue.wsf.

| Operating System | Supported? | Prerequisites |
|---|---|---|
| Microsoft Windows 2000 family | Yes | ■ Microsoft Windows Script Host (WSH) 5.6 or later |
| Microsoft Windows XP Professional | Yes | ■ Windows Management Instrumentation (WMI) |
| Microsoft Windows Server™ 2003 family | Yes | ■ Administrative permission on targeted computers |
|  |  | ■ Network connectivity to each remote computer |

## Description

When you need to distribute a new registry key to multiple computers—say, to configure a new corporate application—you can do so via Group Policy in Microsoft Active Directory®. However, using Group Policy does require you to create an administrative template (.adm) file defining the registry key and values you want to set, which can be a time-consuming and frustrating task. When you want to create only a single key or value, this script offers a somewhat quicker way (which is admittedly less manageable in the long term than a Group Policy, but still has its uses).

Note that this task is actually accomplished by using *two* commands: one to create keys, and the other to create and set values under those keys.

## Performing This Task Manually

The Windows® registry editor (Regedit.exe) provides a graphical user interface for creating and managing registry keys. It also allows you to work with the registries on remote computers, but it doesn't provide any batch functionality, which means you must change each computer individually.

Regedit does allow you to export registry information to a .reg file, which can then be imported to remote computers. However, properly distributing the .reg files and ensuring their integrity can be cumbersome in some environments.

# Example

These scripts allow you to target one computer or multiple computers. For example, to target a single remote computer named ServerA and create a registry key named SOFTWARE\MyKey under HKEY_LOCAL_MACHINE, you would use this code:

```
CreateRegKey.wsf /computer:ServerA /key:SOFTWARE\MyKey
```

Note that these scripts work *only* with HKEY_LOCAL_MACHINE (HKLM). Modifying HKEY_CURRENT_USER (HKCU) is complex when you're working remotely; because these tools use WMI, and because WMI impersonates your credentials on the remote machine, the HKCU you modify will be *yours*, not that of the primary user of the remote machine. To modify the primary user's HKCU, you'd need to modify HKEY_USERS and know the primary user's Security ID (SID).

You can also target a list of computers from a text file. The text file is expected to contain one computer name per line and no other information. Assuming the file is named C:\Computers.txt, you would use this syntax:

```
CreateRegKey.wsf /list:C:\Computers.txt /key:SOFTWARE\MyKey
```

Finally, you can target an entire organizational unit of computer accounts. If your domain contains an OU named West, you would use the following syntax:

```
CreateRegKey.wsf /container:west /key:SOFTWARE\MyKey
```

Note that the */container* argument will work against only the default domain of the computer running the script. In other words, the OU specified must exist within the same domain that the computer running the script belongs to. If the specified OU has nested OUs, you can include their computer accounts as well by specifying one additional argument:

```
CreateRegKey.wsf /container:west /recurse /key:SOFTWARE\MyKey
```

You create and set a new registry value in a similar way:

```
CreateRegValue.wsf /container:west /recurse /key:SOFTWARE\MyKey /valuename:MyValue
/valuesetting:1 /valuetype:DWORD
```

This code creates a new decimal word (DWORD, or numeric) value named *MyValue* under the specified key, and sets the new value equal to 1.

Additional arguments provide more functionality to the command; see the following section titled "Syntax."

# Syntax

The scripts, CreateRegKey.wsf and CreateRegValue.wsf, can be executed as command-line utilities. Set CScript.exe to be your default script processor, as described in Chapter 3, "Working with VBScript."

| | |
|---|---|
| `/list:path`<br>`/computer:name`<br>`/container:name` | One and only one of these is required by the script. Use *list* to target a list of computers contained within a text file. Use *computer* to target a single computer. Use *container* to target an organizational unit within Microsoft Active Directory®. |
| `/recurse` | When used with *container*, also targets computers contained within nested OUs. |
| `/ping` | Verifies the connectivity to all targeted computers prior to attempting a connection. Using this argument will reduce the timeout wait when one or more computers cannot be reached on the network. |
| `/log:path` | Logs unreachable computer names to the specified file. This file can then be used later along with the *list* argument to retry these computers. Requires the *ping* argument. |
| `/verbose` | Causes the script to display more detailed, step-by-step status messages. |
| `/key:keyname` | Required by both CreateRegKey.wsf and CreateRegValue.wsf. Specifies the registry key to create or the key under which a new value should be created. |
| `/valuename:name`<br>`/valuesetting:setting`<br>`/valuetype:{STRING | DWORD}` | Valid and required only for the CreateRegValue.wsf script. Specifies the value name, its setting, and whether it is a STRING or DWORD (numeric) value type. |

You can run these scripts with the */?* parameter to display the command's syntax.

# Under the Hood

Both scripts use the WMI *StdRegProv* provider to connect to the remote registry. For example, CreateRegKey.wsf uses code similar to the following:

```
Dim oReg
Set oReg=GetObject("winmgmts:{impersonationLevel=impersonate}!\\" & sName &
"\root\default:StdRegProv")On Error Resume Next
oReg.CreateKey &H80000002, WScript.Arguments.Named("key")
If Err <> 0 Then
 WScript.Echo " *** Failed to create key on " & sName
Else
 Verbose " Created key on " & sName
End If
```

The *StdRegProv* provider is a piece of software running on the remote machine that ties WMI into that machine's registry. Using the *CreateKey()* method of the provider creates a new registry key on the remote computer. The *&H80000002* value is a constant that specifies the HKLM portion of the registry, which is all these scripts are capable of modifying.

## Troubleshooting

These scripts have the potential to cause two major types of errors. First, a remote computer won't be available. Second, you won't have permission to work with the remote computer's registry. In either case, you'll see an error message that alerts you to the problem for that particular computer. Make sure you have the appropriate permissions and that the computer is reachable via the network from the computer running this script. Unreachable computers can optionally be logged to a text file for a later attempt, and you can speed up the script by specifying the */ping* argument.

Typically, you need to be a local Administrator on each remote computer to modify the HKLM portion of the registry.

## To Learn More

- Learn more about the *StdRegProv* provider at *http://go.microsoft.com/fwlink /?LinkId=29999*.
- You can find a tutorial for using WMI to manage the registry at *http://www. serverwatch.com/tutorials/article.php/1476831*.

# List Registry Permissions

**On the CD**   The sample script can be found on the CD that accompanies this book at \Chap8\ListRegPermission\ListRegPermission.wsf.

| Operating System | Supported? | Prerequisites |
|---|---|---|
| Windows 2000 family | Yes | ■  WSH 5.6 or later |
| Windows XP Professional | Yes | ■  WMI |
| Windows Server 2003 family | Yes | ■  Administrative permission on targeted computers |
| | | ■  Network connectivity to each remote computer |

## Description

Occasionally, you might need to figure out what permissions a particular user has on a given registry key. The ListRegPermission.wsf script is designed to help with that task. However, there are some caveats concerning what this script can accomplish for you; see the next "Under the Hood" section for more details.

## Performing This Task Manually

The Windows registry editor (Regedit.exe) provides a graphical user interface for managing registry keys, enabling you to view the permissions on any given key and check to see which permissions a particular user has. However, even though Regedit allows you to work with the registries on remote computers, it doesn't provide any batch functionality, which means you must check each computer individually.

## Example

This tool allows you to target one computer or multiple computers. When targeting multiple computers, you can request they be listed in a text file or queried from Active Directory. For example, if you want to use the script to target only a single remote computer named ServerA and check a registry key named SOFTWARE\MyKey under HKEY_LOCAL_MACHINE, you would use this code:

```
ListRegPermission.wsf /computer:ServerA /key:SOFTWARE\MyKey /user:joe@domain.com
/password:MyPassw0rd
```

Note that you have to include the user name and password for the user you want to check; more details about this are included in the next "Under the Hood" section.

This script works *only* with HKEY_LOCAL_MACHINE (HKLM). Modifying HKEY_CURRENT_USER (HKCU) is complex when you're working remotely; because these tools use WMI, and because WMI impersonates your credentials on the remote machine, the HKCU you modify will be *yours,* not that of the primary user of the remote machine. To modify the primary user's HKCU, you'd need to modify HKEY_USERS and know the primary user's Security ID (SID).

You can also target a list of computers from a text file. The text file is expected to contain one computer name per line and no other information. Assuming the file is named C:\Computers.txt, you would use this syntax:

```
ListRegPermission.wsf /list:C:\Computers.txt /key:SOFTWARE\MyKey
/user:joe@domain.com /password:MyPassw0rd
```

Finally, you can target an entire organizational unit of computer accounts. If your domain contains an OU named West, you would use the following syntax:

```
ListRegPermission.wsf /container:west /key:SOFTWARE\MyKey /user:joe@domain.com
/password:MyPassw0rd
```

Note that the */container* argument will work against only the default domain of the computer running the script. In other words, the OU specified must exist within the same domain that the computer running the script belongs to. If the specified OU has nested OUs, you can include their computer accounts as well by specifying one additional argument:

```
ListRegPermission.wsf /container:west /recurse /key:SOFTWARE\MyKey
/user:joe@domain.com /password:MyPassw0rd
```

Additional arguments provide more functionality to the command; see the following "Syntax" section.

## Syntax

These scripts can be executed as command-line utilities. Set CScript.exe to be your default script processor, as described in Chapter 3.

| | |
|---|---|
| /list:path<br>/computer:name<br>/container:name | One and only one of these is required by the script. Use */list* to target a list of computers contained within a text file. Use */computer* to target a single computer. Use */container* to target an organizational unit within Active Directory. |
| /recurse | When used with */container,* also targets computers contained within nested OUs. |
| /ping | Verifies the connectivity to all targeted computers prior to attempting a connection. Using this argument will reduce the timeout wait when one or more computers cannot be reached on the network. |

| | |
|---|---|
| /log:path | Logs unreachable computer names to the specified file. This file can then be used later, along with the */list* argument, to retry these computers. Requires the */ping* argument. |
| /verbose | Causes the script to display more detailed, step-by-step status messages. |
| /key:keyname | Required. Specifies the registry key to create or the key under which a new value should be created. |
| /user:name /password:password | The user name and password of the user account whose permissions you want to check. Optional; if you omit these arguments the script will check your permissions on the specified registry key. |
| /output:path | Logs the script's output to a text file specified in *path*. |

You can run these scripts with the */?* parameter to display the command's syntax.

## Under the Hood

This script uses WMI to check the permissions on the given registry key, which does place some limitations on how you can use the script. WMI's *StdRegProv* provider, which provides WMI with an interface to the registry, includes a *CheckAccess()* method. However, *CheckAccess()* doesn't simply return a list of permissions on the registry key; instead, it checks to see whether the user account making the request has a specified permission. Here's a sample of the code used:

```
Set oReg = QueryWMI(sName,"root\default:StdRegProv", WScript.Arguments.Named("user")
, WScript.Arguments.named("password"))
If Err <> 0 Then
 sOutput = sOutput & " *** Could not access key on " & sName & VbCrLf
 sOutput = sOutput & " " & Err.Description & VbCrLf
Else

 oReg.CheckAccess HKEY_LOCAL_MACHINE, WScript.Arguments.Named("key"),
KEY_QUERY_VALUE, bGranted
 If bGranted = True Then
   sOutput = sOutput & " Read value: Granted" & VbCrLf
 Else
   sOutput = sOutput & " Read value: Not Granted" & VbCrLf
 End If
```

The *QueryWMI()* function is used to connect to the targeted computer and issue a query to its WMI service. When you include the */user* and */password* arguments, this connection is made using the user credentials you specify. Thus, the remote computer's WMI service is impersonating the credentials you provided, and the registry *CheckAccess()* method is checking the access for *that* account. If you omit the */user* and */password* arguments, *your* user account is used to make the connection.

The *CheckAccess()* method requires that you specify a registry key as well as a permission that you want to check, such as permission to query the key (represented by KEY_QUERY_VALUE in the preceding script code). This script, then, performs several calls to *CheckAccess()* to check various permissions for the specified user account.

## Troubleshooting

Permissions become a complex issue with this script. To use the script, you must specify a user account that has permissions to both connect to each targeted computer and issue WMI queries to those computers. However, the account you specify is the account whose permissions will be checked in the registry. In other words, you won't be able to check the permissions of any account that does not already have permissions to connect to the targeted computers and issue WMI queries to them. Most of the problems that this script can run into are, therefore, related to permissions. The script will attempt to display any errors that occur so that you can try an alternate user account.

## To Learn More

- Learn more about the *StdRegProv* provider at *http://go.microsoft.com/fwlink /?LinkId=29999*.

- You'll find a tutorial for using WMI to manage the registry at *http://www. serverwatch.com/tutorials/article.php/1476831*.

# List Registry Value

> **On the CD**   The sample script can be found on the CD that accompanies this book at \Chap8\ListRegValue\ListRegValue.wsf.

| Operating System | Supported? | Prerequisites |
|---|---|---|
| Windows 2000 family | Yes | ■ WSH 5.6 or later |
| Windows XP Professional | Yes | ■ WMI |
| Windows Server 2003 family | Yes | ■ Administrative permission on targeted computers |
| | | ■ Network connectivity to each remote computer |

## Description

One common administrative task is to figure out what various computers have for a specific registry value. This ListRegValue.wsf script makes it easy to inventory that information by remotely checking the specified registry value on multiple computers and logging that information to a file for later analysis.

## Performing This Task Manually

The Windows registry editor (Regedit.exe) provides a graphical user interface for managing registry keys, enabling you to view the settings for any given key or value. Although Regedit does allow you to work with the registries on remote computers, it doesn't provide any batch functionality, which means you must check each computer's registry individually.

## Example

This tool allows you to target one computer or multiple computers. When targeting multiple computers, those compters can listed in a text file or queried from Active Directory. For example, if you wanted to use the script to target a single remote computer named ServerA and check a registry key named SOFTWARE\MyKey under HKEY_LOCAL_MACHINE, the tool would check a REG_SZ (string) value named *MyValue*:

```
ListRegValue.wsf /computer:ServerA /key:SOFTWARE\MyKey /valuename:MyValue
/valuetype:string
```

This script works *only* with HKEY_LOCAL_MACHINE (HKLM). Modifying HKEY_CURRENT_USER (HKCU) is complex when you're working remotely.

Because these tools use WMI, and because WMI impersonates your credentials on the remote machine, the HKCU you check will be *yours,* not the primary user of the remote machine. To modify the primary user's HKCU, you'd need to modify HKEY_USERS and know the primary user's Security ID (SID).

You can also target a list of computers from a text file. The text file is expected to contain one computer name per line and no other information. Assuming the file is named C:\Computers.txt, you would use this syntax:

```
ListRegValue.wsf /list:C:\Computers.txt /key:SOFTWARE\MyKey /valuename:MyValue
/valuetype:string
```

Finally, you can target an entire organizational unit of computer accounts. If your domain contains an OU named West, you would use the following syntax:

```
ListRegValue.wsf /container:west /key:SOFTWARE\MyKey /valuename:MyValue
/valuetype:string
```

Note that the */container* argument will work against only the default domain of the computer running the script. In other words, the OU specified must exist within the same domain that the computer running the script belongs to. If the specified OU has nested OUs, you can include their computer accounts as well by specifying one additional argument:

```
ListRegValue.wsf /container:west /recurse /key:SOFTWARE\MyKey /valuename:MyValue
/valuetype:string
```

Additional arguments provide more functionality to the command; see the following section titled "Syntax."

# Syntax

These scripts can be executed as command-line utilities. Set CScript.exe to be your default script processor, as described in Chapter 3.

| | |
|---|---|
| /list:path<br>/computer:name<br>/container:name | One and only one of these is required by the script. Use */list* to target a list of computers contained within a text file. Use */computer* to target a single computer. Use */container* to target an organizational unit within Active Directory. |
| /recurse | When used with */container*, also targets computers contained within nested OUs. |
| /ping | Verifies the connectivity to all targeted computers prior to attempting a connection. Using this argument will reduce the timeout wait when one or more computers cannot be reached on the network. |

| | |
|---|---|
| /log:path | Logs unreachable computer names to the specified file. This file can then be used later, along with the */list* argument, to retry these computers. Requires the */ping* argument. |
| /verbose | Causes the script to display more detailed, step-by-step status messages. |
| /key:keyname | Required. Specifies either the registry key to create or the key under which a new value should be created. |
| /valuename:name /valuetype:{STRING \| DWORD} | Required. Specifies the name and type (STRING or DWORD) of the value you want to inventory. |
| /output:path | Logs the script's output to a text file specified in *path*. |

You can run these scripts with the */?* parameter to display the command's syntax.

## Under the Hood

This script uses WMI to connect to each remote computer and check the specified registry value. The bulk of the script's work is done by the following code:

```
Dim oReg, sValue
Set oReg = QueryWMI(sName,"root\default:StdRegProv","","")
On Error Resume Next
Select Case lcase(WScript.Arguments.Named("valuetype"))
 Case "string"
oReg.GetStringValue(&H80000002, WScript.Arguments.Named("key"), _
 WScript.Arguments.Named("valuename"), sValue)
 Case "dword"
 oReg.GetDWORDValue(&H80000002, WScript.Arguments.Named("key"),WScript.Arguments
.Named("valuename"), _
 sValue)
 Case Else
  WScript.Echo " *** Unknown /valuetype '" & _
   wscript.arguments.named("valuetype") & "' specified."
End Select
If Err <> 0 Then
 WScript.Echo " *** Failed to create value on " & sName
Else
 If WScript.Arguments.Named.Exists("output") Then
  LogFile(WScript.Arguments.Named("output"),sName & "," & svalue,False)
 Else
  WScript.Echo sName & ": " & sValue
 End if
End If
```

The WMI *StdRegProv* registry provider includes a *GetStringValue()* method and a *GetDWORDValue()* method, which are used by the script to retrieve the value you specify. The script provides its own *LogFile()* function, which is used to write information to a text file specified in the */output* argument. Omitting the */output* argument results in the script writing the registry information to the console.

# Troubleshooting

To use this script, you need to have, on each remote computer, permissions to query the registry. Any problems encountered by this script will most likely be related to permissions, and the script will display appropriate error and progress messages to advise you of these problems.

# To Learn More

- Learn more about the *StdRegProv* provider at *http://go.microsoft.com/fwlink /?LinkId=29999*.

- You'll find a tutorial on using WMI to manage the registry at *http://www.serverwatch.com/tutorials/article.php/1476831*.

## Chapter 9

# Other Computer Management Tasks

Administrators are often required to make minor changes to client computers in their environments—minor, of course, until they must be made on a large number of computers. Some of these changes include adjustments to security practices such as modifying local account passwords. Other changes result from troubleshooting efforts and maintenance, such as managing client and server page files.

Tasks automated in this chapter include:

- Changing local account passwords
- Clearing print queues
- Printing test pages on print queues
- Listing running processes
- Starting processes
- Ending processes
- Inventorying page file settings
- Modifying page file settings
- Shutting down and restarting computers
- Modifying Boot.ini files

# Change Local Account Passwords

> **On the CD**   The sample script can be found on the CD that accompanies this book at \Chap9\ChangeLocalPassword\ChangeLocalPassword.wsf.

| Operating System | Supported? | Prerequisites |
|---|---|---|
| Microsoft® Windows® 2000 family | Yes | ■ Microsoft Windows Script Host (WSH) 5.6 or later |
| Microsoft Windows XP Professional | Yes | ■ Windows Management Instrumentation (WMI) |
| Microsoft Windows Server™ 2003 family | Yes | ■ Administrative permission on targeted computers |
| | | ■ Network connectivity to each remote computer |

## Description

One of the best yet most overlooked security practices in a Windows® environment is regularly changing local account passwords, especially for sensitive built-in accounts like Administrator. Domain-based password policies can be used to force a change on a periodic basis, but because local accounts like Administrator are rarely used on many client computers, the password change is never triggered. (Password policies can require a change only when the account is actually used to log on to the computer.) As a result, these local passwords often go unchanged for long periods of time, increasing the likelihood that they will be compromised.

## Performing This Task Manually

Windows provides several means for changing passwords on a single computer. You can use the Computer Management console, for example, to change the password on any local user account. This console can also connect to remote computers and manage their local accounts. From the command line, you can use the NET USER command to modify a password. For example, to change the local Administrator account password, you would use this code:

```
NET USER Administrator NewPassword
```

However, the Windows operating system does not provide a built-in means of changing local accounts on multiple computers at once. (In fact, the primary purpose of a domain is to avoid the need to constantly manage local user accounts on multiple computers.)

# Example

The ChangeLocalPassword.wsf script allows you to target one computer or multiple computers. If you want to use it to target a single remote computer named ServerA and change the password for the Administrator account, you would use this code:

```
ChangeLocalPassword.wsf /computer:ServerA /user:Administrator /password:NewPassword
```

You can also target a list of computers from a text file. The text file is expected to contain one computer name per line and no other information. Assuming the file is named C:\Computers.txt, you would use this syntax:

```
ChangeLocalPassword.wsf /list:C:\Computers.txt /user:Administrator
/password:NewPassword
```

Finally, you can target an entire organizational unit of computer accounts. If your domain contains an OU named West, you would use the following syntax:

```
ChangeLocalPassword.wsf /container:west /user:Administrator /password:NewPassword
```

Note that the *container* argument will work against only the default domain of the computer running the script. In other words, the OU specified must exist within the same domain that the computer running the script belongs to. If the specified OU has nested OUs, you can include their computer accounts as well by specifying one additional argument:

```
ChangeLocalPassword.wsf /container:west /recurse /user:Administrator
/password:NewPassword
```

This is an excellent way to ensure that a consistent local user account password is used across multiple client or server computers. Additional arguments provide more functionality to the command; see the following section titled "Syntax."

# Syntax

This script can be executed as command-line utilities. Set CScript.exe to be your default script processor, as described in Chapter 3, "Working with VBScript."

| | |
|---|---|
| /list:path<br>/computer:name<br>/container:name | One and only one of these is required by the script. Use */list* to target a list of computers contained within a text file. Use */computer* to target a single computer. Use */container* to target an organizational unit within Microsoft Active Directory®. Note that all computer names must be actual computer names; aliases such as *localhost*, as well as IP addresses, will not work. |
| /recurse | When used with */container*, also targets computers contained within nested OUs. |

| /ping | Verifies the connectivity to all targeted computers prior to attempting a connection. Using this argument will reduce the timeout wait when one or more computers cannot be reached on the network. |
|---|---|
| /log:path | Logs unreachable computer names to the specified file. This file can then be used later, along with the */list* argument, to retry these computers. Note that a log is created only when used in conjunction with the */ping* argument. |
| /verbose | Causes the script to display more detailed, step-by-step status messages. |
| /user:username | Required. Specifies the local user account you want to change. |
| /password:password | Required. Specifies the new password for the user account. |

You can run these scripts with the */?* parameter to display the command's syntax.

## Under the Hood

This script uses Active Directory Services Interface (ADSI) to accomplish its work. A common misconception about ADSI is that it works only with Active Directory, but ADSI includes a *WinNT* provider that is designed to work with Microsoft Windows NT® domains as well as local user accounts on standalone and member computers. The main portion of the script code follows:

```
Dim oUser
Set oUser = QueryADSI(sName,"WinNT:// " & sName & "/" &
  WScript.Arguments.Named("user") & ",user")
If Not IsObject(oUser) Then
    WScript.Echo " *** Couldn't retrieve user from " & sName
Else
    On Error Resume Next
    oUser.setpassword WScript.Arguments.Named("password")
    If Err <> 0 Then
        WScript.Echo " *** Couldn't change password on " & sname
        WScript.Echo " " & Err.Description
    Else
        Verbose " Changed password on " & sName
    End If
End If
```

The script uses this *WinNT* provider to connect to each targeted computer and retrieve the specified user account. (The inclusion of ",user" ensures that computer, group, or other objects with similar names are not retrieved by accident.) The returned *User* object supplies a *SetPassword* method that is used to change the password.

# Troubleshooting

This script has the potential to create three major types of errors. First, a remote computer won't be available. Second, you won't have permission to work with the remote computer's users. (Typically, only a member of the Administrators local group has permission to change user passwords.) In either case, you'll see an error message that alerts you to the problem for that computer. Make sure you have the appropriate permissions and that the computer is reachable via the network from the computer running this script. Unreachable computers can optionally be logged to a text file for a later attempt, and you can speed up the script by specifying the */ping* argument.

The third potential problem is that one or more of the targeted computers won't have the user account specified. Although this situation wouldn't normally occur for built-in accounts like Administrator (unless you've inconsistently renamed that account on various computers), it could occur for other local accounts that you might have created. In these instances, the script will return an error and continue trying with the next targeted computer.

## To Learn More

- Learn more about the *WinNT* ADSI provider at *http://msdn.microsoft.com /library/default.asp?url=/library/en-us/adsi/adsi/adsi_winnt_provider.asp*.

- Find more local user account management samples in Microsoft Visual Basic® (VBScript) at *http://www.microsoft.com/technet/scriptcenter/scripts/ds/local /users/default.mspx*.

# Clear Print Queues

 **On the CD** The sample script can be found on the CD that accompanies this book at \Chap9\ClearPrintQueue\ClearPrintQueue.wsf.

| Operating System | Supported? | Prerequisites |
|---|---|---|
| Windows 2000 family | No | ■ WSH 5.6 or later |
| Windows XP Professional | Yes | ■ WMI |
| Windows Server 2003 family | Yes | ■ Administrative permission on targeted computers |
| | | ■ Network connectivity to each remote computer |

## Description

This script, ClearPrintQueue.wsf, will clear documents from one or more print queues on one or more computers. This is typically a troubleshooting or maintenance step performed by an administrator.

## Performing This Task Manually

Windows provides a graphical user interface for managing print queue jobs. Typically, an administrator connects to the printer using the Printers And Faxes folder, and then double-clicks any connected printer to view its queue. Selecting one or more jobs allows these jobs to be paused or cancelled. The NET PRINT command-line utility can also be used to delete individual jobs from remote print queues. However, no built-in means exists for clearing multiple queues at once.

## Example

This tool allows you to target one computer or multiple computers. You can clear all print queues on each targeted computer, or you can choose to clear only one named queue. In the latter case, the queue specified must exist with the same name on each targeted computer. To use the script to target a single remote computer named ServerA and clear all queues, you would use this code:

```
ClearPrintQueue.wsf /computer:ServerA /all
```

You can also target a list of computers from a text file. The text file is expected to contain one computer name per line and no other information. Assuming the file is named C:\Computers.txt, you would use this syntax:

```
ClearPrintQueue.wsf /list:C:\Computers.txt /all
```

Finally, you can target an entire organizational unit of computer accounts. If your domain contains an OU named West, you would use the following syntax:

```
ClearPrintQueue.wsf /container:west /all
```

Note that the */container* argument will work against only the default domain of the computer running the script. In other words, the OU specified must exist within the same domain as that of the computer running the script. If the specified OU has nested OUs, you can include their computer accounts as well by specifying one additional argument:

```
ClearPrintQueue.wsf /container:west /queue:MyQueue
```

Note that this example clears a queue named MyQueue (which is the name of the installed printer), which would exist on each targeted computer. Additional arguments provide more functionality to the command; see following section titled "Syntax."

# Syntax

These scripts can be executed as command-line utilities. Set CScript.exe to be your default script processor, as described in Chapter 3.

| | |
|---|---|
| `/list:path`<br>`/computer:name`<br>`/container:name` | One and only one of these is required by the script. Use */list* to target a list of computers contained within a text file. Use */computer* to target a single computer. Use */container* to target an organizational unit within Active Directory. |
| `/recurse` | When used with */container*, also targets computers contained within nested OUs. |
| `/ping` | Verifies the connectivity to all targeted computers prior to attempting a connection. Using this argument will reduce the timeout wait when one or more computers cannot be reached on the network. |
| `/log:path` | Logs unreachable computer names to the specified file. This file can then be used later, along with the */list* argument, to retry these computers. Note that a log is created only when used in conjunction with the */ping* argument. |
| `/verbose` | Causes the script to display more detailed, step-by-step status messages. |
| `/all`<br>`/queue:queuename` | One of these is required. Use */all* to clear all queues on each targeted computer, or specify a specific queue by using */queue:queuename*. |

You can run these scripts with the */?* parameter to display the command's syntax.

# Under the Hood

This script uses Windows Management Instrumentation (WMI) to connect to each targeted computer. The *Win32_Printer* class is queried (either all instances, representing all queues, or a specific named instance). The following script code performs the work of connecting to the remote queues and clearing them:

```
Dim cQueues, oQueue
If WScript.Arguments.Named.Exists("all") Then
    Set cQueues = QueryWMI(sName,"\root\cimv2","Select * From
  Win32_Printer","","")
Else
    Set cQueues = QueryWMI(sName,"\root\cimv2","Select * From Win32_Printer Where
Name = '" & WScript.arguments.named("queue") & "'","","")
End If
If Not IsObject(cQueues) Then
    WScript.Echo " *** Couldn't retrieve queue(s) from " & sName
Else
    On Error Resume Next
    For Each oQueue In cQueues
        Verbose "Cancelling jobs on " & sName & ": " & oQueue.Name
        oQueue.CancelAllJobs()
        If Err <> 0 Then
            WScript.Echo " *** Error cancelling " & oQueue.name & " on " & sName & ":"
            WScript.Echo " " & Err.Description
        End If
    Next
End If
```

Each instance of the *Win32_Printer* class provides a *CancelAllJobs()* method, which performs the work of canceling all outstanding jobs in that print queue.

# Troubleshooting

This script has the potential for several types of errors. First, a remote computer won't be available. Second, you won't have permission to work with the remote computer's print queues. (Typically, only a member of the Administrators and Power Users or Print Operators groups has permission to cancel all print jobs; ordinary users can typically cancel only their own jobs.) In either case, you'll see an error message that alerts you to the problem for that computer. Make sure you have the appropriate permissions and that the computer is reachable via the network from the computer running this script. Unreachable computers can optionally be logged to a text file for a later attempt, and you can speed up the script by specifying the */ping* argument.

The third potential problem is that one or more of the targeted computers won't have the queue specified (if you use the */queue* argument). In these instances, the script will return an error and continue trying with the next targeted computer. It's also possible for the script to encounter an error while trying to cancel one or more jobs—jobs can become stuck, or the script might be unable to obtain permissions for specified jobs. In these cases, the script will again return an error message and continue trying with the next print queue. However, the script is not designed to retry queues whose jobs have failed to cancel.

## To Learn More

■ Find more VBScript samples for managing printers at *http://
www.microsoft.com/technet/scriptcenter/scripts/printing/default.mspx.*

■ Learn more about the *Win32_Printer* class at *http://msdn.microsoft.com/library
/default.asp?url=/library/en-us/wmisdk/wmi/win32_printer.asp.*

# Print Test Pages

 **On the CD**    The sample script can be found on the CD that accompanies this book at \Chap9\PrintTestPage\PrintTestPage.wsf.

| Operating System | Supported? | Prerequisites |
|---|---|---|
| Windows 2000 family | No | ■  WSH 5.6 or later |
| Windows XP Professional | Yes | ■  WMI |
| Windows Server 2003 family | Yes | ■  Administrative permission on targeted computers |
|  |  | ■  Network connectivity to each remote computer |

## Description

This tool will print test pages, on one or more computers, for all queues or for a named queue. This is a great way to periodically test your queues for proper operation, or a quick way for an administrator or support technician to test a remote print server's queues during troubleshooting.

I've also used this script to quickly identify which physical print devices are connected to a given print server—helpful because some organizations lose track of this information. This script can target all queues on a given print server; print devices producing a test page reveal which devices are connected to a particular server.

## Performing This Task Manually

Windows provides a built-in means for printing test pages on single print queues. To print these pages manually, use this code:

1. Right-click a printer in the Printers And Faxes folder, and select Properties.

2. In the printer's Properties dialog box, click Print Test Page.

A one-page (typically) test is produced that confirms that the printer is working properly and that lists the driver files in use by the printer.

However, Windows provides no built-in means of performing this test on multiple print queues at once.

# Example

This tool allows you to target one computer or multiple computers. You can clear all print queues on each targeted computer, or you can choose to clear only one named queue. In the latter case, the queue specified must exist with the same name on each targeted computer. If you wanted to use the script to target a single remote computer named ServerA and test all queues, you would use this code:

```
PrintTestPage.wsf /computer:ServerA /all
```

You can also target a list of computers from a text file. The text file is expected to contain one computer name per line and no other information. Assuming the file is named C:\Computers.txt, you would use this syntax:

```
PrintTestPage.wsf /list:C:\Computers.txt /all
```

Finally, you can target an entire organizational unit of computer accounts. If your domain contains an OU named West, you would use the following syntax:

```
PrintTestPage.wsf /container:west /all
```

Note that the */container* argument will work against only the default domain of the computer running the script. In other words, the OU specified must exist within the same domain of the computer running the script. If the specified OU has nested OUs, you can include their computer accounts as well by specifying one additional argument:

```
PrintTestPage.wsf /container:west /queue:MyQueue
```

Note that this example tests a queue named MyQueue (which is the name of the installed printer), which must exist on each targeted computer. Additional arguments provide more functionality to the command; see the following section titled "Syntax."

# Syntax

These scripts can be executed as command-line utilities. Set CScript.exe to be your default script processor, as described in Chapter 3.

| | |
|---|---|
| /list:path<br>/computer:name<br>/container:name | One and only one of these is required by the script. Use */list* to target a list of computers contained within a text file. Use */computer* to target a single computer. Use */container* to target an organizational unit within Active Directory. |
| /recurse | When used with */container*, also targets computers contained within nested OUs. |

| | |
|---|---|
| `/ping` | Verifies the connectivity to all targeted computers prior to attempting a connection. Using this argument will reduce the timeout wait when one or more computers cannot be reached on the network. |
| `/log:path` | Logs unreachable computer names to the specified file. This file can then be used later, along with the /list argument, to retry these computers. Note that a log is created only when used in conjunction with the /ping argument. |
| `/verbose` | Causes the script to display more detailed, step-by-step status messages. |
| `/all` `/queue:queuename` | One of these is required. Use /all to test all queues on each targeted computer, or specify a specific queue by using /queue:queuename. |

You can run these scripts with the /? parameter to display the command's syntax.

# Under the Hood

This script uses Windows Management Instrumentation (WMI) to connect to each targeted computer. The *Win32_Printer* class is queried (either all instances representing all queues or a specific named instance). The following script code performs the work of connecting to the remote queues and printing the test page:

```
Dim cQueues, oQueue
If WScript.Arguments.Named.Exists("all") Then
    Set cQueues = QueryWMI(sName,"\root\cimv2","Select * From Win32_Printer","","")
Else
    Set cQueues = QueryWMI(sName,"\root\cimv2","Select * From Win32_Printer Where
Name = '" & WScript.arguments.named("queue") & "'","","")
End If
If Not IsObject(cQueues) Then
    WScript.Echo " *** Couldn't retrieve queue(s) from " & sName
Else
    On Error Resume Next
    For Each oQueue In cQueues
        Verbose "Printing test on " & sName & ": " & oQueue.Name
        oQueue.PrintTestPage()
        If Err <> 0 Then
            WScript.Echo " *** Error printing test to " & oQueue.name & " on "
& sName & ":"
            WScript.Echo " " & Err.Description
        End If
    Next
End If
```

Each instance of the *Win32_Printer* class provides a *PrintTestPage()* method that performs the work of printing a test page to that queue.

# Troubleshooting

This script has the potential to experience several types of errors. First, a remote computer won't be available. Second, you won't have permission to work with the remote computer's print queues. A permissions issue is rare, however, because you're merely printing a document, which all users generally have permissions to do. Any permissions issue you encounter will more likely be a result of connecting to WMI itself, a task that often only Administrators have permission to do. In either case, you'll see an error message that alerts you to the problem for that computer. Make sure you have the appropriate permissions and that the computer is reachable via the network from the computer running this script. Unreachable computers can optionally be logged to a text file for a later attempt, and you can speed up the script by specifying the */ping* argument.

The third potential problem is that one or more of the targeted computers won't have the queue specified (if you use the */queue* argument). In these instances, the script will return an error and continue trying with the next targeted computer. It's also possible for the script to encounter an error while trying to print the test page. This is also rare—Windows typically sends the test page job to the printer much like it would for any other print job. Problems will show up in the printer's queue monitoring window, but problems won't usually result in an error being returned to the script.

## To Learn More

- Find more VBScript samples for managing printers at *http:// www.microsoft.com/technet/scriptcenter/scripts/printing/default.mspx*.

- Learn more about the *Win32_Printer* class at *http://msdn.microsoft.com/library /default.asp?url=/library/en-us/wmisdk/wmi/win32_printer.asp*.

# List Running Processes

> **On the CD**   The sample script can be found on the CD that accompanies this book at \Chap9\ListProcesses\ListProcesses.wsf.

| Operating System | Supported? | Prerequisites |
|---|---|---|
| Windows 2000 family | Yes | ■ WSH 5.6 or later |
| Windows XP Professional | Yes | ■ WMI |
| Windows Server 2003 family | Yes | ■ Administrative permission on targeted computers |
| | | ■ Network connectivity to each remote computer |

## Description

This tool will list all processes running on one or more computers. Optionally, the script's output can be directed to a comma-separated values (CSV) file, providing you with a report of running processes. This file is a useful inventory tool because it allows you to more easily audit the processes running on your computers and look for unauthorized applications, outdated software, and so forth.

Some viruses, spyware, and malware install themselves as innocent-sounding services; I've used this script in the past to quickly inventory multiple computers to see whether any of them were running a process known to be associated with malware or a particular attack.

## Performing This Task Manually

Windows Task Manager provides a list of all processes running on the local computer; command-line tools such as PLIST, RLIST, and TLIST (which have been available in various versions of the Microsoft Windows Resource Kits) also have the capability of listing the processes on a single remote computer. However, there is no built-in means for listing the processes on multiple remote computers.

## Example

This tool allows you to target one computer or multiple computers. To use the script to target a single remote computer named ServerA and list the running processes to the console, you would use the following code:

```
ListProcesses.wsf /computer:ServerA
```

You can also target a list of computers from a text file. The text file is expected to contain one computer name per line and no other information. Assuming the file is named C:\Computers.txt, you would use this syntax:

```
ListProcesses.wsf /list:C:\Computers.txt /output:c:\proclist.csv
```

Note that this syntax outputs the process list to a CSV file named C:\Proclist.csv. This file is especially useful when targeting multiple computers, because the amount of information generated can be awkward to review in a command-line window.

Finally, you can target an entire organizational unit of computer accounts. If your domain contains an OU named West, you would use the following syntax:

```
ListProcesses.wsf /container:west /output:c:\proclist.csv
```

Note that the *container* argument will work against only the default domain of the computer running the script. In other words, the OU specified must exist within the same domain of the computer running the script. If the specified OU has nested OUs, you can include their computer accounts as well by specifying one additional argument:

```
ListProcesses.wsf /container:west /output:c:\proclist.csv
```

Additional arguments provide more functionality to the command; see the following section titled "Syntax."

# Syntax

These scripts can be executed as command-line utilities. Set CScript.exe to be your default script processor, as described in Chapter 3.

| | |
|---|---|
| /list:path<br>/computer:name<br>/container:name | One and only one of these is required by the script. Use */list* to target a list of computers contained within a text file. Use */computer* to target a single computer. Use */container* to target an organizational unit within Active Directory. |
| /recurse | When used with */container*, also targets computers contained within nested OUs. |
| /ping | Verifies the connectivity to all targeted computers prior to attempting a connection. Using this argument will reduce the timeout wait when one or more computers cannot be reached on the network. |
| /log:path | Logs unreachable computer names to the specified file. This file can then be used later, along with the */list* argument, to retry these computers. Note that a log is created only when used in conjunction with the */ping* argument. |
| /verbose | Causes the script to display more detailed, step-by-step status messages. |
| /output:path | Optionally logs the script's output to a CSV file. |

You can run these scripts with the */?* parameter to display the command's syntax.

# Under the Hood

This script uses Windows Management Instrumentation (WMI) to connect to each targeted computer. The *Win32_Process* class is queried (returning all instances, with each instance representing one running process). The following script code performs the work:

```
Dim cProcesses, oProcess, sOutput
Verbose " Connecting to WMI on " & sName
Set cProcesses = QueryWMI(sName,"root\cimv2","Select * From Win32_Process","","")
If Not IsObject(cProcesses) Then
    WScript.Echo " *** Couldn't connect to WMI on " & sName
Else
    For Each oProcess In cProcesses
        sOutput = sName & "," & oProcess.Name & "," & oProcess.CommandLine & ","
& oProcess.ProcessID
        If WScript.Arguments.Named.Exists("output") Then
            LogFile WScript.Arguments.Named("output"),sOutput,False
        Else
            WScript.Echo sOutput
        End If
    Next
End If
```

The variable *sOutput* is used to contain information about each process, including its name, process ID, and the command-line used to execute the process. The *sOutput* variable is then printed in the command-line window or, if you use the */output* argument, to the specified CSV file.

# Troubleshooting

This script has the potential to result in two types of errors. First, a remote computer won't be available. Second, you won't have permission to work with the remote computer's processes. (Typically, only a member of the Administrators group has permission to do so.) In either case, you'll see an error message that alerts you to the problem for that computer. Make sure you have the appropriate permissions and that the computer is reachable via the network from the computer running this script. Unreachable computers can optionally be logged to a text file for a later attempt, and you can speed up the script by specifying the */ping* argument.

# To Learn More

- Find more VBScript samples for managing and monitoring processes at *http://www.microsoft.com/technet/scriptcenter/scripts/os/process/default.mspx*.

- Learn more about the *Win32_Process* class at *http://msdn.microsoft.com/library /default.asp?url=/library/en-us/wmisdk/wmi/win32_process.asp*.

# Start a Process

**On the CD**   The sample script can be found on the CD that accompanies this book at \Chap9\StartProcess\StartProcess.wsf.

| Operating System | Supported? | Prerequisites |
|---|---|---|
| Windows 2000 family | Yes | ■ WSH 5.6 or later |
| Windows XP Professional | Yes | ■ WMI |
| Windows Server 2003 family | Yes | ■ Administrative permission on targeted computers |
| | | ■ Network connectivity to each remote computer |

## Description

This tool will start a new process, using the specified command line, on one or more computers. The results of this tool will differ somewhat depending on the precise circumstances in which you run the script. For example, when a user starts a new process (such as an application) using Microsoft Windows Explorer, the process runs under the user's normal security context and is visible on the user's desktop. Processes started by other users, however, are generally prevented from interacting with the logged-on user's desktop. Because this script uses *your* credentials to connect to remote computers, the processes you start will usually be running under your security context on the remote computer and might not be visible to the user logged on to that computer. So you might not be able to use this script to, for example, open a new instance of Microsoft Notepad, which will be visible to the logged-on user. Consider this tool to be more appropriate for starting new background maintenance tasks (such as disk defragmenters), which require no user interaction.

The lack of user interaction can also pose problems. If you start a process that requires some user interaction, but the process is not visible to the logged-on user, the process might "hang" while it waits for a response to a dialog box or some other interactive element. Try to avoid remotely starting processes that might require such interaction.

## Performing This Task Manually

Windows includes a command-line tool named Rexec, which can start a process on a remote computer. The following, for example, will run a process named MyProcess.exe on a computer named Client1:

```
Rexec Client1 MyProcess.exe
```

However, Rexec is unable to target multiple computers simultaneously.

# Example

This tool allows you to target one computer or multiple computers. If you wanted to use the script to target a single remote computer named ServerA and start a process named MyProcess.exe, you would use the following code:

```
StartProcess.wsf /computer:ServerA /cmd:MyProcess.exe
```

Note that the *cmd* argument requires a complete path to the process you want started unless the process specified is in the system search path (which generally includes the Windows and Windows\System32 directories).

You can also target a list of computers from a text file. The text file is expected to contain one computer name per line and no other information. Assuming the file is named C:\Computers.txt, you would use this syntax:

```
StartProcess.wsf /list:C:\Computers.txt /cmd:MyProcess.exe
```

Finally, you can target an entire organizational unit of computer accounts. If your domain contains an OU named West, you would use the following syntax:

```
StartProcess.wsf /container:west /cmd:MyProcess.exe
```

Note that the *container* argument will work against only the default domain of the computer running the script. In other words, the OU specified must exist within the same domain of the computer running the script. If the specified OU has nested OUs, you can include their computer accounts as well by specifying one additional argument:

```
StartProcess.wsf /container:west /cmd:MyProcess.exe
```

Additional arguments provide more functionality to the command; see the following section titled "Syntax."

# Syntax

These scripts can be executed as command-line utilities. Set CScript.exe to be your default script processor, as described in Chapter 3.

| | |
|---|---|
| /list:path<br>/computer:name<br>/container:name | One and only one of these is required by the script. Use */list* to target a list of computers contained within a text file. Use */computer* to target a single computer. Use */container* to target an organizational unit within Active Directory. |
| /recurse | When used with */container*, also targets computers contained within nested OUs. |

| | |
|---|---|
| /ping | Verifies the connectivity to all targeted computers prior to attempting a connection. Using this argument will reduce the timeout wait when one or more computers cannot be reached on the network. |
| /log:path | Logs unreachable computer names to the specified file. This file can then be used later, along with the */list* argument, to retry these computers. Note that a log is created only when used in conjunction with the */ping* argument. |
| /verbose | Causes the script to display more detailed, step-by-step status messages. |
| /cmd:path | Required. Complete path and file name of the executable to start. This path can be a UNC, and each targeted computer will load the executable from that UNC and execute it locally. |

You can run these scripts with the */?* parameter to display the command's syntax.

## Under the Hood

This script uses Windows Management Instrumentation (WMI) to connect to each targeted computer. The entire *Win32_Process* class is retrieved rather than a specific instance of that class; the class itself provides a *Create()* method that creates a new instance of the class with the specified parameters. One return parameter is the new process's process ID, which the script will output to the command-line window if you specify the */verbose* argument.

```
Dim oProcesses, ErrResult, iID
Verbose " Connecting to WMI on " & sName
On Error Resume Next
Set oProcess = GetObject("winmgmts:\\" & sName & "\root\cimv2:Win32_Process")
If Err <> 0 Then
    WScript.Echo " *** Couldn't connect to WMI on " & sName
    LogBadConnect(sName)
Else
    ErrResult = oProcess.Create(WScript.Arguments.Named("cmd"),Null,Null,iID)
    If ErrResult = 0 Then
        Verbose " Created ID " & iID & " on " & sName
    Else
        WScript.Echo " *** Couldn't start on " & sname & ": " & ErrResult
    End If
End if
```

## Troubleshooting

This script has the potential to result in several types of errors. First, a remote computer won't be available. Second, you won't have permission to start remote processes. Generally, local Administrator permissions are required to start remote processes via WMI. In either case, you'll see an error message that alerts you to the problem for that computer. Make sure you have the appropriate permissions and that the computer is reachable via the network from the computer running this script. Unreachable computers can optionally be logged to a text file for a later attempt, and you can speed up the script by specifying the */ping* argument.

The third potential problem is that the targeted computers will be unable to access the executable you specify. This will result in the script displaying an error, which will likely occur for all targeted computers. In most environments, WMI will attempt to access the specified executable using *your* credentials, so if you must, specify a UNC or local file path to which your user account has at least Read and Execute privileges.

## To Learn More

- Find more VBScript samples for managing and monitoring processes at *http:// www.microsoft.com/technet/scriptcenter/scripts/os/process/default.mspx*.

- Learn more about the *Win32_Process* class at *http://msdn.microsoft.com /library/default.asp?url=/library/en-us/wmisdk/wmi/win32_process.asp*.

# End a Process

> **On the CD**   The sample script and be found on the CD that accompanies this book at \Chap9\EndProcess\EndProcess.wsf.

| Operating System | Supported? | Prerequisites |
|---|---|---|
| Windows 2000 family | Yes | ■  WSH 5.6 or later |
| Windows XP Professional | Yes | ■  WMI |
| Windows Server 2003 family | Yes | ■  Administrative permission on targeted computers |
| | | ■  Network connectivity to each remote computer |

## Description

This tool will end a named process on one or more computers. This is an excellent way to stop undesired processes that might be running. Note that you must provide the name of each process, which is sometimes slightly different from the name of its command-line executable. The name sometimes includes a file name extension, such as .exe, but not always; I recommend using the *ListProcesses* script, described in this chapter, to list the processes on a representative computer. That script lists, among other details, each process's name.

## Performing This Task Manually

Windows Task Manager can be used to end individual tasks (processes) on the local computer. A KILL command-line utility has also been included with various versions of the Windows Resource Kits; this tool can be used to end processes either by name (in some versions) or by process ID number (often requiring a second tool like PLIST or TLIST to discover the process number). Windows doesn't provide a built-in means for terminating processes on multiple computers at once.

## Example

This tool allows you to target one computer or multiple computers. If you wanted to use the script to target a single remote computer named ServerA and terminates a process named MyProcess.exe, you would use this code:

```
EndProcess.wsf /computer:ServerA /name:MyProcess.exe
```

You can also target a list of computers from a text file. The text file is expected to contain one computer name per line and no other information. Assuming the file is named C:\Computers.txt, you would use this syntax:

```
EndProcess.wsf /list:C:\Computers.txt /name:MyProcess.exe
```

Finally, you can target an entire organizational unit of computer accounts. If your domain contains an OU named West, you would use the following syntax:

```
EndProcess.wsf /container:west /name:MyProcess.exe
```

Note that the *container* argument will work against only the default domain of the computer running the script. In other words, the OU specified must exist within the same domain as that of the computer running the script. If the specified OU has nested OUs, you can include their computer accounts as well by specifying one additional argument:

```
EndProcess.wsf /container:west /name:MyProcess.exe
```

Additional arguments provide more functionality to the command; see the following section titled "Syntax."

# Syntax

These scripts can be executed as command-line utilities. Set CScript.exe to be your default script processor, as described in Chapter 3.

| | |
|---|---|
| `/list:path`<br>`/computer:name`<br>`/container:name` | One and only one of these is required by the script. Use */list* to target a list of computers contained within a text file. Use */computer* to target a single computer. Use */container* to target an organizational unit within Active Directory. |
| `/recurse` | When used with */container*, also targets computers contained within nested OUs. |
| `/ping` | Verifies the connectivity to all targeted computers prior to attempting a connection. Using this argument will reduce the timeout wait when one or more computers cannot be reached on the network. |
| `/log:path` | Logs unreachable computer names to the specified file. This file can then be used later, along with the */list* argument, to retry these computers. Note that a log is created only when used in conjunction with the */ping* argument. |
| `/verbose` | Causes the script to display more detailed, step-by-step status messages. |
| `/name:processname` | Required. Identifies the name of the process to terminate. This must be the actual process name, which might include a file name extension for some processes. |

You can run these scripts with the */?* parameter to display the command's syntax.

# Under the Hood

This script uses Windows Management Instrumentation (WMI) to connect to each targeted computer. The *Win32_Process* class is queried for the specified instance. The following script code performs the work of connecting to the remote computer and terminating the selected process:

```
Dim cProcesses, oProcess
Set cProcesses = QueryWMI(sName,"root\cimv2","Select * from Win32_Process Where Name
 = '" & wscript.arguments.named("name") & "'","","")
If Not IsObject(cProcesses) Then
    WScript.Echo " *** Could not retrieve process (or process does not exist) on "
& sName
Else
    For Each oProcess In cProcesses
        On Error Resume Next
        oProcess.Terminate()
        If Err <> 0 Then
            WScript.Echo " *** Error terminating on " & sName
            WScript.Echo " " & Err.Description
        Else
            Verbose " Terminated on " & sName
        End If
    Next
End If
```

Each instance of the *Win32_Process* class provides a *Terminate()* method that attempts to end the process.

# Troubleshooting

This script has the potential to result in several types of errors. First, a remote computer won't be available. Second, you won't have permission to work with the remote computer's processes (typically, only a member of the Administrators group will have permission to terminate a process). In either case, you'll see an error message that alerts you to the problem for that computer. Make sure you have the appropriate permissions and that the computer is reachable via the network from the computer running this script. Unreachable computers can optionally be logged to a text file for a later attempt, and you can speed up the script by specifying the */ping* argument.

The third potential problem is that one or more of the targeted computers won't have the process. In these instances, the script will return an error and continue trying with the next targeted computer. It's also possible for the script to encounter an error while trying to terminate the process; some processes can be configured, for security reasons, to resist termination by administrators, whereas other processes might encounter an error while terminating and fail to terminate properly. In these cases, the script will display an error code and continue trying the next targeted computer.

Note that terminating a process is not the same as ending it cleanly. Terminating a process will often result in the loss of whatever data the process was working with; you should terminate processes only when you're certain that doing so will not destabilize Windows, other processes or services, or result in a loss of important data.

## To Learn More

- Find more VBScript samples for managing and monitoring processes at *http:// www.microsoft.com/technet/scriptcenter/scripts/os/process/default.mspx.*

- Learn more about the *Win32_Process* class at *http://msdn.microsoft.com/library /default.asp?url=/library/en-us/wmisdk/wmi/win32_process.asp.*

# List Page Files

 **On the CD**   The sample script can be found on the CD that accompanies this book at \Chap9\ListPageFile\ListPageFile.wsf.

| Operating System | Supported? | Prerequisites |
|---|---|---|
| Windows 2000 family | Yes | ■ WSH 5.6 or later |
| Windows XP Professional | Yes | ■ WMI |
| Windows Server 2003 family | Yes | ■ Administrative permission on targeted computers |
| | | ■ Network connectivity to each remote computer |

## Description

This tool will list the page file properties for all page files on one or more computers. For each page file, you are shown its host drive, initial size, and maximum size. Optionally, the tool can save this information to a CSV file for long-term archiving or reporting. This is a useful way to quickly check a number of computers to ensure that their page files are optimally configured or configured to meet your organization's policies.

## Performing This Task Manually

In the Windows operating system, your primary means of managing the page file is by using the Properties dialog box of My Computer (specifically, the Advanced tab). Follow these steps to view page file settings:

1. Right-click My Computer.

2. Select Properties to open the System Properties dialog box.

3. Select the Advanced tab.

4. Under the Performance section, click Settings to display the Performance Options dialog box.

5. Select the Advanced tab.

6. Under the Virtual Memory section, click Change to display the Virtual Memory dialog box.

Using this procedure to review the page file settings of multiple computers, however, can be tedious.

# Example

This tool allows you to target one computer or multiple computers. If you wanted to use the script to target a single remote computer named ServerA and display its page file settings in the command-line window, you would use this code:

```
ListPageFile.wsf /computer:ServerA
```

You can also target a list of computers from a text file. The text file is expected to contain one computer name per line and no other information. Assuming the file is named C:\Computers.txt, you would use this syntax:

```
ListPageFile.wsf /list:C:\Computers.txt /output:C:\MyFile.csv
```

Note that this saves the output to a CSV file, which can be easier to review than the command-line window when targeting multiple computers. Finally, you can target an entire organizational unit of computer accounts. If your domain contains an OU named West, you would use the following syntax:

```
ListPageFile.wsf /container:west /output:C:\MyFile.csv
```

Note that the *container* argument will work against only the default domain of the computer running the script. In other words, the OU specified must exist within the same domain as that of the computer running the script. If the specified OU has nested OUs, you can include their computer accounts as well by specifying one additional argument:

```
ListPageFile.wsf /container:west /output:C:\MyFile.csv
```

Additional arguments provide more functionality to the command; see the following section titled "Syntax."

# Syntax

These scripts can be executed as command-line utilities. Set CScript.exe to be your default script processor, as described in Chapter 3.

| | |
|---|---|
| /list:path<br>/computer:name<br>/container:name | One and only one of these is required by the script. Use */list* to target a list of computers contained within a text file. Use */computer* to target a single computer. Use */container* to target an organizational unit within Active Directory. |
| /recurse | When used with */container*, also targets computers contained within nested OUs. |
| /ping | Verifies the connectivity to all targeted computers prior to attempting a connection. Using this argument will reduce the timeout wait when one or more computers cannot be reached on the network. |

| | |
|---|---|
| /log:path | Logs unreachable computer names to the specified file. This file can then be used later, along with the */list* argument, to retry these computers. Note that a log is created only when used in conjunction with the */ping* argument. |
| /verbose | Causes the script to display more detailed, step-by-step status messages. |
| /output:path | Saves the script's output to a CSV file specified in *path*. |

You can run these scripts with the */?* parameter to display the command's syntax.

## Under the Hood

This script uses Windows Management Instrumentation (WMI) to connect to each targeted computer. All instances of the *Win32_PageFile* class are queries, and specific properties of each instance are used in the script's output. The main work of the script is performed by this code:

```
Dim cFiles, oFile, sOutput
Verbose " Connecting to WMI on " & sName
Set cFiles = QueryWMI(sName,"root\cimv2","Select * From Win32_PageFile","","")
If Not IsObject(cFiles) Then
    WScript.Echo " *** Couldn't connect to WMI on " & sName
Else
    For Each oFile In cFiles
        sOutput = sName & "," & oFile.Drive & "," & oFile.InitialSize & ","
& oFile.MaximumSize
        If WScript.Arguments.Named.Exists("output") Then
            LogFile WScript.Arguments.Named("output"),sOutput,False
        Else
            WScript.Echo sOutput
        End If
    Next
End If
```

## Troubleshooting

This script has the potential to result in two types of errors. First, a remote computer won't be available. Second, you won't have permission to work with the remote computer's page files. In either case, you'll see an error message that alerts you to the problem for that computer. Make sure you have the appropriate permissions and that the computer is reachable via the network from the computer running this script. Unreachable computers can optionally be logged to a text file for a later attempt, and you can speed up the script by specifying the */ping* argument.

## To Learn More

- Find more VBScript samples for managing page files at *http://www.microsoft.com/technet/scriptcenter/scripts/os/pagefile/default.mspx*.

- Learn more about the *Win32_PageFile* class at *http://msdn.microsoft.com/library/default.asp?url=/library/en-us/wmisdk/wmi/win32_pagefile.asp*.

# Modify Page File Settings

**On the CD**   The sample script can be found on the CD that accompanies this book at \Chap9\ModifyPageFile\ModifyPageFile.wsf.

| Operating System | Supported? | Prerequisites |
|---|---|---|
| Windows 2000 family | Yes | ■  WSH 5.6 or later |
| Windows XP Professional | Yes | ■  WMI |
| Windows Server 2003 family | Yes | ■  Administrative permission on targeted computers |
| | | ■  Network connectivity to each remote computer |

## Description

This tool will modify the initial and maximum sizes for all page files on one or more computers. This is a useful, quick way to reconfigure multiple computers to have consistent page file settings.

## Performing This Task Manually

In Windows, your primary means of managing the page file is by using the Properties dialog box of My Computer (specifically, the Advanced tab). Follow these steps to view page file settings:

1. Right-click My Computer.

2. Select Properties to open the System Properties dialog box.

3. Select the Advanced tab.

4. Under the Performance section, click Settings to display the Performance Options dialog box.

5. Select the Advanced tab.

6. Under the Virtual Memory section, click Change to display the Virtual Memory dialog box.

Using this procedure to modify the page file settings of multiple computers, however, can be tedious.

## Example

This tool allows you to target one computer or multiple computers. You must specify the /initsize and /maxsize parameters, which both accept a size in megabytes (MB). If you wanted to use the script to target a single remote computer named ServerA and set its page file to have an initial size of 128 MB and a maximum size of 384 MB, you would use this code:

```
ModifyPageFile.wsf /computer:ServerA /initsize:128 /maxsize:384
```

Note that for computers with multiple page files (many administrators, for example, create page files on multiple physical drives to help spread the page file workload), each page file will be configured to have the initial and maximum size you specify.

You can also target a list of computers from a text file. The text file is expected to contain one computer name per line and no other information. Assuming the file is named C:\Computers.txt, you would use this syntax:

```
ModifyPageFile.wsf /list:C:\Computers.txt /initsize:128 /maxsize:384
```

Finally, you can target an entire organizational unit of computer accounts. If your domain contains an OU named West, you would use the following syntax:

```
ModifyPageFile.wsf /container:west /initsize:128 /maxsize:384
```

Note that the */container* argument will work against only the default domain of the computer running the script. In other words, the OU specified must exist within the same domain as that of the computer running the script. If the specified OU has nested OUs, you can include their computer accounts as well by specifying one additional argument:

```
ModifyPageFile.wsf /container:west /initsize:128 /maxsize:384
```

Additional arguments provide more functionality to the command; see the following section titled "Syntax."

## Syntax

These scripts can be executed as command-line utilities. Set CScript.exe to be your default script processor, as described in Chapter 3.

| | |
|---|---|
| `/list:path`<br>`/computer:name`<br>`/container:name` | One and only one of these is required by the script. Use */list* to target a list of computers contained within a text file. Use */computer* to target a single computer. Use */container* to target an organizational unit within Active Directory. |
| `/recurse` | When used with */container*, also targets computers contained within nested OUs. |
| `/ping` | Verifies the connectivity to all targeted computers prior to attempting a connection. Using this argument will reduce the timeout wait when one or more computers cannot be reached on the network. |

| | |
|---|---|
| /log:path | Logs unreachable computer names to the specified file. This file can then be used later, along with the */list* argument, to retry these computers. Note that a log is created only when used in conjunction with the */ping* argument. |
| /verbose | Causes the script to display more detailed, step-by-step status messages. |
| /initsize:MB | Required. Specifies the initial page file size in megabytes. |
| /maxsize:MB | Required. Specifies the maximum page file size in megabytes. |

You can run these scripts with the */?* parameter to display the command's syntax.

# Under the Hood

This script uses Windows Management Instrumentation (WMI) to connect to each targeted computer. The following code performs the main work of this script:

```
Dim cFiles, oFile
Verbose " Connecting to WMI on " & sName
Set cFiles = QueryWMI(sName,"root\cimv2","Select * From Win32_PageFileSetting","","")
If Not IsObject(cFiles) Then
    WScript.Echo " *** Couldn't connect to WMI on " & sName
Else
    For Each oFile In cFiles
        Verbose "Changing on " & sName
        On Error Resume Next
        oFile.InitialSize = WScript.Arguments.Named("initsize")
        If Err <> 0 Then
            WScript.Echo " *** Error setting initsize on " & sName
            WScript.Echo " " & Err.Description
        Else
            Verbose " Set initsize on " sName
        End If
        oFile.MaximumSize = WScript.Arguments.Named("maxsize")
        If Err <> 0 Then
            WScript.Echo " *** Error setting maxsize on " & sName
            WScript.Echo " " & Err.Description
        Else
            Verbose " Set maxsize on " sName
        End If
        oFile.Put_
        If Err <> 0 Then
            WScript.Echo " *** Error setting sizes on " & sName
            WScript.Echo " " & Err.Description
        Else
            Verbose " Set sizes on " sName
        End If

    Next
End If
```

Notice that the *Win32_PageFile* class is retrieved from each computer, and the class's *InitialSize* and *MaximumSize* properties are modified. These are some of the very few WMI properties that can be directly read and written by a script; most WMI properties are read-only, and you make changes by using methods of the class. In the example in the preceding code, you must use the class's *Put_()* method to save the changes made to the properties.

## Troubleshooting

This script has the potential to result in several types of errors. First, a remote computer won't be available. Second, you won't have permission to work with the remote computer's page files. (Typically, only a member of the Administrators group has permission to do so.) In either case, you'll see an error message that alerts you to the problem for that computer. Make sure you have the appropriate permissions and that the computer is reachable via the network from the computer running this script. Unreachable computers can optionally be logged to a text file for a later attempt, and you can speed up the script by specifying the */ping* argument.

The third potential problem is that one or more of the targeted computers won't have the disk space needed to support the page file sizes you specify. Be very careful to not specify a page file that would exceed the available disk space; Chapter 10, "File, Disk, and Volume Management," includes tools to help you automate the process of inventorying available drive space on multiple computers.

## To Learn More

- Find more VBScript samples for managing page files at *http:// www.microsoft.com/technet/scriptcenter/scripts/os/pagefile/default.mspx*.
- Learn more about the *Win32_PageFile* class at *http://msdn.microsoft.com /library/default.asp?url=/library/en-us/wmisdk/wmi/win32_pagefile.asp*.

# Shut Down or Restart Computers

> **On the CD** The sample script can be found on the CD that accompanies this book at \Chap9\ShutdownRestart\ShutdownRestart.wsf.

| Operating System | Supported? | Prerequisites |
|---|---|---|
| Windows 2000 family | Yes | ■ WSH 5.6 or later |
| Windows XP Professional | Yes | ■ WMI |
| Windows Server 2003 family | Yes | ■ Administrative permission on targeted computers |
| | | ■ Network connectivity to each remote computer |

## Description

This tool will shut down, restart, log off, or power off multiple computers. The power off functionality must be supported in the computers' hardware and BIOS; if it is not, the power off command will be interpreted as a simple shutdown command. This tool will, by default, issue *normal* commands for shut down, restart, and so forth, meaning individual applications could intercept and abort the command. This tool can optionally *force* the specified operation, which will give applications a fixed amount of time in which to shut down properly, and then it can terminate any applications that fail to do so.

## Performing This Task Manually

Windows provides well-known means for performing shutdown, restart, and logoff operations for an individual computer from the graphical user interface. The Windows Support Tools (and some versions of the Windows Resource Kits) also include a Shutdown.exe command-line utility, which can be used to shut down or restart a single remote computer. There are no built-in means to target multiple computers at once, however.

## Example

This tool allows you to target one computer or multiple computers. If you wanted to use the script to target a single remote computer named ServerA and shut it down, you would use this code:

```
ShutdownRestart.wsf /computer:ServerA /action:shutdown
```

You can also target a list of computers from a text file. The text file is expected to contain one computer name per line and no other information. Assuming the file is named C:\Computers.txt, you would use this syntax:

```
ShutdownRestart.wsf /list:C:\Computers.txt /action:shutdown
```

Finally, you can target an entire organizational unit of computer accounts. If your domain contains an OU named West, you would use the following syntax:

```
ShutdownRestart.wsf /container:west /action:shutdown
```

Note that the *container* argument will work against only the default domain of the computer running the script. In other words, the OU specified must exist within the same domain as that of the computer running the script. If the specified OU has nested OUs, you can include their computer accounts as well by specifying one additional argument:

```
ShutdownRestart.wsf /container:west /action:shutdown
```

Additional arguments provide more functionality to the command; see the following section titled "Syntax."

# Syntax

These scripts can be executed as command-line utilities. Set CScript.exe to be your default script processor, as described in Chapter 3.

| | |
|---|---|
| `/list:path`<br>`/computer:name`<br>`/container:name` | One and only one of these is required by the script. Use */list* to target a list of computers contained within a text file. Use */computer* to target a single computer. Use */container* to target an organizational unit within Active Directory. |
| `/recurse` | When used with */container*, also targets computers contained within nested OUs. |
| `/ping` | Verifies the connectivity to all targeted computers prior to attempting a connection. Using this argument will reduce the timeout wait when one or more computers cannot be reached on the network. |
| `/log:path` | Logs unreachable computer names to the specified file. This file can then be used later, along with the */list* argument, to retry these computers. Note that a log is created only when used in conjunction with the */ping* argument. |
| `/verbose` | Causes the script to display more detailed, step-by-step status messages. |
| `/action:command` | Required. *Command* must be one of these: *restart, logoff, shutdown*, or *poweroff*. |
| `/force` | Forces the command specified in */action*, preventing an application or process from aborting the specified command. |

You can run these scripts with the */?* parameter to display the command's syntax.

# Under the Hood

This script uses Windows Management Instrumentation (WMI) to connect to each targeted computer. The *Win32_OperatingSystem* class is queried because that class provides methods for performing a shutdown. The following script code performs the work of connecting to the remote computers and performing the specified command:

```
Dim cSystems, oSystem, iAction
Select Case lcase(WScript.Arguments.Named("action"))
    Case "shutdown"
        iAction = 1
    Case "restart"
        iAction = 2
    Case "logoff"
        iAction = 0
    Case "poweroff"
        iAction = 8
    Case Else
        WScript.Echo "*** Unknown action " & WScript.Arguments.Named("action")
End Select
If WScript.Arguments.Named.Exists("force") Then
    iAction = iAction + 4
End If
Verbose " Connecting to WMI on " & sName
Set cSystems = QueryWMI(sName,"root\cimv2","Select * From Win32_OperatingSystem",
"","")
If Not IsObject(cSystems) Then
    WScript.Echo " *** Couldn't connect to WMI on " & sName
Else
    For Each oSystem In cSystems
        On Error Resume Next
        oSystem.Win32Shutdown(iAction)
        If Err <> 0 Then
            WScript.Echo " *** Couldn't perform action on " & sName
            WScript.Echo " " & Err.Description
        Else
            Verbose "Successful on " & sName
        End If
    Next
End If
```

The *Win32_OperatingSystem* class also has a *Shutdown()* method, but this script uses the more flexible *Win32Shutdown()* method, which supports additional commands such as power off as well as the ability to force the specified command.

## Troubleshooting

In this script, other than connectivity issues (which can be avoided by specifying the */ping* argument to test for connectivity), only a lack of permissions will result in an error. Typically, members of a computer's local Administrators group have permissions to initiate remote shutdown, restart, poweroff, or logoff.

## To Learn More

- Learn more about the *Win32_OperatingSystem* class and its *Win32Shutdown()* method at *http://msdn.microsoft.com/library /default.asp?url=/library/en-us/wmisdk/wmi/win32shutdown_method_ in_class_win32_operatingsystem.asp.*

- Read more about the Shutdown.exe command-line tool.
  - Windows 2000: *http://support.microsoft.com/default.aspx?scid=kb; en-us;317371.*
  - Windows Server 2003: *http://www.microsoft.com/resources/documentation /WindowsServ/2003/standard/proddocs/en-us/Default.asp?url=/resources /documentation/WindowsServ/2003/standard/proddocs/en-us /shutdown.asp.*

# Modify Boot.ini Files

> **On the CD**   The sample script can be found on the CD that accompanies this book at \Chap9\ModifyBootIni\ModifyBootIni.wsf.

| Operating System | Supported? | Prerequisites |
|---|---|---|
| Windows 2000 family | Yes | ■ WSH 5.6 or later |
| Windows XP Professional | Yes | ■ WMI |
| Windows Server 2003 family | Yes | ■ Administrative permission on targeted computers |
| | | ■ Network connectivity to each remote computer |

## Description

This tool will modify the Boot.ini file on one more computers so that it has a new startup delay time. This delay time specifies how long the Windows operating system selection screen is displayed before Windows starts the default operating system.

Many Windows computers will not display an operating system selection screen. When only one operating system and the Recovery Console is not installed, Boot.ini contains only one entry, and Windows always starts that entry without displaying the selection screen. However, it is a best practice (at least on servers) to install the Recovery Console, which will cause the selection screen to be displayed when the server starts. Consistently configuring the delay time on this screen will make your servers more predictable and easier to manage in the event the Recovery Console is needed.

## Performing This Task Manually

To manually modify the startup delay:

1. Right-click My Computer.

2. Select Properties to display the System Properties dialog box.

3. Select the Advanced tab.

4. Under the Startup And Recovery section, click Settings to display the Startup And Recovery dialog box.

5. Modify the Time to display a list of operating systems values as desired. (The default is 30 seconds.)

# Example

This tool allows you to target one computer or multiple computers. If you wanted to use the script simply to target a single remote computer named ServerA and set its startup delay to 45 seconds, you would use this code:

```
ModifyBootIni.wsf /computer:ServerA /delay:45
```

You can also target a list of computers from a text file. The text file is expected to contain one computer name per line and no other information. Assuming the file is named C:\Computers.txt, you would use this syntax:

```
ModifyBootIni.wsf /list:C:\Computers.txt /delay:45
```

Finally, you can target an entire organizational unit of computer accounts. If your domain contains an OU named West, you would use the following syntax:

```
ModifyBootIni.wsf /container:west /delay:45
```

Note that the *container* argument will work against only the default domain of the computer running the script. In other words, the OU specified must exist within the same domain as that of the computer running the script. If the specified OU has nested OUs, you can include their computer accounts as well by specifying one additional argument:

```
ModifyBootIni.wsf /container:west /delay:45
```

Additional arguments provide more functionality to the command; see the following section titled "Syntax."

# Syntax

These scripts can be executed as command-line utilities. Set CScript.exe to be your default script processor, as described in Chapter 3.

| | |
|---|---|
| `/list:path`<br>`/computer:name`<br>`/container:name` | One and only one of these is required by the script. Use */list* to target a list of computers contained within a text file. Use */computer* to target a single computer. Use */container* to target an organizational unit within Active Directory. |
| `/recurse` | When used with */container*, also targets computers contained within nested OUs. |
| `/ping` | Verifies the connectivity to all targeted computers prior to attempting a connection. Using this argument will reduce the timeout wait when one or more computers cannot be reached on the network. |

| | |
|---|---|
| /log:path | Logs unreachable computer names to the specified file. This file can then be used later, along with the */list* argument, to retry these computers. Note that a log is created only when used in conjunction with the */ping* argument. |
| /verbose | Causes the script to display more detailed, step-by-step status messages. |
| /delay:seconds | Required. Specifies the number of seconds to display the operating system selection screen before starting the default entry. |

You can run these scripts with the */?* parameter to display the command's syntax.

## Under the Hood

This script uses Windows Management Instrumentation (WMI) to connect to each targeted computer. The *Win32_ComputerSystem* class provides access to major properties of the Boot.ini file, as shown in this portion of the script:

```
Dim cSystems, oSystem, sOutput
Verbose " Connecting to WMI on " & sName
Set cSystems = QueryWMI(sName,"root\cimv2","Select * From Win32_ComputerSystem","","")
If Not IsObject(cSystems) Then
    WScript.Echo " *** Couldn't connect to WMI on " & sName
Else
    For Each oSystem In cSystems
        On Error Resume Next
        oSystem.SystemStartupDelay = WScript.Arguments.Named("delay")
        oSystem.Put_
        If Err <> 0 Then
            WScript.Echo " *** Error changing " & sName
            WScript.Echo " " & Err.Description
        Else
            Verbose " Changed " & sName
        End If
    Next
End If
```

The *SystemStartupDelay* property—one of the few writable WMI properties—configures the startup delay; the *Put_()* method is required to save the changes to this property.

## Troubleshooting

This script has the potential to result in two types of errors. First, a remote computer won't be available. Second, you won't have permission to work with the remote computer's Boot.ini properties. (Typically, only a member of the Administrators group will have permission to do so.) In either case, you'll see an error message that alerts you to the problem for that computer. Make sure you have the appropriate permissions and that the computer is reachable via the network from the computer running this script. Unreachable computers can optionally be logged to a text file for a later attempt, and you can speed up the script by specifying the */ping* argument.

## To Learn More

- Find more VBScript samples for managing startup and shutdown properties at *http://www.microsoft.com/technet/scriptcenter/scripts/desktop/state/default.mspx.*

- Learn more about remote access to the *Win32_ComputerSystem* class at *http:// msdn.microsoft.com/library/default.asp?url=/library/en-us/wmisdk/wmi /accessing_a_remote_wmi_win32_computersystem_object.asp.*

# Part III
# Disk and File Management Tasks

Chapter 10

# File, Disk, and Volume Management

File, disk, and volume management can often be one of the most tedious kinds of management in a Microsoft® Windows® environment. The widespread use of the Windows® operating system as a file server means that many organizations have hundreds or thousands of megabytes of files. Thus, any management task that must affect more than a handful of files can become laborious and time-consuming.

Tasks automated in this chapter include:

- Taking ownership of multiple files
- Compressing and uncompressing folders on file servers
- Inventorying free disk space
- Inventorying disk properties
- Inventorying partitions (logical disks)
- Defragmenting drives on multiple servers
- Scheduling a regular disk defragmentation on multiple servers

# Taking Ownership of Files

> **On the CD**    The sample script can be found on the CD that accompanies this book at \Chap10\TakeOwnership\TakeOwnership.wsf.

| Operating System | Supported? | Prerequisites |
|---|---|---|
| Microsoft Windows 2000 family | Yes | ■ Windows Script Host (WSH) 5.6 or later |
| Microsoft Windows XP Professional | Yes | ■ Windows Management Instrumentation (WMI) |
| Microsoft Windows Server™ 2003 family | Yes | ■ Administrative permission on targeted computers |
| | | ■ Network connectivity to each remote computer |

## Description

Most organizations routinely make the Administrator account the owner of all files not belonging to a particular user. Ownership of files by the Administrator account helps ensure consistent permissions and recoverability for files across the organization. On file servers where quotas are enabled, having files owned by the Administrator account enables those files to be excluded from an individual user's quota, which is commonly desired for files that are shared by a project team, by a department, or by the entire company. This script, TakeOwnership.wsf, enables you to quickly take ownership of multiple files on multiple servers, improving consistency and manageability.

## Performing This Task Manually

Windows provides a well-known graphical user interface for taking ownership of files, including multiple files located within a folder hierarchy. To take ownership of files manually, follow these steps:

1. Right-click a folder or file.

2. Select Properties to display the file (or folder) Properties dialog box.

3. Select the Security tab and click Advanced to display the Advanced Security Settings dialog box.

4. Select the Owner tab.

5. In the Change Owner To list box, select the new owner for the file or folder. Select the Replace Owner On Subcontainers And Objects check box to make the change effective for files and subfolders within a folder.

6. Click OK twice.

This technique does not, however, work across multiple servers. You can perform this task remotely, one server at a time, by accessing remote files through a shared folder or by logging onto the remote server using Remote Desktop (if enabled).

# Example

This tool allows you to target one computer or multiple computers. If you wanted to use it to target a single remote computer named ServerA and take ownership of all files in the C:\Shares folder, you would use this code:

```
TakeOwnership.wsf /computer:ServerA /folder:C:\Shares
```

Notice that the */folder* argument requires you to provide a local file path, not a UNC. The preceding code will therefore take ownership of the C:\Shares folder on the computer named ServerA.

You can also target a list of computers from a text file. The text file is expected to contain one computer name per line and no other information. Assuming the file is named C:\Computers.txt, you would use this syntax:

```
TakeOwnership.wsf /list:C:\Computers.txt /folder:C:\Shares
```

Finally, you can target an entire organizational unit (OU) of computer accounts. If your domain contains an OU named West, you would use the following syntax:

```
TakeOwnership.wsf /container:west /folder:C:\Shares
```

Note that the */container* argument will work against only the default domain of the computer running the script. In other words, the OU specified must exist within the same domain as that of the computer running the script. If the specified OU has nested OUs, you can include their computer accounts as well by specifying one additional argument:

```
TakeOwnership.wsf /container:west /recurse /folder:C:\Shares
```

This script always assigns ownership to your user account. Additional arguments provide more functionality to the command; see the following section titled "Syntax."

# Syntax

These scripts can be executed as command-line utilities. Set CScript.exe to be your default script processor, as described in Chapter 3, "Working with VBScript."

| | |
|---|---|
| /list:path<br>/computer:name<br>/container:name | One and only one of these is required by the script. Use /list to target a list of computers contained within a text file. Use /computer to target a single computer. Use /container to target an organizational unit within Microsoft Active Directory®. |
| /recurse | When used with /container, also targets computers contained within nested OUs. |
| /ping | Verifies the connectivity to all targeted computers prior to attempting a connection. Using this argument will reduce the timeout wait when one or more computers cannot be reached on the network. |
| /log:path | Logs unreachable computer names to the specified file. This file can then be used later, along with the /list argument, to retry these computers. Note that a log is created only when used in conjunction with the /ping argument. |
| /verbose | Causes the script to display more detailed, step-by-step status messages. |
| /folder:path | Required. Specifies the local path of the folder to take ownership of. Must exist on all targeted servers. |

You can run these scripts with the /? parameter to display the command's syntax.

# Under the Hood

This script uses a straightforward Windows Management Instrumentation (WMI) query to retrieve the instance of the *Win32_Directory* class corresponding to the folder path you specify. The script then executes the instance's *TakeOwnership()* method, which assigns ownership to the user account that was used to execute the script.

```
Dim cFolders, errResults, oFolder
Set cFolders = QueryWMI(sName,"root\cimv2","Select * From Win32_Directory where
name = '" & _
 Replace(WScript.Arguments.Named("folder"),"\","\\") & "'", "", "")
If Not IsObject(cFolders) Then
    WScript.Echo "Couldn't retrieve folder from " & sName
Else
    For Each oFolder In cFolders
        Verbose " Taking ownership on " & sName
        errResults = oFolder.TakeOwnership()
        Verbose " Result on " & sName & ": " & errResults
    Next
End If
```

Notice that the script handles the conversion of the folder path you specify to the format required by WMI; specifically, backslashes (which are treated as special characters by WMI) are doubled, ensuring they will be recognized as part of the folder path. This conversion is accomplished through the use of the *Replace()* function.

## Troubleshooting

As with most scripts, this script can run into a couple of common errors. First, one or more targeted computers might not be available, a condition the script can handle properly. You can reduce the script's execution time by including the */ping* argument, which tests connectivity prior to trying to execute the WMI query. The second possible error is that you won't have permission to take ownership of the files involved. This is unusual if you're running the script as an administrator, but the script will detect this error, display a message, and continue running.

It's also possible that one or more targeted servers won't contain the folder you've specified. This script's primary value is in ensuring consistent ownership across file servers that are already more or less consistently configured; for example, all your file servers might house their shared folders under a root \Shares folder, which could in turn be targeted by this script. However, on less consistently configured servers, the script will display a message and skip any server not containing the specified folder.

## To Learn More

- Learn more about the *Win32_Directory* class and its *TakeOwnership()* method at *http://msdn.microsoft.com/library/default.asp?url=/library/en-us/wmisdk/wmi/takeownership_method_in_class_win32_directory.asp*.

- Find more local folder managament samples in Microsoft Visual Basic® (VBScript) at *http://www.microsoft.com/technet/scriptcenter/scripts/storage/folders/default.mspx*.

# Compress or Uncompress Files and Folders

**On the CD**   The sample script can be found on the CD that accompanies this book at \Chap10\CompressDecompress\CompressDecompress.wsf.

| Operating System | Supported? | Prerequisites |
|---|---|---|
| Windows 2000 family | Yes | ■ WSH 5.6 or later |
| Windows XP Professional | Yes | ■ WMI |
| Windows Server 2003 family | Yes | ■ Administrative permission on targeted computers |
| | | ■ Network connectivity to each remote computer |

## Description

Many organizations use the native file compression features offered by Windows to reduce disk space utilization on crowded file servers. This script enables you to consistently apply or remove file compression on a folder that exists on multiple file servers. This script works best for file servers that are consistently configured—for example, servers that contain all their shared folders under a root \Shares folder. This script is designed to target local file paths rather than shared folders, enabling you to apply or remove folder compression at any level of the folder hierarchy.

## Performing This Task Manually

Windows provides a well-known graphical user interface for managing file compression, including multiple files located within a folder hierarchy. To manually manage file compression, follow these steps:

1. Right-click a folder or file.

2. Select Properties to display the file (or folder) Properties dialog box.

3. Click Advanced to display the Advanced Attributes dialog box.

4. Select (or clear) the Compress Contents To Save Disk Space check box.

This technique does not, however, work across multiple servers. You can perform this task remotely, one server at a time, by accessing remote files through a shared folder or by logging on to the remote server using Remote Desktop (if enabled).

# Example

This tool allows you to target one computer or multiple computers. If you wanted to use it to target a single remote computer named ServerA and compress all files in the C:\Shares folder, you would use this code:

```
CompressDecompress.wsf /computer:ServerA /folder:C:\Shares /mode:compress
```

Notice that the */folder* argument requires you to provide a local file path, not a UNC. Using the local file path compresses the C:\Shares folder on the computer named ServerA.

You can also target a list of computers from a text file. The text file is expected to contain one computer name per line and no other information. Assuming the file is named C:\Computers.txt, you would use this syntax:

```
CompressDecompress.wsf /list:C:\Computers.txt /folder:C:\Shares /mode:compress
```

Finally, you can target an entire organizational unit of computer accounts. If your domain contains an OU named West, you would use the following syntax:

```
CompressDecompress.wsf /container:west /folder:C:\Shares /mode:compress
```

Note that the */container* argument will work against only the default domain of the computer running the script. In other words, the OU specified must exist within the same domain as that of the computer running the script. If the specified OU has nested OUs, you can include their computer accounts as well by specifying one additional argument:

```
CompressDecompress.wsf /container:west /recurse /folder:C:\Shares /mode:compress
```

Additional arguments provide more functionality to the command; see the following section titled "Syntax."

# Syntax

These scripts can be executed as a command-line utility. Set CScript.exe to be your default script processor, as described in Chapter 3.

| | |
|---|---|
| `/list:path`<br>`/computer:name`<br>`/container:name` | One and only one of these is required by the script. Use */list* to target a list of computers contained within a text file. Use */computer* to target a single computer. Use */container* to target an organizational unit within Active Directory. |
| `/recurse` | When used with */container*, also targets computers contained within nested OUs. |

| | |
|---|---|
| /ping | Verifies the connectivity to all targeted computers prior to attempting a connection. Using this argument will reduce the timeout wait when one or more computers cannot be reached on the network. |
| /log:path | Logs unreachable computer names to the specified file. This file can then be used later, along with the */list* argument, to retry these computers. Note that a log is created only when used in conjunction with the */ping* argument. |
| /verbose | Causes the script to display more detailed, step-by-step status messages. |
| /folder:path | Required. Specifies the local path of the folder to take ownership of. Must exist on all targeted servers. |
| /mode:compress\|decompress | Required. Specifies whether to compress or decompress the folder specified. |

You can run these scripts with the */?* parameter to display the command's syntax.

# Under the Hood

This script uses a straightforward Windows Management Instrumentation (WMI) query to retrieve the instance of the *Win32_Directory* class corresponding to the folder path you specify. The script then executes the instance's *Compress()* or *Uncompress()* method, which performs the associated compression action.

```
Dim cFolders, errResults, oFolder
Set cFolders = QueryWMI(sName,"root\cimv2","Select * From Win32_Directory where
name = '" & _
 Replace(WScript.Arguments.Named("folder"),"\","\\") & "'", "","")
If Not IsObject(cFolders) Then
    WScript.Echo "Couldn't retrieve folder from " & sName
Else
    For Each oFolder In cFolders
        Select Case lcase(WScript.Arguments.Named("mode"))
            Case "compress"
                errresult = oFolder.compress
                Verbose " Compress on " & sName & ": " & errResult
            Case "decompress"
                errResult = oFolder.uncompress
                Verbose " Decompress on " & sName & ": " & errResult
            Case Else
                WScript.Echo "Unknown /mode specified"
        End Select
    Next
End If
```

Notice that the script handles the conversion of the folder path you specify to the format required by WMI; specifically, backslashes (which are treated as special characters by WMI) are doubled, ensuring they will be recognized as part of the folder path. This conversion is accomplished through the use of the *Replace()* function.

# Troubleshooting

As with most scripts, this script can run into a couple of common errors. First, one or more targeted computers might not be available, a condition the script can handle properly. You can reduce the script's execution time by including the */ping* argument, which tests connectivity prior to trying to execute the WMI query. The second possible error is that you won't have permission to manage compression of the files involved. This is unusual if you're running the script as an administrator, but the script will detect this error, display a message, and continue running.

It's also possible that one or more targeted servers won't contain the folder you've specified. This script's primary value is in ensuring consistent compression settings across file servers that are already more or less consistently configured; for example, all your file servers might house their shared folders under a root \Shares folder, which could in turn be targeted by this script. However, on less consistently configured servers, the script will display a message and skip any server not containing the specified folder.

# To Learn More

- Learn more about the *Win32_Directory* class and its *Compress()* method at *http://msdn.microsoft.com/library/default.asp?url=/library/en-us/wmisdk/wmi/ compress_method_in_class_win32_directory.asp*.

- Find more local folder management samples in VBScript at *http:// www.microsoft.com/technet/scriptcenter/scripts/storage/folders/default.mspx*.

# List Free Disk Space

> **On the CD** The sample script can be found on the CD that accompanies this book at \Chap10\ListFreeDiskSpace\ListFreeDiskSpace.wsf.

| Operating System | Supported? | Prerequisites |
|---|---|---|
| Windows 2000 family | Yes | ■ WSH 5.6 or later |
| Windows XP Professional | Yes | ■ WMI |
| Windows Server 2003 family | Yes | ■ Administrative permission on targeted computers |
| | | ■ Network connectivity to each remote computer |

## Description

Without using third-party tools, quickly obtaining a free disk report from multiple computers can sometimes be difficult. Being able to do so is certainly useful for servers, but it's also useful for client computers, because it allows you to quickly determine which computers might need additional maintenance to free up disk space. This script can target multiple computers and create a formatted report of available disk space one ach drive within each computer.

## Performing This Task Manually

Microsoft Windows Explorer provides a view that shows free space on each configured logical disk. You can also right-click any disk within Windows Explorer and select Properties to display a pie chart of free and used disk space on that disk. However, these techniques do not allow you to easily target remote computers or multiple computers, and they do not produce formatted reports.

## Example

This tool allows you to target one computer or multiple computers. If you wanted to use it to target a single remote computer named ServerA and display its free disk space in the command-line window, you would use this code:

```
FreeDiskSpace.wsf /computer:ServerA
```

You can also target a list of computers from a text file. The text file is expected to contain one computer name per line and no other information. Assuming the file is named C:\Computers.txt, you would use this syntax:

```
FreeDiskSpace.wsf /list:C:\Computers.txt /output:C:\Report.csv
```

Note that this saves the free disk space report to a comma-separated values (CSV) file named C:\Report.csv, which can be easier to review than the command-line window display.

Finally, you can target an entire organizational unit of computer accounts. If your domain contains an OU named West, you would use the following syntax:

```
FreeDiskSpace.wsf /container:west /output:C:\Report.csv
```

Note that the */container* argument will work against only the default domain of the computer running the script. In other words, the OU specified must exist within the same domain as that of the computer running the script. If the specified OU has nested OUs, you can include their computer accounts as well by specifying one additional argument:

```
FreeDiskSpace.wsf /container:west /recurse /output:C:\Report.csv
```

Additional arguments provide more functionality to the command; see the following section titled "Syntax."

# Syntax

These scripts can be executed as command-line utilities. Set CScript.exe to be your default script processor, as described in Chapter 3.

| | |
|---|---|
| `/list:path`<br>`/computer:name`<br>`/container:name` | One and only one of these is required by the script. Use */list* to target a list of computers contained within a text file. Use */computer* to target a single computer. Use */container* to target an organizational unit within Active Directory. |
| `/recurse` | When used with */container*, also targets computers contained within nested OUs. |
| `/ping` | Verifies the connectivity to all targeted computers prior to attempting a connection. Using this argument will reduce the timeout wait when one or more computers cannot be reached on the network. |
| `/log:path` | Logs unreachable computer names to the specified file. This file can then be used later, along with the */list* argument, to retry these computers. Note that a log is created only when used in conjunction with the */ping* argument. |
| `/output:path` | Saves the free disk space information to a CSV file specified in *path*. |

You can run these scripts with the */?* parameter to display the command's syntax.

# Under the Hood

This script uses a straightforward Windows Management Instrumentation (WMI) query to retrieve all instances of the *Win32_LogicalDisk* class and display their free space. The script uses the *Size* and *FreeSpace* properties to calculate the percentage of free disk space, which is also included in the script's output.

```
Dim cDrives, oDrive, sOutput
Verbose " Connecting to WMI on " & sName
Set cDrives = QueryWMI(sName,"root\cimv2","Select * From Win32_LogicalDisk WHERE
DriveType = 3","","")
If Not IsObject(cDrives) Then
    WScript.Echo " *** Couldn't connect to WMI on " & sName
Else
    For Each oDrive In cDrives
        sOutput = sName & "," & oDrive.DeviceID & "," & oDrive.Size & ","
& oDrive.FreeSpace & "," & Int((oDrive.FreeSpace / oDrive.Size) * 100) & "%"
        If WScript.Arguments.Named.Exists("output") Then
            LogFile WScript.Arguments.Named("output"),sOutput,False
        Else
            WScript.Echo sOutput
        End If
    Next
End If
```

# Troubleshooting

As with most scripts, this script can run into a couple of common errors. First, one or more targeted computers might not be available, a condition the script can handle properly. You can reduce the script's execution time by including the */ping* argument, which tests connectivity prior to trying to execute the WMI query.

The second possible error is that you won't have permission to examine the drives involved. This is unusual if you're running the script as an administrator, but the script will detect this error, display a message, and continue running.

# To Learn More

- Learn more about the *Win32_LogicalDisk* class at *http://msdn.microsoft.com/ library/default.asp?url=/library/en-us/wmisdk/wmi/win32_logicaldisk.asp*.

- Find more disk management samples in VBScript at *http://www.microsoft.com/ technet/scriptcenter/scripts/storage/disks/drives/default.mspx*.

# Inventory Disks

**On the CD**   The sample script can be found on the CD that accompanies this book at \Chap10\InventoryDrives\InventoryDrives.wsf.

| Operating System | Supported? | Prerequisites |
|---|---|---|
| Windows 2000 family | Yes | ■  WSH 5.6 or later |
| Windows XP Professional | Yes | ■  WMI |
| Windows Server 2003 family | Yes | ■  Administrative permission on targeted computers |
| | | ■  Network connectivity to each remote computer |

## Description

Obtaining a quick inventory of your computers' hard disks can be difficult if you aren't using a systems management tool like Microsoft Systems Management Server (SMS). This script can scan multiple computers and create a report of their hard disks, including device IDs, interface type, manufacturer, model, size, and cylinder and head configuration. Not all information will be available for all drives; some drive manufacturers don't expose certain information in a way that Windows can access.

## Performing This Task Manually

Windows Device Manager displays this type of information, although typically in less detail than this script can provide. You can use Device Manager to target remote computers, but only one computer at a time. Some of the physical configuration information provided by this script—such as cylinder and head information—is often most easily obtained through computers' BIOS setup screens, a technique that is unfortunately available only when you're physically in front of the computer.

## Example

This tool allows you to target one computer or multiple computers. Suppose you want to use it to target a single remote computer named ServerA and inventory its drives to the command-line window:

```
InventoryDrives.wsf /computer:ServerA
```

You can also target a list of computers from a text file. The text file is expected to contain one computer name per line and no other information. Assuming the file is named C:\Computers.txt, you would use this syntax:

```
InventoryDrives.wsf /list:C:\Computers.txt /output:C:\Drives.csv
```

Note that this will create a comma-separated values (CSV) file named C:\Drives.csv containing the drive inventory for the targeted computers.

Finally, you can target an entire organizational unit of computer accounts. If your domain contains an OU named West, you would use the following syntax:

```
InventoryDrives.wsf /container:west /output:C:\Drives.csv
```

The *container* argument will work only in the default domain of the computer running the script. In other words, the OU specified must exist within the same domain as that of the computer running the script. If the specified OU has nested OUs, you can include their computer accounts as well by specifying one additional argument:

```
InventoryDrives.wsf /container:west /recurse /output:C:\Drives.csv
```

Additional arguments provide additional functionality to the command; see the following section titled "Syntax."

## Syntax

These scripts can be executed as a command-line utility. Set CScript.exe to be your default script processor, as described in Chapter 3.

| | |
|---|---|
| `/list:path`<br>`/computer:name`<br>`/container:name` | One and only one of these is required by the script. Use */list* to target a list of computers contained within a text file. Use */computer* to target a single computer. Use */container* to target an organizational unit within Active Directory. |
| `/recurse` | When used with */container*, also targets computers contained within nested OUs. |
| `/ping` | Verifies the connectivity to all targeted computers prior to attempting a connection. Using this argument will reduce the timeout wait when one or more computers cannot be reached on the network. |
| `/log:path` | Logs unreachable computer names to the specified file. This file can then be used later, along with the */list* argument, to retry these computers. Note that a log is created only when used in conjunction with the */ping* argument. |
| `/verbose` | Causes the script to display more detailed, step-by-step status messages. |
| `/output:path` | Saves the drive inventory to a CSV file specified in *path*. |

You can run these scripts with the */?* parameter to display the command's syntax.

## Under the Hood

This script uses a straightforward Windows Management Instrumentation (WMI) query to retrieve all instances of the *Win32_DiskDrive* class from each targeted computer. Select properties from each instance are displayed in the command-line window or written to a CSV file (if you specify the */output* argument).

```
Dim cDrives, oDrive, sOutput
Verbose " Connecting to WMI on " & sName
Set cDrives = QueryWMI(sName,"root\cimv2","Select * From Win32_DiskDrive","","")
If Not IsObject(cDrives) Then
    WScript.Echo " *** Couldn't connect to WMI on " & sName
Else
    For Each oDrive In cDrives
        sOutput = sName & "," & oDrive.DeviceID & "," & oDrive.interfacetype & ","
& oDrive.manufacturer & "," & oDrive.model & "," & oDrive.name & ","
& oDrive.partitions & "," & oDrive.size & "," & oDrive.status & ","
& oDrive.totalcylinders & "," & oDrive.totalheads & "," & oDrive.totalsectors & ","
& oDrive.totaltracks & "," & oDrive.trackspercylinder
        If WScript.Arguments.Named.Exists("output") Then
            LogFile WScript.Arguments.Named("output"),sOutput,False
        Else
            WScript.Echo sOutput
        End If
    Next
End If
```

You can easily modify this script to display or save additional properties from the *Win32_DiskDrive* class.

## Troubleshooting

As with most scripts, this script can run into a couple of common errors. First, one or more targeted computers might not be available, a condition the script can handle properly. You can reduce the script's execution time by including the */ping* argument, which tests connectivity prior to trying to execute the WMI query.

The second possible error is that you won't have permission to inventory the drives' properties. This is unusual if you're running the script as an administrator, but the script will detect this error, display a message, and continue running.

## To Learn More

- Learn more about the *Win32_DiskDrive* class at *http://msdn.microsoft.com/library/default.asp?url=/library/en-us/wmisdk/wmi/win32_diskdrive.asp*.

- Find more physical disk management samples in VBScript at *http://www.microsoft.com/technet/scriptcenter/scripts/storage/disks/drives/default.mspx*.

# Inventory Logical Drives

**On the CD** The sample script can be found on the CD that accompanies this book at \Chap10\InventoryPartitions\InventoryPartitions.wsf.

| Operating System | Supported? | Prerequisites |
|---|---|---|
| Windows 2000 family | Yes | ■ WSH 5.6 or later |
| Windows XP Professional | Yes | ■ WMI |
| Windows Server 2003 family | Yes | ■ Administrative permission on targeted computers |
| | | ■ Network connectivity to each remote computer |

## Description

Most organizations maintain documentation about the logical disk configuration of their servers, but they rarely maintain documentation for their client computers. Such detailed configuration information can be invaluable when troubleshooting problems, planning upgrades, and so forth. This script can target multiple computers and create a complete inventory of their logical disk configuration. The information can be displayed in a command-line window for immediate use, or written to a comma-separated values (CSV) file for reporting and archival.

## Performing This Task Manually

Windows Explorer provides an easy way of examining the logical drives on a single computer but provides no ready means of displaying this information for remote computers or for multiple computers. Viewing the contents of My Computer (double-click My Computer to open it) will display all configured logical disks and their basic properties.

## Example

This script, InventoryPartitions.wsf, allows you to target one computer or multiple computers. If you wanted to use it to target a single remote computer named ServerA and take an inventory of its logical disks, you would use this code:

```
InventoryPartitions.wsf /computer:ServerA
```

You can also target a list of computers from a text file. The text file is expected to contain one computer name per line and no other information. Assuming the file is named C:\Computers.txt, you would use this syntax:

```
InventoryPartitions.wsf /list:C:\Computers.txt /output:C:\Report.csv
```

Note that this code will write the inventory information to a CSV file named C:\Report.csv, which is more useful than having the code write the information to the command-line window when you're targeting multiple computers. Finally, you can target an entire organizational unit of computer accounts. If your domain contains an OU named West, you would use the following syntax:

```
InventoryPartitions.wsf /container:west /output:C:\Report.csv
```

Note that the *container* argument will work only in the default domain of the computer running the script. In other words, the OU specified must exist within the same domain as that of the computer running the script. If the specified OU has nested OUs, you can include their computer accounts as well by specifying one additional argument:

```
InventoryPartitions.wsf /container:west /recurse /output:C:\Report.csv
```

This script always assigns ownership to your user account. Additional arguments provide more functionality to the command; see the following section titled "Syntax."

# Syntax

These scripts can be executed as command-line utilities. Set CScript.exe to be your default script processor, as described in Chapter 3.

| | |
|---|---|
| `/list:path` `/computer:name` `/container:name` | One and only one of these is required by the script. Use */list* to target a list of computers contained within a text file. Use */computer* to target a single computer. Use */container* to target an organizational unit within Active Directory. |
| `/recurse` | When used with */container*, also targets computers contained within nested OUs. |
| `/ping` | Verifies the connectivity to all targeted computers prior to attempting a connection. Using this argument will reduce the timeout wait when one or more computers cannot be reached on the network. |
| `/log:path` | Logs unreachable computer names to the specified file. This file can then be used later, along with the */list* argument, to retry these computers. Note that a log is created only when used in conjunction with the */ping* argument. |
| `/verbose` | Causes the script to display more detailed, step-by-step status messages. |
| `/output:path` | Saves the logical disk inventory to a CSV file specified in *path*. |

You can run these scripts with the */?* parameter to display the command's syntax.

# Under the Hood

This script uses a straightforward Windows Management Instrumentation (WMI) query to retrieve all instances of the *Win32_LogicalDisk* class. Each instance corresponds to a single configured logical disk, including removable drives. Various properties of each instance are displayed or saved to a file.

```
Dim cDrives, oDrive, sOutput
Verbose " Connecting to WMI on " & sName
Set cDrives = QueryWMI(sName,"root\cimv2","Select * From Win32_LogicalDisk","","")
If Not IsObject(cDrives) Then
    WScript.Echo " *** Couldn't connect to WMI on " & sName
Else
    For Each oDrive In cDrives
        sOutput = sName & "," & oDrive.DeviceID & "," & oDrive.DriveType & ","
& oDrive.FileSystem & "," & oDrive.MediaType & "," & oDrive.Size & ","
& oDrive.Status & "," & oDrive.VolumeName
        If WScript.Arguments.Named.Exists("output") Then
            LogFile WScript.Arguments.Named("output"),sOutput,False
        Else
            WScript.Echo sOutput
        End If
    Next
End If
```

You can modify this script to display additional properties of the *Win32_LogicalDisk* class, if desired.

# Troubleshooting

As with most scripts, this script can run into a couple of common errors. First, one or more targeted computers might not be available, a condition the script can handle properly. You can reduce the script's execution time by including the */ping* argument, which tests connectivity prior to trying to execute the WMI query. The second possible error is that you won't have permission to inventory the logical disks on a targeted computer. This is unusual if you're running the script as an administrator, but the script will detect this error, display a message, and continue running.

# To Learn More

- Learn more about the *Win32_LogicalDisk* class at *http://msdn.microsoft.com/ library/default.asp?url=/library/en-us/wmisdk/wmi/win32_logicaldisk.asp*.

- Find more logical disk management samples in VBScript at *http:// www.microsoft.com/technet/scriptcenter/scripts/storage/disks/drives/ default.mspx*.

# Defragment Disks

> **On the CD**   The sample script can be found on the CD that accompanies this book at \Chap10\DefragDrives\DefragDrives.wsf.

| Operating System | Supported? | Prerequisites |
|---|---|---|
| Windows 2000 family | No | ■  WSH 5.6 or later |
| Windows XP Professional | No | ■  WMI |
| Windows Server 2003 family | Yes | ■  Administrative permission on targeted computers |
| | | ■  Network connectivity to each remote computer |

## Description

This script allows you to analyze and, if necessary, defragment the drives on multiple computers. Regular disk defragmentation can improve computer performance, although starting a defragmentation process on multiple computers can sometimes be time-consuming.

## Performing This Task Manually

Windows provides a graphical Disk Defragmenter tool (from the Start menu, select All Programs, Accessories, System Tools) as well as a command-line Defrag.exe tool. Neither tool permits you to target multiple computers simultaneously.

## Example

This tool allows you to target one computer or multiple computers. If you wanted to use it to target a single remote computer named ServerA and defragment all drives which require defragmentation:

```
DefragDrives.wsf /computer:ServerA
```

Note that any drive not recommended by Windows for defragmentation will be skipped automatically. You can add the */analyze* argument to return just a fragmentation report:

```
DefragDrives.wsf /computer:ServerA /analyze
```

You can also target a list of computers from a text file. The text file is expected to contain one computer name per line and no other information. Assuming the file is named C:\Computers.txt, you would use this syntax:

```
DefragDrives.wsf /list:C:\Computers.txt
```

Finally, you can target an entire organizational unit of computer accounts. If your domain contains an OU named West, you would use the following syntax:

```
DefragDrives.wsf /container:west
```

Note that the *container* argument will work only in the default domain of the computer running the script. In other words, the OU specified must exist within the same domain as that of the computer running the script. If the specified OU has nested OUs, you can include their computer accounts as well by specifying one additional argument:

```
DefragDrives.wsf /container:west /recurse
```

This script will always skip drives that are not recommended by Windows for defragmentation; there is no facility provided to force defragmentation on a drive that doesn't currently require it. Additional arguments provide more functionality to the command; see the following section titled "Syntax."

## Syntax

These scripts can be executed as command-line utilities. Set CScript.exe to be your default script processor, as described in Chapter 3.

| | |
|---|---|
| /list:path<br>/computer:name<br>/container:name | One and only one of these is required by the script. Use */list* to target a list of computers contained within a text file. Use */computer* to target a single computer. Use */container* to target an organizational unit within Active Directory. |
| /recurse | When used with */container*, also targets computers contained within nested OUs. |
| /ping | Verifies the connectivity to all targeted computers prior to attempting a connection. Using this argument will reduce the timeout wait when one or more computers cannot be reached on the network. |
| /log:path | Logs unreachable computer names to the specified file. This file can then be used later, along with the */list* argument, to retry these computers. Note that a log is created only when used in conjunction with the */ping* argument. |
| /verbose | Causes the script to display more detailed, step-by-step status messages. |
| /analyze | Skips defragmentation on all drives and instead returns a fragmentation report for all drives. |

You can run these scripts with the */?* parameter to display the command's syntax.

## Under the Hood

This script uses a straightforward Windows Management Instrumentation (WMI) query to retrieve all instances of the *Win32_Volume* class. The script uses the *DefragAnalysis()* method to return a fragmentation report for each instance. This method sets a variable, *bDefrag*, to True if a defragmentation is recommended. If the */analyze* argument is specified, the analysis report is displayed and no other action is taken; otherwise, drives requiring defragmentation are defragmented. The following script does the work:

```
Dim cVols, errResults, oVol, bDefrag, oReport
Set cVols = QueryWMI(sName,"root\cimv2","Select * From Win32_Volume", "", "")
If Not IsObject(cVols) Then
    WScript.Echo "Couldn't retrieve volumes from " & sName
    LogBadConnect(sName)
Else
    For Each oVol In cVols
        bDefrag = true
        If WScript.Arguments.Named.Exists("analyze") Then
            Verbose " Analyzing volume " & ovol.name & " on " & sName
            errResult = oVol.DefragAnalysis(bDefrag,oReport)
        End If
        If bDefrag = True Then
            Verbose " Defragmenting " & oVol.name & " on " & sName
            errResult = oVol.Defrag()
            Verbose " Result: " & errResult
        End If
    Next
End If
```

Note that all analysis and defragmentation occurs locally on each targeted computer; the process is simply started and monitored by the script. Very little network bandwidth is required for this script to execute.

## Troubleshooting

As with most scripts, this script can run into a couple of common errors. First, one or more targeted computers might not be available, a condition the script can handle properly. You can reduce the script's execution time by including the */ping* argument, which tests connectivity prior to trying to execute the WMI query. The second possible error is that you won't have permission to defragment the drives. This is unusual if you're running the script as an administrator, but the script will detect this error, display a message, and continue running.

It's also possible that an error can occur during the defragmentation. The script will attempt to handle these errors, usually displaying the error information and moving on to the next drive or computer.

## To Learn More

- Learn more about the *Win32_Volume* class at *http://msdn.microsoft.com/library/default.asp?url=/library/en-us/wmisdk/wmi/win32_volume.asp*.

- Find more VBScript defragmentation examples at *http://www.microsoft.com/technet/scriptcenter/scripts/storage/disks/drives/default.mspx*.

# Schedule Disk Defragmentation

> **On the CD**   The sample script can be found on the CD that accompanies this book at \Chap10\ScheduleDefrag\ScheduleDefrag.wsf.

| Operating System | Supported? | Prerequisites |
|---|---|---|
| Windows 2000 family | No | ■ WSH 5.6 or later |
| Windows XP Professional | Yes | ■ WMI |
| Windows Server 2003 family | Yes | ■ Administrative permission on targeted computers |
| | | ■ Network connectivity to each remote computer |

## Description

This script gives you the ability to create a consistent disk defragmentation schedule for multiple computers, including client computers running Windows XP. Rather than using VBScript or WMI to perform the defragmentation, this script uses VBScript to create a new scheduled task in Windows Scheduled Tasks, and configures that task to run the command-line Defrag.exe tool on a regular basis (by default, at 1:00 A.M. UTC on the fifth day of each month).

## Performing This Task Manually

You can accomplish this task on a per-computer basis by using Windows Scheduled Tasks to schedule a task that executes Defrag.exe on a regular basis. This script automates the creation of this scheduled task on multiple computers.

## Example

This tool allows you to target one computer or multiple computers. If you wanted to use it to target a single remote computer named ServerA and schedule the defragmentation for volume C, you would use this code:

```
ScheduleDefrag.wsf /computer:ServerA /volume:C
```

You can also specify the */force* argument, which creates a scheduled task that *always* performs the defragmentation on schedule. Without the */force* argument, the scheduled task will always analyze disk fragmentation but begin an actual defragmentation process only when one is recommended by Windows.

```
ScheduleDefrag.wsf /computer:ServerA /force /volume:C
```

You can also target a list of computers from a text file. The text file is expected to contain one computer name per line and no other information. Assuming the file is named C:\Computers.txt, you would use this syntax:

```
ScheduleDefrag.wsf /list:C:\Computers.txt /volume:C
```

Finally, you can target an entire organizational unit of computer accounts. If your domain contains an OU named West, you would use the following syntax:

```
ScheduleDefrag.wsf /container:west /volume:C
```

Note that the *container* argument will work against only the default domain of the computer running the script. In other words, the OU specified must exist within the same domain as that of the computer running the script. If the specified OU has nested OUs, you can include their computer accounts as well by specifying one additional argument:

```
ScheduleDefrag.wsf /container:west /recurse /volume:C
```

Additional arguments provide more functionality to the command; see the following section titled "Syntax."

# Syntax

These scripts can be executed as command-line utilities. Set CScript.exe to be your default script processor, as described in Chapter 3.

| | |
|---|---|
| /list:path<br>/computer:name<br>/container:name | One and only one of these is required by the script. Use */list* to target a list of computers contained within a text file. Use */computer* to target a single computer. Use */container* to target an organizational unit within Active Directory. |
| /recurse | When used with */container*, also targets computers contained within nested OUs. |
| /ping | Verifies the connectivity to all targeted computers prior to attempting a connection. Using this argument will reduce the timeout wait when one or more computers cannot be reached on the network. |
| /log:path | Logs unreachable computer names to the specified file. This file can then be used later, along with the */list* argument, to retry these computers. Note that a log is created only when used in conjunction with the */ping* argument. |
| /verbose | Causes the script to display more detailed, step-by-step status messages. |
| /volume:letter | Required. Specifies the volume to defragment, identified by drive letter. |
| /force | Forces a defragmentation rather than analyzing and performing a defragmentation only when recommended by Windows. |

You can run these scripts with the */?* parameter to display the command's syntax.

## Under the Hood

This script uses a straightforward Windows Management Instrumentation (WMI) query to create the new scheduled task. The following script code performs the work:

```
Dim sCmd, oWMI, oJob, errResult, iJob
If WScript.Arguments.Named.Exists("force") Then
    sCmd = "defrag.exe " & WScript.Arguments.Named("volume") & ": -f"
Else
    sCmd = "defrag.exe " & WScript.Arguments.Named("volume") & ":"
End If
On Error Resume Next
Verbose "Connecting to " & sName
Set oWMI = GetObject("winmgmts:{impersonationLevel=impersonate}!\\" & sName &
"\root\cimv2")
If Err <> 0 Then
    WScript.Echo " ** Couldn't connect to WMI on " & sName
    LogBadConnect(sName)
Else
    Verbose " Scheduling job on " & sName
    Set oJob = oWMI.Get("Win32_ScheduledJob")
    errResult = oJob.Create(sCmd, "********100000.000000-000", True , ,5 , , iJob)
    Verbose " result on " & sName & ": " & errResult
End If
```

The schedule is specified in the *Create()* method. To change the time (which is always measured in UTC, not in local time), change the "*100000*" portion of the *Create()* method. In other words, to configure 12:00 A.M. UTC, use "*120000*" instead. To change the execution day from the fifth day, change the *16* in the *Create()* method to another number: Use 1 for the 1st, 2 for the 2nd, 4 for the 3rd, 8 for the 4th, and so forth; each successive day of the month is the next power of two.

Note that this script does not check for an existing schedule; it just creates a new scheduled task. Targeting a computer multiple times will result in multiple identical scheduled tasks. This can be useful if, for example, you target the C volume in one run and the D volume in another, but it can create scheduling conflicts if you target the same volume in multiple runs of the script.

## Troubleshooting

As with most scripts, this script can run into a couple of common errors. First, one or more targeted computers might not be available, a condition the script can handle properly. You can reduce the script's execution time by including the */ping* argument, which tests connectivity prior to trying to execute the WMI query. The second possible error is that you won't have permission to work with scheduled tasks on the remote computers. This is unusual if you're running the script as an administrator, but the script will detect this error, display a message, and continue running.

This script provides no feedback on the defragmentation process; this script just creates the scheduled task.

## To Learn More

- Learn more about the *Win32_ScheduledJob* class at *http://msdn.microsoft.com/ library/default.asp?url=/library/en-us/wmisdk/wmi/win32_scheduledjob.asp.*

- Find more VBScript scheduled task management samples at *http:// www.microsoft.com/technet/scriptcenter/scripts/os/tasks/default.mspx.*

Chapter 11
# File Server Management

Microsoft® Windows®–based file servers offer a number of useful features for almost any environment, including shared folders and disk quotas. However, managing these features for a number of servers can be unnecessarily time-consuming.

Tasks automated in this chapter include:

- Listing disk quota usage for users across multiple servers
- Listing the users who have a shared file open
- Listing all disk quota entries and their status across multiple servers
- Enabling or disabling disk quotas on multiple servers
- Creating shared folders on multiple servers
- Copy shared folder permissions from one shared folder to another
- Managing shared folder permissions and removing shared folders
- Modifying file and folder permissions

# List Disk Usage

> **On the CD**   The sample script can be found on the CD that accompanies this book
> at \Chap11\ListDiskUsagePerUser\ListDiskUsagePerUser.wsf.

| Operating System | Supported? | Prerequisites |
|---|---|---|
| Microsoft Windows 2000 family | No | ■  Windows Script Host (WSH) 5.6 or later |
| Microsoft Windows XP Professional | Yes | ■  Windows Management Instrumentation (WMI) |
| Microsoft Windows Server™ 2003 family | Yes | ■  Administrative permission on targeted computers |
|  |  | ■  Network connectivity to each remote computer |

## Description

Any file server that has disk quotas enabled keeps track of the amount of disk space
utilized by each user. A user's disk utilization consists of the total disk space occupied
by files that are owned by that user. This script, ListDiskUsagePerUser.wsf, lists all
disk space used by all users. This script retrieves its information from disk quotas, so
it can be used only on file servers where disk quotas have been enabled (other servers
will report no disk utilization at all). You don't need to have disk quotas enforcing a
limit; they simply have to be enabled so that disk utilization statistics are maintained.

This script can output its information to a comma-separated values (CSV) file.
Because the script can target multiple file servers at once, the CSV output is perhaps
the most useful way to use this script. Once the CSV file is created, you can import it
into an application like Microsoft Excel and determine aggregate disk space usage
for individual users across multiple servers, create chargeback data for internal disk
utilization accounting in your organization, and so forth.

## Performing This Task Manually

Windows provides a graphical user interface for viewing quotas on a single computer.
To view quotas in this way, follow these steps:

1.  Right-click a volume in My Computer, and then click Properties.

2.  In the volume's Properties dialog box, select the Quota tab.

3.  Click Quota Entries.

Windows will display a Quota Entries dialog box listing all current quotas. Even if a quota limit is not enforced, Windows still tracks per-user disk utilization whenever the quota system is enabled for a volume.

# Example

This tool allows you to target one computer or multiple computers. If you wanted to use it to target a single remote computer named ServerA, you would use this syntax:

```
ListDiskUsagePerUser.wsf /computer:ServerA
```

You can also target a list of computers from a text file. The text file is expected to contain one computer name per line and no other information. Assuming the file is named C:\Computers.txt, you would use this syntax:

```
ListDiskUsagePerUser.wsf /list:C:\Computers.txt /output:C:\Usage.csv
```

Notice that this command writes the information to a file named C:\Usage.csv.

Finally, you can target an entire organizational unit of computer accounts. If your domain contains an OU named West, you would use the following syntax:

```
ListDiskUsagePerUser.wsf /container:west /output:C:\Usage.csv
```

Note that the *container* argument will work against only the default domain of the computer running the script. In other words, the OU specified must exist within the same domain as that of the computer running the script. If the specified OU has nested OUs, you can include their computer accounts as well by specifying one additional argument:

```
ListDiskUsagePerUser.wsf /container:west /recurse /output:C:\Usage.csv
```

# Syntax

This script can be executed as a command-line utility. Set CScript.exe to be your default script processor, as described in Chapter 3, "Working with VBScript."

| | |
|---|---|
| /list:path<br>/computer:name<br>/container:name | One and only one of these is required by the script. Use */list* to target a list of computers contained within a text file. Use */computer* to target a single computer. Use */container* to target an organizational unit within Microsoft Active Directory®. |
| /recurse | When used with */container*, also targets computers contained within nested OUs. |

| `/ping` | Verifies the connectivity to all targeted computers prior to attempting a connection. Using this argument will reduce the timeout wait when one or more computers cannot be reached on the network. |
| `/log:path` | Logs unreachable computer names to the specified file. This file can then be used later, along with the /list argument, to retry these computers. Note that a log is created only when used in conjunction with the /ping argument. |
| `/verbose` | Causes the script to display more detailed, step-by-step status messages. |
| `/output:path` | Specifies the path and file name of a file to which the script will write its information, rather than displaying that information in the command-line window. |

You can run this script with the /? parameter to display the command's syntax.

## Under the Hood

This script uses a straightforward Windows Management Instrumentation (WMI) query to retrieve all instances of the *Win32_DiskQuota* class and display (or write to a file) selected properties of those instances:

```
Dim cQuotas, oQuota, sOutput
Verbose " Connecting to WMI on " & sName
Set cQuotas = QueryWMI(sName,"root\cimv2","Select * From Win32_DiskQuota","","")
If Not IsObject(cQuotas) Then
    WScript.Echo " *** Couldn't connect to WMI on " & sName
Else
    For Each oQuota In cQuotas
        sOutput = sName & "," & oQuota.QuotaVolume & "," & oQuota.User & ","
& oQuota.DiskSpaceUsed
        If WScript.Arguments.Named.Exists("output") Then
            LogFile WScript.Arguments.Named("output"),sOutput,False
        Else
            WScript.Echo sOutput
        End If
    Next
End If
```

In the event that a server without quotas enabled is targeted, the script will not retrieve any instances of the *Win32_DiskQuota* class from that server, making it appear in the output as if no disk space is being utilized on that server.

## Troubleshooting

As with most scripts, this script can run into a couple of common errors. First, one or more targeted computers might not be available, a condition the script can handle properly. You can reduce the script's execution time by including the /ping argument, which tests connectivity prior to trying to execute the WMI query. The second possible error is that you won't have permission to view quota information. This is unusual if you're running the script as an administrator, but the script will detect this error, display a message, and continue running.

It's also possible that one or more targeted servers won't have the disk quota system enabled. In those cases, no information will be returned, but no error should occur.

## To Learn More

- Learn more about the *Win32_DiskQuota* class at *http://msdn.microsoft.com /library/default.asp?url=/library/en-us/wmisdk/wmi/win32_diskquota.asp*.
- Find more disk quota management samples in Microsoft Visual Basic® Script (VBScript) at *http://www.microsoft.com/technet/scriptcenter/scripts/storage /quotas/default.mspx*.

# List Open File Users

**On the CD**   The sample script can be found on the CD that accompanies this book at \Chap11\ShowOpenFileUsers\ShowOpenFileUsers.wsf.

| Operating System | Supported? | Prerequisites |
|---|---|---|
| Windows 2000 family | Yes | ■  WSH 5.6 or later |
| Windows XP Professional | Yes | ■  WMI |
| Windows Server 2003 family | Yes | ■  Administrative permission on targeted computers |
| | | ■  Network connectivity to each remote computer |

## Description

When maintaining a file server, it can sometimes be frustrating to try to move, open, or delete a file, only to see an error message indicating that the file has been opened by another user. This experience can be especially common on a busy file server because multiple users might have the file open. Determining which users have the file open can be difficult, but the ShowOpenFileUsers.wsf script takes care of this task by quickly listing all users who have a particular file open through a shared folder.

## Performing This Task Manually

The Computer Management console—which can be used to target remote computers as well as the local one—lists open files and sessions. Just expand the Shared Folders node and click the Open Files node to see a list. However, scanning this list for a specific file and finding its users can be time-consuming. And possibly, by the time you find the file you're interested in, that file's status and the users who have it open will have changed.

## Example

The script requires only two arguments: the name of the file server containing the file, and the path of the file itself. For example:

```
ShowOpenFileUsers.wsf /server:Server1 /file:C:\Shares\Sales\Report.xls
```

Note that the file path must be the local path of the file because the file sits on the server. You cannot specify a Universal Naming Convention (UNC)—for example, \\Server1\Sales\Report.xls. Also keep in mind that the script can list only those files that are currently held open through the Server service, meaning files that are currently opened through a shared folder. Review the information in the next "Troubleshooting" section for more details, especially if the script doesn't seem to be returning the information you expect.

## Syntax

This script can be executed as a command-line utility. Set CScript.exe to be your default script processor, as described in Chapter 3.

| | |
|---|---|
| /file:path | Specifies the local file path of the file to check. This must start with a local volume letter, followed by a colon and a complete local path to the file itself. Example: C:\Shares\Sales\Report.xls. UNC paths are not acceptable. |
| /server:name | Specifies the name of the file server to check. |

You can run this script with the */?* parameter to display the command's syntax.

## Under the Hood

This script uses the Microsoft Windows NT® ADSI provider to connect to the specified server's Server service. The Server service makes file sharing possible, and it maintains a list of all currently-opened resources. The script queries the entire list of opened resources and scans through that list looking for the file you specified. The following script does the work:

```
For Each oResource In oFileService.Resources
    ' does this resource match the one we're looking for?
    If oResource.Path = WScript.Arguments.Named("file") Then

        ' we found the file - show who's got it
        bFoundNone = False
        WScript.Echo " User: " & oResource.User
    End If
Next
' if we didn't find the file open, display a msg
If bFoundNone = True Then
    WScript.Echo "Didn't find that file currently opened by anyone."
End If
```

Because the Server service tracks files by their local path (for example, C:\SharedFiles \Sales\Report.xls rather than \\Server1\Sales\Report.xls), you must remember to specify this local path in the */file* argument of the script.

## Troubleshooting

A number of situations can make this script appear as though it is not working correctly. Always remember that this script can display only those files that are currently opened through a shared folder. Files that have been opened locally on the server, or through a Remote Desktop or Terminal Services session, will not be listed by the script because those open files don't consume resources through the Server service (which is what this script queries). The script also will not display files that are opened by services on the server, because those opened files aren't consuming Server service resources.

Additionally, keep in mind that some applications don't maintain an open file connection. For example, if you open a text file in Microsoft Notepad, Notepad opens the file, reads its contents, and then immediately closes the file. The file does not remain open while you view or edit it in Notepad, and so this script will not report that file as open unless you happen to run the script during the split second when Notepad is actually reading the file's contents.

The errors that can occur with this script are generally limited to connectivity and permissions.

## To Learn More

- Find more file management scripts in the ScriptVault at *http://www.scriptinganswers.com*.

- Read about managing file resources through ADSI at *http://support.microsoft.com/default.aspx?scid=kb;en-us;234234*.

- Read the ADSI WinNT Provider documentation at *http://msdn.microsoft.com/library/default.asp?url=/library/en-us/adsi/adsi/adsi_winnt_provider.asp*.

# List Disk Quotas

> **On the CD**   The sample script can be found on the CD that accompanies this book at \Chap11\QuotaReport\QuotaReport.wsf.

| Operating System | Supported? | Prerequisites |
|---|---|---|
| Windows 2000 family | No | ■ WSH 5.6 or later |
| Windows XP Professional | Yes | ■ WMI |
| Windows Server 2003 family | Yes | ■ Administrative permission on targeted computers |
| | | ■ Network connectivity to each remote computer |

## Description

If you're using the disk quota support integrated into the Windows operating system, you might from time to time want to generate a report of all existing quotas, their current status, the amount of disk space consumed, and so forth. These reports can be useful for both maintenance and troubleshooting purposes, but Windows does not provide a built-in means of obtaining this information across a number of servers. This script, QuotaReport.wsf, provides the functionality you need.

## Performing This Task Manually

Windows provides a graphical user interface for viewing quotas on a single computer. To view the quotas on a single computer, follow these steps:

1.  Right-click a volume in My Computer, and then click Properties.

2.  In the volume's Properties dialog box, select the Quota tab.

3.  Click Quota Entries.

Windows will display the Quota Entries dialog box listing all current quotas. Even if a quota limit is not enforced, Windows tracks per-user disk utilization whenever the quota system is enabled for a volume.

## Example

This tool allows you to target one computer or multiple computers. If you wanted to use it to target a single remote computer named ServerA, you would use this code:

```
QuotaReport.wsf /computer:ServerA
```

You can also target a list of computers from a text file. The text file is expected to contain one computer name per line and no other information. Assuming the file is named C:\Computers.txt, you would use this syntax:

```
QuotaReport.wsf /list:C:\Computers.txt /output:C:\Usage.csv
```

Notice that this command writes the information to a file named C:\Usage.csv.

Finally, you can target an entire organizational unit of computer accounts. If your domain contains an OU named West, you would use the following syntax:

```
QuotaReport.wsf /container:west /output:C:\Usage.csv
```

Note that the *container* argument will work against only the default domain of the computer running the script. In other words, the OU specified must exist within the same domain as that of the computer running the script. If the specified OU has nested OUs, you can include their computer accounts as well by specifying one additional argument:

```
QuotaReport.wsf /container:west /recurse /output:C:\Usage.csv
```

# Syntax

This script can be executed as a command-line utility. Set CScript.exe to be your default script processor, as described in Chapter 3.

| | |
|---|---|
| /list:path<br>/computer:name<br>/container:name | One and only one of these is required by the script. Use */list* to target a list of computers contained within a text file. Use */computer* to target a single computer. Use */container* to target an organizational unit within Active Directory. |
| /recurse | When used with */container*, also targets computers contained within nested OUs. |
| /ping | Verifies the connectivity to all targeted computers prior to attempting a connection. Using this argument will reduce the timeout wait when one or more computers cannot be reached on the network. |
| /log:path | Logs unreachable computer names to the specified file. This file can then be used later, along with the */list* argument, to retry these computers. Note that a log is created only when used in conjunction with the */ping* argument. |
| /verbose | Causes the script to display more detailed, step-by-step status messages. |
| /output:path | Specifies the path and file name of a file to which the script will write its information, rather than displaying that information in the command-line window. |

You can run this script with the */?* parameter to display the command's syntax.

# Under the Hood

This script uses WMI to retrieve all instances of the *Win32_DiskQuota* class for a given volume, and then displays (or writes to a file) selected properties from each class. The following code does the core work:

```
Dim cQuotas, oQuota, sOutput
Verbose " Connecting to WMI on " & sName
Set cQuotas = QueryWMI(sName,"root\cimv2","Select * From Win32_DiskQuota","","")
If Not IsObject(cQuotas) Then
    WScript.Echo " *** Couldn't connect to WMI on " & sName
Else
    For Each oQuota In cQuotas
        sOutput = sName & "," & oQuota.QuotaVolume & "," & oQuota.User & ","
& oQuota.DiskSpaceUsed & "," & oQuota.Limit & "," & oQuota.WarningLimit & ","
& oQuota.Status
        If WScript.Arguments.Named.Exists("output") Then
            LogFile WScript.Arguments.Named("output"),sOutput,False
        Else
            WScript.Echo sOutput
        End If
    Next
End If
```

This script is similar to the earlier ListDiskUsagePerUser.wsf script, but this script returns more information from the *Win32_DiskQuota* class, making it more useful for monitoring systems in which a quota limit and warning limit have been established.

# Troubleshooting

As with most scripts, this script can run into a couple of common errors. First, one or more targeted computers might not be available, a condition the script can handle properly. You can reduce the script's execution time by including the */ping* argument, which tests connectivity prior to trying to execute the WMI query. The second possible error is that you won't have permission to view quota information. This is unusual if you're running the script as an administrator, but the script will detect this error, display a message, and continue running.

It's also possible that one or more targeted servers won't have the disk quota system enabled. In those cases, no information will be returned, but no error should occur.

You might occasionally see results from this script that do not match the graphical user interface for quota management. Keep in mind that the disk quota information is updated nearly in real time, so it is possible—probable, even, on a busy file server—for the statistics to constantly change. As a result, running the script and then looking at the graphical user interface might yield different results; even running the script twice in succession might produce different results.

## To Learn More

- Learn more about the *Win32_DiskQuota* class at *http://msdn.microsoft.com /library/default.asp?url=/library/en-us/wmisdk/wmi/win32_diskquota.asp*.

- Find more disk quota management samples in VBScript at *http:// www.microsoft.com/technet/scriptcenter/scripts/storage/quotas/default.mspx*.

# Enable or Disable Disk Quotas

> **On the CD**   The sample script can be found on the CD that accompanies this book at \Chap11\EnableDisableQuotas\EnableDisableQuotas.wsf.

| Operating System | Supported? | Prerequisites |
|---|---|---|
| Windows 2000 family | No | ■ WSH 5.6 or later |
| Windows XP Professional | Yes | ■ WMI |
| Windows Server 2003 family | Yes | ■ Administrative permission on targeted computers |
| | | ■ Network connectivity to each remote computer |

## Description

You might want to enable or disable the disk quota system on multiple file servers at once. For example, you might want to temporarily enable the system so that you can obtain a report of per-use disk utilization, and then disable the system because you don't plan to use it again for some time. This script, EnableDisableQuotas.wsf, provides you with the ability to quickly turn the disk quota system on or off on any number of computers at once.

## Performing This Task Manually

Windows provides a graphical user interface for managing quotas on a single computer. To manage quotas using this graphical interface, follow these steps:

1. Right-click a volume in My Computer, and then click Properties.

2. In the volume's Properties dialog box, select the Quota tab.

3. Select the appropriate option to enable or disable the quota system. An icon will indicate whether the system is enabled (green), disabled (red), or in the process of being enabled (yellow).

## Example

This tool allows you to target one computer or multiple computers. If you wanted to use it to target a single remote computer named ServerA, you would use this syntax:

```
EnableDisableQuotas.wsf /computer:ServerA /volume:C /enable:yes
```

This example enables quotas on the C: volume for ServerA.

You can also target a list of computers from a text file. The text file is expected to contain one computer name per line and no other information. Assuming the file is named C:\Computers.txt, you would use this syntax:

```
EnableDisableQuotas.wsf /list:C:\Computers.txt /volume:C /enable:yes
```

This example enables the quota system on the C: volume of every targeted computer.

Finally, you can target an entire organizational unit of computer accounts. If your domain contains an OU named West, you would use the following syntax:

```
EnableDisableQuotas.wsf /container:west /volume:D /enable:no
```

This example disables the quota system on the D: volume of every targeted computer.

Note that the *container* argument will work against only the default domain of the computer running the script. In other words, the OU specified must exist within the same domain as that of the computer running the script. If the specified OU has nested OUs, you can include their computer accounts as well by specifying one additional argument:

```
EnableDisableQuotas.wsf /container:west /recurse /volume:D /enable:no
```

## Syntax

This script can be executed as a command-line utility. Set CScript.exe to be your default script processor, as described in Chapter 3.

| | |
|---|---|
| /list:path<br>/computer:name<br>/container:name | One and only one of these is required by the script. Use */list* to target a list of computers contained within a text file. Use */computer* to target a single computer. Use */container* to target an organizational unit within Active Directory. |
| /recurse | When used with */container*, also targets computers contained within nested OUs. |
| /ping | Verifies the connectivity to all targeted computers prior to attempting a connection. Using this argument will reduce the timeout wait when one or more computers cannot be reached on the network. |
| /log:path | Logs unreachable computer names to the specified file. This file can then be used later, along with the */list* argument, to retry these computers. Note that a log is created only when used in conjunction with the */ping* argument. |
| /verbose | Causes the script to display more detailed, step-by-step status messages. |

| /volume:letter | Specifies the volume on which to enable or disable quotas; this must be a single letter only, with no colons. |
| /enable:[ YES \| NO ] | Specify *yes* to enable the quota system on the specified volume, or *no* to disable the system. |

You can run this script with the */?* parameter to display the command's syntax.

# Under the Hood

This script uses WMI to retrieve the *Win32_QuotaSetting* instance that corresponds to the specified volume. The main work is done by the following code:

```
Dim cQuotas, oQuota
Verbose " Connecting to WMI on " & sName
Set cQuotas = QueryWMI(sName,"root\cimv2","Select * From Win32_QuotaSetting Where
VolumePath = '" & wscript.arguments.named("volume") & ":\\'","","")
If Not IsObject(cQuotas) Then
    WScript.Echo " *** Couldn't connect to WMI, or volume not present, on " & sName
Else
    For Each oQuota In cQuotas
        If lcase(WScript.Arguments.Named("enable")) = "yes" Then
            oQuota.State = 1
            Verbose "  Enabled disk quotas on " & sName
        Else
            oQuota.State = 0
            Verbose "  Disabled disk quotas on " & sName
        End If
        oQuota.Put_
    Next
End If
```

You could modify this script to enable or disable quotas on *all* volumes—simply remove the following text from the script:

```
Where VolumePath = '" & wscript.arguments.named("volume") & ":\\'
```

You will still need to specify a */volume* argument when running the script (further modification would be required to remove the need for the argument), but the script will essentially ignore the argument and enable or disable quotas on every volume on every targeted server.

# Troubleshooting

As with most scripts, this script can run into a couple of common errors. First, one or more targeted computers might not be available, a condition the script can handle properly. You can reduce the script's execution time by including the */ping* argument, which tests connectivity prior to trying to execute the WMI query. The second possible error is that you won't have permission to view quota information. This is unusual if you're running the script as an administrator, but the script will detect this error, display a message, and continue running.

It's also possible that one or more targeted servers won't be able to enable the disk quota system. If you accidentally target a Windows 2000 Server computer, for example, an error might occur because those computers do not support WMI-based management of disk quotas, even though they do have a disk quota system.

## To Learn More

- Learn more about the *Win32_QuotaSetting* class at *http://msdn.microsoft.com /library/default.asp?url=/library/en-us/wmisdk/wmi/win32_quotasetting.asp*.

- Find more disk quota management samples in VBScript at *http:// www.microsoft.com/technet/scriptcenter/scripts/storage/quotas/default.mspx*.

# Create Shared Folders

> **On the CD**   The sample script can be found on the CD that accompanies this book at \Chap11\ShareFolder\ShareFolder.wsf.

| Operating System | Supported? | Prerequisites |
|---|---|---|
| Windows 2000 family | Yes | ■  WSH 5.6 or later |
| Windows XP Professional | Yes | ■  WMI |
| Windows Server 2003 family | Yes | ■  Administrative permission on targeted computers |
| | | ■  Network connectivity to each remote computer |

## Description

This script, ShareFolder.wsf, shares a folder on one or more computers. Although the script can target multiple servers, that functionality is most often used when you have multiple file servers hosting the same content (and are perhaps load-balancing or directing content to those servers using the Distributed File System [DFS]). The script works fine against a single computer, as well, making it easy to remotely create shared folders.

This script creates shared folders that have the default security permissions; under Windows Server 2003, for example, the default share permissions grant Read permission to the Everyone group.

## Performing This Task Manually

Any folder can be manually shared by following these steps:

1. Right-click the folder.

2. Select Properties.

3. On the Sharing tab of the Properties dialog box, select Share This Folder.

Performing this task on remote computers, however, can be tedious and might require the use of Remote Desktop or another remote-control technique. Performing this task on multiple remote computers can be even more time-consuming.

# Example

This tool allows you to target one computer or multiple computers. If you wanted to use it to target a single remote computer named ServerA, you would use this code:

```
ShareFolder.wsf /computer:ServerA /sharename:Sales /folder:D:\Shares\Sales
/maxconn:100 /desc:SalesDepartment
```

This example shares the D:\Shares\Sales folder as Sales, with a maximum of 100 connections, the default share permissions (which is not configurable), and a description of "SalesDepartment". Descriptions with spaces, for example, "Sales Department", must be enclosed in quotation marks.

You can also target a list of computers from a text file. The text file is expected to contain one computer name per line and no other information. Assuming the file is named C:\Computers.txt, you would use this syntax:

```
ShareFolder.wsf /list:C:\Computers.txt /sharename:Sales /folder:D:\Shares\Sales
/maxconn:100 /desc:"Sales Department"
```

Finally, you can target an entire organizational unit of computer accounts. If your domain contains an OU named West, you would use the following syntax:

```
ShareFolder.wsf /container:west /sharename:Sales /folder:D:\Shares\Sales
/maxconn:100 /desc:"Sales Department"
```

Note that the *container* argument will work against only the default domain of the computer running the script. In other words, the OU specified must exist within the same domain as that of the computer running the script. If the specified OU has nested OUs, you can include their computer accounts as well by specifying one additional argument:

```
ShareFolder.wsf /container:west /recurse /sharename:Sales /folder:D:\Shares\Sales
/maxconn:100 /desc:"Sales Department"
```

# Syntax

This script can be executed as a command-line utility. Set CScript.exe to be your default script processor, as described in Chapter 3.

| | |
|---|---|
| /list:path<br>/computer:name<br>/container:name | One and only one of these is required by the script. Use */list* to target a list of computers contained within a text file. Use */computer* to target a single computer. Use */container* to target an organizational unit within Active Directory. |
| /recurse | When used with */container*, also targets computers contained within nested OUs. |

| | |
|---|---|
| `/ping` | Verifies the connectivity to all targeted computers prior to attempting a connection. Using this argument will reduce the timeout wait when one or more computers cannot be reached on the network. |
| `/log:path` | Logs unreachable computer names to the specified file. This file can then be used later, along with the */list* argument, to retry these computers. Note that a log is created only when used in conjunction with the */ping* argument. |
| `/verbose` | Causes the script to display more detailed, step-by-step status messages. |
| `/sharename:name` | Specifies the share name to create. |
| `/maxconn:number` | Specifies the maximum number of connections for the new share. |
| `/desc:description` | Specifies a description for the new share. If the description will contain spaces, the text must be enclosed in quotation marks. |
| `/folder:path` | Specifies the folder path to share. |

You can run this script with the */?* parameter to display the command's syntax.

## Under the Hood

This script uses WMI to create a new shared folder. The following code performs the bulk of the work:

```
Dim oWMIService, oShare, errReturn
On Error Resume Next
Set oWMIService = GetObject("winmgmts:{impersonationLevel=impersonate}!\\" & sName &
"\root\cimv2")
If Err <> 0 Then
 WScript.Echo "** Couldn't connect to WMI on " & sName
Else
 Verbose "   Createing share on " & sName
 Set oShare = oWMIService.Get("Win32_Share")
 errReturn = oShare.Create (WScript.Arguments.Named("folder"), WScript.Arguments.
Named("sharename"), 0, WScript.Arguments.Named("maxconn"), WScript.Arguments.
Named("desc"))
 Verbose "   Status on " & sName & ": " errReturn
End if
```

The script allows the operating system of the targeted computer to determine the share permissions: Windows 2000 Server prior to Service Pack 3, for example, applies Full Control permission to the Everyone group, whereas Windows Server 2003 applies only Read permission to the Everyone group. You can modify the share permissions manually, or you can use a tool such as Permcopy.exe, discussed next in this chapter.

# Troubleshooting

This script can run into several possible errors. It's possible that the folder specified might not exist, which will cause an error that the script can deal with. It's also possible that the share name specified might already exist. The script can usually handle this and move on to the next targeted computer. Or, you might not have permission to create shared folders on a targeted computer. The script will usually display an error and continue running.

The script is not designed to target clustered file servers. Although the script can properly share a folder on a cluster node's local storage, the script cannot create clustered file shares. Targeting an active cluster node will result in a non-clustered share being created; targeting an inactive node (one without access to the folder path specified) will result in an error.

## To Learn More

- Learn more about the *Win32_Share* class at *http://msdn.microsoft.com/library /default.asp?url=/library/en-us/wmisdk/wmi/win32_share.asp*.

# Copy Shared Folder Permissions

Permcopy.exe is included in the Windows Server 2003 Resource Kit Tools.

| Operating System | Supported? | Prerequisites |
|---|---|---|
| Windows 2000 family | No | ■ WSH 5.6 or later |
| Windows XP Professional | Yes | ■ WMI |
| Windows Server 2003 family | Yes | ■ Administrative permission on targeted computers |
| | | ■ Network connectivity to each remote computer |

## Description

Permcopy.exe is a *Windows Server 2003 Resource Kit* command-line tool that can be used to copy shared folder permissions. It is an excellent way to automate share folder configuration, as it provides faster operation and better consistency. For example, I recommend maintaining a set of empty template shared folders that contain no files but have permissions appropriate for various needs within your environment (such as specific projects and classes of user). When a new share is created, the permissions can easily be copied from one of these templates to the new share.

## Performing This Task Manually

Any folder can be manually shared by doing the following:

1. Right-click the folder.

2. Select Properties.

3. On the Sharing tab of the Properties dialog box, select Share This Folder.

Once created, shared folder permissions can be modified from within this same dialog box by clicking the Permissions button and assigning the desired permissions.

## Example

Permcopy.exe is easy to use:

```
PermCopy.exe \\Server1 Sales \\Server2 Finance
```

This code copies the permissions from the shared folder \\Server1\Sales to the shared folder \\Server2\Finance. Note that there is no backslash between the server and share names.

# Syntax

This tool is a command-line utility. Its syntax is straightforward:

```
PermCopy.exe \\sourceserver sourceshare \\targetserver targetshare
```

In this syntax, *sourceserver* is the name of the server containing *sourceshare,* which is the share from which you will copy permissions; and *targetserver* is the destination server containing *targetshare*, which is the share to which permissions will be copied.

You can run this tool with the */?* parameter to display the command's syntax.

# Under the Hood

Permcopy.exe does not attempt to validate the permissions it copies. In general, this means you can copy only permissions that are in the same security context. For example, it is inadvisable to copy permissions from a server in one domain to a server in another, or from a domain member server to a standalone (non-member) server. Permissions assigned to built-in accounts (Administrator, Guest, and so forth) can be freely copied between standalone (non-member) computers because these accounts utilize *well-known* security identifiers that are valid on all computers running Windows.

# Troubleshooting

Permcopy.exe should not be used to copy permissions to an administrative share (the default shares created by the operating system for each attached drive, such as C$). Doing so will generally result in a service locking up and the permissions being incorrectly copied. See *http://www.microsoft.com/resources/documentation/WindowsServ/ 2003/all/techref/en-us/Default.asp?url=/Resources/Documentation/windowsserv/ 2003/all/techref/en-us/permcopy_remarks.asp* for more details.

Permcopy.exe cannot create shared folders; if the specified source or target share does not exist, an error will occur.

# To Learn More

■ Learn more about the Permcopy.exe tool syntax at *http://www.microsoft.com /resources/documentation/WindowsServ/2003/all/techref/en-us/Default.asp?url= /Resources/Documentation/windowsserv/2003/all/techref/en-us /permcopy_syntax.asp*.

■ Read more about copying files, shares, and permissions at *http://www.microsoft .com/windowsserver2003/upgrading/nt4/tooldocs/msfsc.mspx*, which discusses the Microsoft File Server Migration Toolkit.

# Manage Shared Folder Permissions and Removing Shared Folders

Download Rmtshare.exe from *ftp://ftp.microsoft.com/bussys/winnt/winnt-public /reskit/nt40/i386/RMTSHAR.EXE.*

| Operating System | Supported? | Prerequisites |
|---|---|---|
| Windows 2000 family | Yes | ■ WSH 5.6 or later |
| Windows XP Professional | Yes | ■ WMI |
| Windows Server 2003 family | Yes | ■ Administrative permission on targeted computers |
| | | ■ Network connectivity to each remote computer |

## Description

Rmtshare.exe was originally a part of the *Microsoft Windows NT 4.0 Resource Kit*; since then, Microsoft has released the tool into the public domain and made it available for download from their Internet FTP site. The tool works with current versions of Windows, and provides the ability to list share permissions, change share permissions, and perform other tasks with shares located on remote servers.

**Note**   Rmtshar.exe has also been distributed as Rmtshare.exe. I'll refer to it as Rmtshar.exe in this section; if your copy is named Rmtshare, modify the examples appropriately.

## Performing This Task Manually

Any folder can be manually shared by doing the following:

1. Right-click the folder.

2. Select Properties.

3. On the Sharing tab of the Properties dialog box, select Share This Folder.

Once created, shared folder permissions can be modified from within this same dialog box by clicking the Permissions button and assigning the desired permissions.

## Example

This tool is a command-line utility, and it has many functions. To display all shares on a remote server, you would use this code:

```
RMTSHARE \\server
```

To display details of a specific share:

```
RMTSHARE \\server\sharename
```

To add a new shared folder:

```
RMTSHARE \\server\sharename=drive:path options
```

Options include:

```
/USERS:number
/UNLIMITED
/REMARK:"text"
/GRANT user:perm
/REMOVE user
```

For example, to create a share named \\Server1\MyShare, for the folder C:\MyFolder, with unlimited connections and Read permissions for the Everyone group, you would use this code:

```
RMTSHARE \\Server1\MyShare=C:\MyFolder /UNLIMITED /GRANT Everyone:Read
```

To edit an existing share, specify the share and any of the preceding options to modify permissions or change the share's connections:

```
RMTSHARE \\server\sharename options
```

To remove a shared folder (but not the underlying files and folders):

```
RMTSHARE \\server\sharename /DELETE
```

## Syntax

Rmtshare.exe has a fairly straightforward syntax.

| | |
|---|---|
| \\server | Specifies a server; with no other arguments, lists the shares on the server. |
| \\server\share | Specifies a server and share; with no other arguments, lists the details of the specified share. You might include any of the following options to modify the share: /USERS, /UNLIMITED, /REMARK, /GRANT, /REMOVE, and /DELETE. |
| \\server\share=path | Creates a new shared folder for the specified path. You might include any of the following options: /USERS, /UNLIMITED, /REMARK, /GRANT, and /REMOVE. |
| /USERS:number | Specifies the number of user connections the share will allow. |
| /UNLIMITED | Specifies that the share allow unlimited user connections. |
| /REMARK:"text" | Specifies a description for the share. |

| /GRANT user:perm | Adds a user or group to the share's access control list, along with the specified permission (Read, Full Control, or Write). |
| --- | --- |
| /REMOVE user | Removes a user or group (and their permissions) from the share's access control list. |
| /DELETE | When used with an existing share, removes the share. |

You can run this tool with the */?* parameter to display the command's syntax.

## Under the Hood

Rmtshare.exe uses remote procedure calls (RPCs) to connect to remote servers. Computers that have a local firewall enabled (particularly Windows XP client computers) might not allow incoming RPC connections, and so Rmtshare.exe might not work. Otherwise, Rmtshare.exe is a fairly straightforward tool for managing shares on remote computers.

Rmtshare.exe can be scripted, in the form of batch files, to affect multiple computers at once. However, share details are rarely applied identically to multiple computers, and so you will most likely use Rmtshare.exe as a convenient tool for managing shares on remote computers.

## Troubleshooting

Having sufficient permissions to manage remote shares is, of course, required when using Rmtshare.exe. Other than permissions or potential connectivity issues, Rmtshare.exe will rarely encounter problems.

One trick with the tool is that long file paths must be enclosed in double quotation marks. For example:

```
RMTSHARE \\Server1\MyShare="C:\Program Files"
```

Failure to do so will result in Rmtshare.exe trying to share C:\Program (which will fail if the folder doesn't exist) and treating Files as a separate argument, which will cause an error.

## To Learn More

■ Read about Share.vbs, an alternative means of managing remote shared folders (although not their permissions), at *http://www.microsoft.com/Resources /documentation/SBS/2000/all/reskit/en-us/sbrkapxf.mspx*.

■ Read more about Rmtshare.exe at *http://www.jsiinc.com/SUBM/tip6300 /rh6353.htm*.

# Modify File and Folder Permissions

Xcacls.exe is included in the Windows Server 2003 Resource Kit Tools.

| Operating System | Supported? | Prerequisites |
|---|---|---|
| Windows 2000 family | Yes | ■ WSH 5.6 or later |
| Windows XP Professional | Yes | ■ WMI |
| Windows Server 2003 family | Yes | ■ Administrative permission on targeted computers |
| | | ■ Network connectivity to each remote computer |

## Description

Managing file and folder permissions can be complicated, especially when you need to modify permissions on a large number of files and folders at once. Microsoft provides the Xcacls.exe tool, which can be used to automate permissions changes.

Another tool, Cacls.exe, is included with all recent versions of Windows. However, Cacls.exe provides less flexibility and cannot apply the full set of permissions available through the graphical user interface. Xcacls.exe is more flexible and can work with the entire set of possible permissions.

## Performing This Task Manually

Every file and folder on an NTFS volume can have its permissions manually modified. Just right-click the file or folder, select Properties, and then select the Security tab of the Properties dialog box. On this tab you can control which users and groups have access to a file or folder. By clicking the Advanced button, you can also modify advanced permissions, including permissions inheritance of folders.

## Example

At its most basic, Xcacls.exe can be used to completely replace the access control list (ACL) on a file or folder (or on a set of files and folders). This removes all previous permissions and replaces them with whatever you specify, so it is critical that you specify the correct permissions. It is entirely possible to lock yourself out of files and folders by having Xcacls.exe replace the existing permissions with ones that do not include your user account or groups. For example:

```
xcacls *.* /g administrator:rw /y
```

This will replace the permissions on all files in the current folder, granting the administrator read/write permissions. The /y argument suppresses a confirmation prompt that reminds you that you are replacing all effective permissions on the files.

Xcalcs.exe has a more powerful mode in which it *edits* the existing ACL rather than replacing it entirely:

```
xcacls *.* /g TestUser:rwed;rw /e
```

This modifies the ACL of all files in the current folder, granting the TestUser account read, write, execute, and delete permissions on new files, as well as read and write permissions on any existing files, *without* modifying any other permissions that are already in the ACL.

# Syntax

Xcacls.exe has a somewhat complex syntax, which fits with the tool's flexibility.

| | |
|---|---|
| `Folder or file` | Required. If used with no other options, lists the existing ACL. |
| `/t` | Applies changes to the current folder and all subfolders, including all files contained therein. |
| `/e` | Edits, rather than replaces, the existing ACL. |
| `/x` | Edits, rather than replaces, the existing ACL, and edits only ACL entries corresponding to the specified user or group. |
| `/c` | Continues processing (that is, it skips the denied file) if access is denied to a specified file or folder. |
| `/g User:Perm;Spec` | Grants a permission. *User* is the user or group to grant permission to. In the case of a file, only *Perm* is necessary. In the case of a folder, *Perm* specifies file inheritance for the folder. |
| `/r User` | Removes the specified user or group from the ACL. |
| `/p User:Perm;Spec` | Replaces the access rights for the specified user or group. *Perm* and *Spec* work the same as they do for the */g* argument. |
| `/d User` | Denies the specified user access to the file or folder. |
| `/y` | Suppresses the warning confirmation normally displayed when replacing permissions. |

You can run this tool with the */?* parameter to display the command's syntax.

Valid permission codes include:

| | |
|---|---|
| *R* | Read |
| *C* | Change (write) |
| *F* | Full Control |
| *P* | Change Permissions (special access) |
| *O* | Take Ownership (special access) |
| *X* | Execute (special access) |
| *E* | Read (special access) |
| *W* | Write (special access) |
| *D* | Delete (special access) |

# Under the Hood

Xcacls.exe is designed to work against only the local server. It can be scripted, in the form of batch files, to affect multiple folder hierarchies at once. However, modifying permissions in this fashion can be dangerous if an error is made. I strongly recommend testing Xcacls.exe commands before using them on production servers, as there is no Undo function in the event you make a mistake.

# Troubleshooting

Having sufficient permissions to manage file and folder security is, of course, required when using Xcacls.exe. If the tool encounters an error, it will stop processing further files and folders unless you specify the /c argument. Other than permissions issues, Xcacls.exe will rarely encounter problems.

# To Learn More

- Read the official documentation on Xcacls.exe at *http://www.microsoft.com /resources/documentation/WindowsServ/2003/all/techref/en-us/Default.asp?url= /Resources/Documentation/windowsserv/2003/all/techref/en-us/xcacls_syntax.asp.*

- Read the documentation on Cacls.exe, a somewhat easier version of Xcacls.exe that is included with the Windows operating system, at *http://www.microsoft .com/resources/documentation/WindowsServ/2003/standard/proddocs/en-us /Default.asp?url=/resources/documentation/WindowsServ/2003/standard/proddocs /en-us/cacls.asp.*

# Part IV
# Security and Network Management Tasks

Chapter 12

# General Network and Server Management Tasks

Network management tasks aren't always the ones you need to perform on multiple computers, but they are often the ones you need to perform frequently or in a hurry (perhaps while troubleshooting a problem), or with great accuracy. Automation can help make information available quickly in time of need, can perform configuration changes with great accuracy, and can make frequently performed tasks less tedious.

Tasks automated in this chapter include:

- Listing the holders of Flexible Single Master Operations (FSMO) roles
- Creating DHCP scopes
- Modifying DHCP scope options
- Creating static DNS records
- Creating print queues

# List FSMO Role Holders

> **On the CD**    The sample script can be found on the CD that accompanies this book at \Chap12\ListFSMOs\ListFSMOs.wsf.

| Operating System | Supported? | Prerequisites |
|---|---|---|
| Microsoft® Windows® 2000 family | No | ■ Windows Script Host (WSH) 5.6 or later |
| Microsoft Windows XP Professional | Yes | ■ Windows Management Instrumentation (WMI) |
| Microsoft Windows Server™ 2003 family | Yes | ■ Administrative permission on targeted computers |
| | | ■ Network connectivity to each remote computer |

## Description

Microsoft Active Directory® defines five Flexible Single Master Operations (FSMO) roles, which provide specialized services for various domain and forest functions. Each FSMO role is initially held by the first domain controller in the first forest you create; you can manually reassign these roles to other domain controllers. When troubleshooting domain problems, it can be useful to know which domain controllers hold which FSMO roles. For example, the Schema Master role is required to make changes to the Active Directory schema; if you are attempting to make changes to the schema and having problems, figuring out which domain controller holds the Schema Master role is a good first troubleshooting step. If, for example, that domain controller is unavailable or unreachable, you'll know why you're having problems.

## Performing This Task Manually

The management tools for Active Directory provide a way to discover which domain controllers hold each FSMO role. The various roles' current holders can be viewed by using different tools.

- To view the current Schema Master by using the Active Directory Schema console, with the console open, right-click Active Directory Schema and select Operations Master.

- To view the current Domain Naming Master by using the Active Directory Domains and Trusts console, with the console open, right-click Active Directory Domains And Trusts and select Operations Master.

- To view all other FSMO roles by using the Active Directory Users and Computers console, with the console open, right-click Active Directory Users And Computers, point to All Tasks, and then select Operations Master.

Note that you can also manually change the role holder for each FSMO role using the preceding steps. After selecting Operations Master, you'll see the current role holder and a Change button, which allows you to select a new role holder.

# Example

This script requires no command-line arguments. Simply run it:

```
ListFSMOs.wsf
```

The script will work for only the default domain of the computer on which the script is run, displaying the domain and forestwide roles for that default domain. This script will not work when run from a computer that is not a member of a domain.

# Syntax

This script has no command-line arguments. Set CScript.exe to be your default script processor, as described in Chapter 3, "Working with VBScript." You can run this script by using the /? parameter to display the command's syntax.

# Under the Hood

This script uses Microsoft Active Directory Services Interface (ADSI) to query the FSMO role holders from the domain. One very important limitation of this script is that it can list only the FSMO role holders that are known to and accepted by the domain controller to which the script connects, which is generally the domain controller that authenticated the computer running the script. In a normal, properly functioning domain, all domain controllers will agree on which domain controllers hold which FSMO roles. However, it is possible for a domain to become damaged, in which case disagreement can occur. For example, suppose you take the PDC Emulator role holder offline, and then instruct another domain controller to seize the PDC Emulator role. If you then return the original PDC Emulator role holder to the network, the network will believe that this original role holder is the one and only PDC Emulator; the remaining domain controllers in the domain will believe the *new* holder is the one and only PDC Emulator. In this situation, this script will return different results when querying the original PDC Emulator (which believes it is the official role holder) and any other domain controller (which believes the new role holder is the official one).

An example of how the script works is shown in the following code:

```
Set oRootDSE = GetObject("LDAP://rootDSE")
If Err <> 0 Then
    WScript.Echo "Could not connect to the domain."
    WScript.Quit
End If


' Schema Master
Set oSchema = GetObject("LDAP://" & oRootDSE.Get("schemaNamingContext"))
sSchemaMaster = oSchema.Get("fSMORoleOwner")
Set oNtds = GetObject("LDAP://" & sSchemaMaster)
Set oComputer = GetObject(oNtds.Parent)
WScript.Echo "Forest :        Schema Master: " & oComputer.Name
```

The first line of code connects to the domain; the last five lines of code query the Schema Master role holder name and display that information on the command line. The script repeats this process to obtain the other four FSMO role holder names.

## Troubleshooting

The most common problem with this script is its inability to connect to the domain, which usually occurs only on a computer that is not a member of a domain at all. On a domain member computer, this script rarely has a problem; even if it is unable to connect to the computer's preferred domain controller, it will automatically attempt to contact another domain controller to obtain the FSMO information.

## To Learn More

- Learn more about the FSMO roles and how to manually view their holders and transfer holders at *http://support.microsoft.com/default.aspx? kbid=324801&product=winsvr2003*.

- Read more about the FSMO roles and their function within Active Directory by referring to the Windows Server 2003 Help and Support Center.

# Create DHCP Scope

> **On the CD**    The sample script can be found on the CD that accompanies this book at \Chap12\CreateDHCPScopes\CreateDHCPScopes.wsf.

| Operating System | Supported? | Prerequisites |
|---|---|---|
| Windows 2000 family | No | ■ WSH 5.6 or later |
| Windows XP Professional | No | ■ WMI |
| Windows Server 2003 family | Yes | ■ Administrative permission on targeted computers |
| | | ■ Network connectivity to each remote computer |

## Description

The Dynamic Host Configuration Protocol (DHCP) server included with Microsoft Windows Server 2003 is designed to support one or more *scopes*, which are ranges of IP addresses, from which addresses are issued to DHCP clients. Creating new scopes is typically performed through the DHCP Server console, a graphical administrative tool. However, using the console to configure a new server with a large number of scopes can be time-consuming and error-prone. Windows Server 2003 provides a scriptable command-line tool, Netsh, that can be used to create new scopes from the command line. However, this tool can be complex and difficult to use manually. The CreateDHCPScopes.wsf script automates the Netsh tool, enabling easier bulk creation of multiple DHCP scopes.

## Performing This Task Manually

Using the DHCP Server console to create a new scope is a straightforward task. Typically, a new scope includes a range of IP addresses that define the scope as well as one or more scope options. Most environments define only a router option for the scope and define global rather than scope options for name resolution servers.

You can also use the Netsh command to manually configure a new scope. For example, the following will create a new scope named MyScope for the 192.168.1.0/24 subnet, on a DHCP server at 192.168.12.2:

```
Netsh dhcp server 192.168.12.2 add scope 192.168.1.0 255.255.255.0 MyScope
ScopeComment
```

Additional steps are required to add an IP address range and any scope options to the newly created scope.

# Example

This script can be executed as follows:

```
CreateDHCPScopes.wsf /server:192.168.12.2 /scope:192.168.1 /name:MyScope
```

The script assumes a 24-bit subnet mask and assumes that the router for this subnet is at the .1 host address. It assigns an IP address range from .10 through .254 for use by DHCP clients. The new scope has the following properties:

- A subnet mask of 255.255.255.0
- A name of MyScope
- A router option (DHCP option value 003) of 192.168.1.1
- An IP address range from 192.168.1.10 through 192.168.1.254

The scope is created on a DHCP server at address 192.168.12.2. After creating the scope, adding the IP address range, and specifying the router scope option, the script activates the scope.

# Syntax

This script has several command-line arguments, which are described in the following table. Set CScript.exe to be your default script processor, as explained in Chapter 3.

| | |
|---|---|
| `/server:address` | Specifies the name or IP address of the DHCP server. This must be a Windows Server 2003 server running the Windows DHCP Service. |
| `/scope:address` | Specifies the subnet address for the new scope. This must be only three octets. For example, to create a scope for 192.168.5.0/24, specify */scope:192.168.5*. |
| `/name:string` | Specifies the name of the new scope. |

You can run this script by using the */?* parameter to display the script's syntax.

# Under the Hood

This script uses the Windows Script Host's *WshShell* object (specifically, the object's *Run()* method) to execute the Netsh command. The following script code does most of the work:

```
Dim sCmd
sCmd = "netsh dhcp server " & WScript.Arguments.Named("server") & _
 " add scope " & WScript.Arguments.Named("scope") & ".0 255.255.255.0 " & _
 WScript.Arguments.Named("name") & " ScriptedScope"
GoRun sCmd
```

```
'create scope range
sCmd = "netsh dhcp server " & WScript.Arguments.Named("server") & _
 " scope " & WScript.Arguments.Named("name") & _
 " add iprange " & WScript.Arguments.Named("scope") & ".10 " & _
 WScript.Arguments.Named("scope") & ".254"
GoRun sCmd

'create router Option
sCmd = "netsh dhcp server " & WScript.Arguments.Named("server") & _
 " scope " & WScript.Arguments.Named("name") & _
 " set optionvalue 003 IPADDRESS " & WScript.Arguments.Named("scope") & ".1"
GoRun sCmd

'activate scope
sCmd = "netsh dhcp server " & WScript.Arguments.Named("server") & _
 " scope " & WScript.Arguments.Named("name") & _
 " set state active"
GoRun sCmd

WScript.Echo "Commands completed"
```

You can make changes to some of the script's code so that you can change some of the script's basic operations. At the beginning of the script, the following code specifies how the new scope will be created:

```
sStart = "10"
sFinish = "254"
sRouter = "1"
```

Change *sStart* from *10* and *sFinish* from *254* to other values to change the IP address range included in the scope. For example, to have the script always create scopes with IP address ranges from .12 through .100, change *sStart* to 12 and *sFinish* to 100. If your routers are typically configured to use a .2 host address, change *sRouter* to 2, and each new scope's router option will use the .2 host address.

This script is most useful in environments in which each subnet is configured in a standardized fashion—that is, client addresses issued from range *x* to *y*, router at host address *z*, and all subnets configured to use Class C (24-bit) subnet masks.

## Troubleshooting

Because the Netsh command is not a scriptable COM object, it can't provide detailed feedback when a command fails. For this reason, troubleshooting this script can be difficult. Thus, you need to ensure that you have sufficient permissions to create scopes on the targeted DHCP server and that you provide acceptable values for the script's arguments. The script runs the Netsh command four times to create the scope, add the IP address range, create the router option, and activate the scope; each time, the Netsh command output will appear in a command-line window, where you might also be prompted for user credentials if necessary.

## To Learn More

- Learn more about using the Netsh command to create DHCP scopes at *http://www.microsoft.com/resources/documentation/WindowsServ/2003 /standard/proddocs/en-us/Default.asp?url=/resources/documentation /WindowsServ/2003/standard/proddocs/en-us/netsh_dhcp_example.asp.*

- Read more about Windows Server 2003 DHCP Server at *http:// www.microsoft.com/technet/prodtechnol/windowsserver2003/serverroles /dhcpserver/default.mspx.*

# Modify DHCP Options

This sample script is built into Windows Server 2003.

| Operating System | Supported? | Prerequisites |
|---|---|---|
| Windows 2000 family | No | ■ WSH 5.6 or later |
| Windows XP Professional | No | ■ WMI |
| Windows Server 2003 family | Yes | ■ Administrative permission on targeted computers |
| | | ■ Network connectivity to each remote computer |

## Description

Windows DHCP servers support a number of server and scope options. These options are used to pass IP configuration information to DHCP clients. Specifically, *server options* are passed to all DHCP clients obtaining an address from the server, whereas *scope options* are passed only to clients obtaining an address for the associated scope. Thus, the options passed to a client are all options for that client's issuing scope and all server options.

Automating the maintenance of DHCP options can make network configuration changes easier. For example, if your company has multiple DHCP servers (not uncommon in large environments), they might all be configured to issue the same DNS server addresses to clients (also a common scenario). Should those DNS server addresses change, automation can help ensure that the change is consistently and quickly applied to all DHCP servers.

## Performing This Task Manually

Most administrators manage server and scope options from within the DHCP Server console, a graphical user interface. The interface makes changing multiple options for a single server or scope easy, but making the same changes in multiple scopes or on multiple servers can be time-consuming and error-prone.

## Example

The Netsh command-line tool provides a means to modify DHCP server and scope options from the command line. By using the tool in a batch file, you can automate the process of changing multiple scopes or servers simultaneously.

To change a server option, run:

```
Netsh dhcp server a.a.a.a set optionvalue xxx datatype data
```

Where:

- *A.a.a.a* is the IP address of the DHCP server; alternately, you might specify \\*servername* to use the server's name.

- *Xxx* is the number option code you want to change.

- *Datatype* is the type of data contained within the option. This might be BYTE, WORD, DWORD, STRING, or IPADDRESS. IPADDRESS is perhaps the most common.

- *Data* is the actual data to be assigned to the option, such as an IP address.

Changing a scope option is similar to changing a server option—you simply identify the scope in addition to the server:

```
Netsh dhcp server a.a.a.a scope scope set optionvalue xxx datatype data
```

For example, to set the Router option (whose option code is 003) to 192.168.1.1 for a scope 192.168.1.0 on the DHCP server at 192.168.12.2, you would run this code:

```
Netsh dhcp server 192.168.12.2 scope 192.168.1.0 set optionvalue 003
IPADDRESS 192.168.1.1
```

Common option codes and their data types include:

- **002–Time Offset** DWORD. Specify the offset in seconds.
- **003–Router** IPADDRESS. Can provide multiple addresses separated by spaces.
- **004–Time Server** IPADDRESS
- **006–DNS Servers** IPADDRESS
- **015–DNS Domain Name** STRING
- **044–WINS/NBNS Servers** IPADDRESS
- **046–WINS/NBT Node Type** DWORD

Note that not all DHCP clients support all the preceding options, but they can all be assigned to the DHCP server for those clients that do support them.

Turning the Netsh command into an automation tool is simple—just create a new text file with a .bat file name extension. If, for example, you need to change the DNS server option to 192.168.7.54 on three servers, the .bat file would contain the following:

```
Netsh server \\server1 set optionvalue 006 IPADDRESS 192.168.7.54
Netsh server \\server2 set optionvalue 006 IPADDRESS 192.168.7.54
Netsh server \\server2 set optionvalue 006 IPADDRESS 192.168.7.54
```

> **Tip**   Using the Copy and Paste features in Microsoft Notepad makes it easier to duplicate this line three times and reduces the chance you will introduce a typo when manually creating the second and third lines.

Saving and double-clicking the .bat file will make your change on all three servers.

## Syntax

| | |
|---|---|
| `Server address` | Specifies the name or IP address of the DHCP server. This must be a Windows Server 2003 server running the Windows DHCP Service. When specifying a name, use the format \\*servername*. |
| `Scope scope` | Specifies the scope when changing a scope option. |
| `Optionvalue code type value` | Specifies the option code for the option you want to change or set, the type (DWORD, WORD, STRING, IPADDRESS, or BYTE), and the value to change (or set) the option to. |

## Under the Hood

The Netsh command provides a great deal of command-line network configuration functionality. It primarily relies on remote procedure calls (RPCs) to connect to remote servers and perform its work; firewalled servers might block these ports, which is a consideration when using this tool.

## Troubleshooting

Netsh provides excellent feedback when errors occur, and the most common errors are syntax-related. Before creating a .bat file containing multiple Netsh commands, take a moment to test a sample command against a nonproduction DHCP server to verify the command's accuracy and operation; then create your .bat file based on that tested command.

## To Learn More

- Learn more about Netsh scripting at *http://www.brienposey.com/kb /netsh_scripting.asp*.

- Read more about DHCP-specific uses of Netsh at *http://www.microsoft.com /resources/documentation/windows/xp/all/proddocs/en-us/netsh_dhcp.mspx*.

- Read the complete list of industry-standard DHCP options at *http:// www.iana.org/assignments/bootp-dhcp-parameters*.

# Create DNS Host Records

**On the CD**   The sample script can be found on the CD that accompanies this book at \Chap12\CreateARecords\CreateARecords.wsf.

| Operating System | Supported? | Prerequisites |
|---|---|---|
| Windows 2000 family | Yes, with the optional DNS WMI Provider installed | ■ WSH 5.6 or later ■ WMI ■ Administrative permission on targeted computers ■ Network connectivity to each remote computer |
| Windows XP Professional | No | |
| Windows Server 2003 family | Yes | |

## Description

Although most Windows-based environments utilize Dynamic DNS (DDNS) to register host records, many environments still require the use of static host records in DNS for computers and devices that are not DDNS-capable (such as legacy devices and many non-Microsoft operating systems). This script, CreateARecords.wsf, automates the process of creating host records for both IP and IPv6 addresses (stored in DNS A and AAAA records, respectively).

Manual record creation is also necessary on systems where DDNS has been disabled. DDNS is often disabled on DNS servers that connect to the Internet, because having DDNS enabled presents a potential security risk. This script is also useful for these situations and does not require DDNS to be enabled.

**Note**   This script functions only with the Windows Server 2003 DNS Service. It can also work with the Microsoft Windows 2000 Server DNS Service, provided the DNS server has the Windows Management Instrumentation (WMI) provider installed. See the "Learn More" links at the end of this section for more information about this provider and its installation procedures.

## Performing This Task Manually

Administrators typically use the DNS Server console when they need to manually create records. The procedure for creating A (IP address) and AAAA (IPv6 address) records is similar. To create an A record, right-click the zone in which the records should be created and select New Host (A). In the New Host dialog box, type the host name and IP address, and click Add Host to save the information. The graphical user interface is not difficult to use, but creating records in bulk can be time-consuming.

# Example

This script is designed to read host names and addresses from a text file in which the host name, IP address, and IPv6 address (optional) are separated by commas. A sample text file might look like this:

```
Server1,192.168.0.12,3ffe:ffff:0100:f101:0210:a4ff:fee3:9566
Server2,192.168.7.43,3ffe:ffff:100:f101:210:a4ff:fee3:9566
Server3,192.168.7.216,3ffe:ffff:100:f101::1
```

As shown in the preceding text file example, both full and abbreviated IPv6 addresses are acceptable. The file does not contain a header row. If you don't want to specify IPv6 addresses, omit that information.

> **Note**  When specifying IPv6 addresses, you typically provide the address that any client can use to reach the server. Link-local addresses are not usually registered with DNS, for example, because they are valid only on the computer's local subnet. Private addresses (typically routable within an intranet) and global addresses (which are routable on the Internet) are suitable for DNS registration.

Running the script requires you to specify the text file path and name, as well as the DNS server name (or address) and whether you want IPv6 records created:

```
CreateARecords.wsf /dns:MyDNSServer /list:C:\hosts.csv /ipv6 /domain:company.com
```

You must also specify the domain in which the records will be created, and the DNS server specified must host a writable (primary) copy of that domain's zone. Note that specifying the */ipv6* argument will cause errors if the input file does not contain IP *and* IPv6 addresses for each host.

# Syntax

This script has several command-line arguments, which are listed in the following table. Set CScript.exe to be your default script processor, as described in Chapter 3.

| | |
|---|---|
| /dns:name | Specifies the name or IP address of the Windows DNS server. |
| /list:file | Specifies the path and file name of the text file containing the hosts and IP addresses to be added. |
| /domain:name | Specifies the name of the domain in which the records should be created. |
| /ipv6 | Specifies that both IP and IPv6 records should be added to DNS for each host. |

You can run this script with the */?* parameter to display the script's syntax.

# Under the Hood

This script uses WMI to connect to a DNS server and create new records. The following code performs the bulk of the work:

```
Do Until oTS.AtEndOfStream
    sData = Split(oTS.ReadLine,",")
    sName = sData(0)
    sAddress = sData(1)

    'Create AAAA records
    if wscript.Arguments.Named.Exists("ipv6") Then
        sIPv6Address = sData(2)
        Set oItem = oWMIService.Get("MicrosoftDNS_AAAAType")
        WScript.Echo  " Creating AAAA record for " & sName
        errResult = oItem.CreateInstanceFromPropertyData (sDNSServer, sDomain, sName,
 1, 600, sIPv6Address)
        If errResult <> 0 Then
            WScript.Echo " ** Error: " & Err.Description
        End If
    End If

    'Create A records
    Set oItem = oWMIService.Get("MicrosoftDNS_AType")
    WScript.Echo  " Creating A record for " & sName
    errResult = oItem.CreateInstanceFromPropertyData (sDNSServer, sDomain, sName, 1,
 600, sAddress)
    If errResult <> 0 Then
        WScript.Echo " ** Error: " & Err.Description
    End If
Loop
```

The variable *oWMIService* is set to an instance of the DNS server's WMI service, which provides the interface for querying and creating DNS records. The WMI namespace used, *root\MicrosoftDNS*, is available only when the DNS WMI provider is installed (which is always the case on computers running Windows Server 2003 and the Microsoft DNS service).

# Troubleshooting

Several things can go wrong with this script, although the most common problem concerns permissions. The user account running the script must have permission to create new DNS records on the DNS server specified.

Other problems generally come from the DNS server itself. For example, the DNS server might not allow a record to be created if an existing record with the same name exists; the outcome depends on how the permissions on that record are configured. The DNS server might also be configured to disallow certain record types (unlikely with A records but more likely with AAAA records, which are less commonly used). In all cases, the script will display an error message if the DNS server returns one.

Other errors usually result from improperly formatted input files. Always check to make sure your input file's format matches the example shown earlier and that the first line of the file contains a host name and an IP address, and not a header row.

## To Learn More

- Learn more about the DNS WMI provider at *http://msdn.microsoft.com/library /default.asp?url=/library/en-us/dns/dns/dns_wmi_provider_overview.asp.*

- Get DNS WMI scripting examples from *http://msdn.microsoft.com/library /default.asp?url=/library/en-us/dns/dns/dns_wmi_provider_scripting_ examples.asp.*

- Download and install the DNS WMI provider from *http://msdn.microsoft.com /library/default.asp?url=/library/en-us/dns/dns/installing_the_provider.asp* (for Windows 2000 Server only; the provider is preinstalled on Windows Server 2003).

- Learn more about IPv6 at *http://www.ipv6.org/.*

# Create Print Queues

> **On the CD**   The sample script can be found on the CD that accompanies this book at \Chap12\CreatePrintQueues\CreatePrintQueues.wsf.

| Operating System | Supported? | Prerequisites |
|---|---|---|
| Windows 2000 family | No | ■ WSH 5.6 or later |
| Windows XP Professional | Yes | ■ WMI |
| Windows Server 2003 family | Yes | ■ Administrative permission on targeted computers |
| | | ■ Network connectivity to each remote computer |

## Description

This script, CreatePrintQueues.wsf, is used to create multiple print queues. (A print queue is referred to as a *printer* in Microsoft Windows terminology. The physical hardware is referred to as a *print device*.) Because an administrator rarely needs to create the same kind of print queue on multiple computers, this script is designed to create multiple printers on a single computer. This can be useful for restoring a print server that contains multiple queues, or for migrating a print server's queues to a new server.

## Performing This Task Manually

Creating a printer involves using the Printers And Faxes folder, which is accessible from Control Panel. In the Printers And Faxes folder, an Add A Printer link is provided, which launches a wizard that collects the necessary information to set up the new printer. This process can be cumbersome and time-consuming when you need to set up multiple printers, so the script streamlines it. The script can also automatically enable the sharing of printers so that they are available to network users. However, the script uses the default share permissions for newly shared printers and does not provide a facility for specifying custom shared printer permissions.

## Example

This script provides two basic modes of operation. The first mode reads the existing printers on a server and writes their information into a text file. The second mode reads a text file—such as the kind created by the first mode—and creates printers based on the data contained within the file.

The first mode is executed like this:

```
CreatePrintQueues.wsf /server:Server1 /output:C:\Printers.csv
```

This code will connect to a server named Server1 and write its printer information to a file named Printers.csv. This file is a comma-separated values (CSV) file formatted as follows:

```
DriverName,PortName,DeviceID,Location,Network,Shared,ShareName
```

The second mode of the script reads a CSV file formatted in that fashion and creates printers:

```
CreatePrintQueues.wsf /server:Server2 /input:C:\Printers.csv
```

Keep in mind that this script does not install printer drivers; it simply creates queues that reference those drivers. For example, the script is capable of creating a queue for a Brand X print device, but it cannot install the Brand X device drivers. All device drivers needed to create the queues listed in the input file must be installed before running the script.

# Syntax

This script has several command-line arguments, which are listed in the following table. Set CScript.exe to be your default script processor, as described in Chapter 3.

| | |
|---|---|
| /server:name | Specifies the name or IP address of the server to target. |
| /input:file | Specifies the path and file name of the CSV text file containing the printer information; cannot be used in conjunction with *output*. |
| /output:file | Specifies the path and file name of the CSV text file that will contain the printer information; cannot be used in conjunction with *input*. |

You can run this script with the */?* parameter to display the script's syntax.

# Under the Hood

The following code snippet is used to inventory existing printers and write their information to a file:

```
Set oTS = oFSO.CreateTextFile(WScript.Arguments.Named("output"),True)
If Err <> 0 Then
    WScript.Echo "** Could not open output file"
    WScript.Echo Err.Description
    WScript.Quit
End If

Set cPrinters = oWMI.ExecQuery("Select * From Win32_Printer")
For Each oPrinter In cPrinters
    sData = oPrinter.DriverName
    sData = sData & "," & oPrinter.PortName
    sData = sData & "," & oPrinter.DeviceID
    sData = sData & "," & oPrinter.Location
    sData = sData & "," & oPrinter.Network
```

```
        sData = sData & "," & oPrinter.Shared
        sData = sData & "," & oPrinter.ShareName
        WScript.Echo sData
        oTS.WriteLine sData
Next
```

This is a simple WMI query for all available instances of the *Win32_Printer* class. Using the script's */input* argument runs the following code, which reads information from a file and creates new printers by spawning instances of the *Win32_Printer* class:

```
sData = ots.ReadLine
sData=Split(sData,",")
Set oPrinter = oWMI.Get("Win32_Printer").SpawnInstance_
oPrinter.DriverName = sData(0)
oPrinter.PortName   = sData(1)
oPrinter.DeviceID   = sData(2)
oPrinter.Location = sData(3)
oPrinter.Network = sData(4)
oPrinter.Shared = sData(5)
oPrinter.ShareName = sData(6)
oPrinter.Put_
If Err <> 0 Then
    WScript.Echo "** Error creating " & sData(0)
    WScript.Echo Err.Description
End If
```

The script expects the data in the input file to be within acceptable ranges and properly formatted. Use the */output* switch to generate a sample file if you plan to manually create your own input files.

This script works best with networked printers that are accessed via TCP/IP printing (also called LPD/LPR or IP printing). Other types of printers might require local printer port configurations, which the script cannot automatically create.

## Troubleshooting

To run this script, you must have permission to create new printers on the targeted server. The script will not be able to create all printer types. Those using specialized ports, those using drivers that are not installed, and some printers utilizing USB connectivity will often cause errors. You can edit the file produced with the */output* argument to remove any printers that you do not want created or that are causing problems. If a printer cannot be created, the script will try to obtain and display error information. Removing the printer from the input file will prevent the error from recurring.

## To Learn More

- Find more Microsoft Visual Basic® Script (VBScript) samples that deal with printers and print queues at *http://www.microsoft.com/technet/scriptcenter /scripts/printing/servers/default.mspx.*

Chapter 13

# Security Management Tasks

Many of the chapters in this book address security-related management tasks, and this chapter will bring together many tasks that are specific to security, including security log management and Public Key Infrastructure (PKI) management. For the PKI tasks in particular, I'll tend to direct you to existing command-line tools rather than providing scripts. That's because you typically perform PKI tasks on a single computer rather than on multiple computers, although you might want to schedule the tasks to run repetitively—functionality that command-line tools excel at.

In addition, the PKI-related tasks that you would want to perform on multiple computers usually need to be performed for the primary user of those computers, which often means working with the users' profiles. This is difficult to do remotely because by default remote scripts work with the profile of the person running the script, not with the profile of the remote computer's primary user. Command-line tools can be easily added to logon scripts, which makes easier the automation of tasks that deal with individual user profiles.

Tasks automated in this chapter include:

- Archiving and clearing the security log on multiple computers
- Backing up the keys for a Certificate Authority (CA)

- Restoring the keys for a CA
- Backing up a CA and its database
- Restoring a CA and its database
- Publishing a Certificate Revocation List (CRL)
- Requesting a CA certificate renewal

# Archive and Clear Security Logs

**On the CD**  The sample script for this task can be found on the CD that accompanies this book at \Chap13\ArchiveLogs\ArchiveLogs.wsf.

| Operating System | Supported? | Prerequisites |
|---|---|---|
| Microsoft® Windows® 2000 family | Yes | ■ Windows Script Host (WSH) 5.6 or later |
| Microsoft Windows XP Professional | Yes | ■ Windows Management Instrumentation (WMI) |
| Microsoft Windows Server™ 2003 family | Yes | ■ Administrative permission on targeted computers |
| | | ■ Network connectivity to each remote computer |

## Description

The Security event log in Windows contains detailed information about auditing events (if you enabled auditing) and other security-related system events. Many organizations have policies that require security logs to be archived for a period of time as an audit trail; some organizations might even be required by law or industry practices to retain this information. This script, ArchiveLogs.wsf, is designed to create an archive of the security logs. When archiving a log, the script also clears it, making room for new events.

## Performing This Task Manually

To manually archive an event log, open the Event Viewer console, right-click the Security event log, and select Save Log File As. You can select Clear All Events to clear the log. The Event Viewer console allows you to connect to remote computers to perform this task, but doing so for multiple remote computers can be time-consuming.

## Example

This tool allows you to target one computer or multiple computers. If you wanted to use it to target a single remote computer named ServerA, you would use this code:

```
ArchiveLogs.wsf /computer:ServerA /path:C:\Archive
```

You can also target a list of computers from a text file. The text file is expected to contain one computer name per line and no other information. Assuming the file is named C:\Computers.txt, you would use this syntax:

```
ArchiveLogs.wsf /list:C:\Computers.txt /path:C:\Archive
```

Finally, you can target an entire organizational unit of computer accounts. If your domain contains an OU named West, you would use the following syntax:

```
ArchiveLogs.wsf /container:west /path:C:\Archive
```

Note that the *container* argument will work against only the default domain of the computer running the script. In other words, the OU specified must exist within the same domain of the computer running the script. If the specified OU has nested OUs, you can include their computer accounts as well by specifying one additional argument:

```
ArchiveLogs.wsf /container:west /recurse /path:C:\Archive
```

# Syntax

This script can be executed as a command-line utility. Set CScript.exe to be your default script processor, as described in Chapter 3, "Working with VBScript."

| | |
|---|---|
| /list:path<br>/computer:name<br>/container:name | One and only one of these is required by the script. Use */list* to target a list of computers contained within a text file. Use */computer* to target a single computer. Use */container* to target an organizational unit within Microsoft Active Directory®. |
| /recurse | When used with */container*, also targets computers contained within nested OUs. |
| /ping | Verifies the connectivity to all targeted computers prior to attempting a connection. Using this argument will reduce the timeout wait when one or more computers cannot be reached on the network. |
| /log:path | Logs unreachable computer names to the specified file. This file can then be used later, along with the */list* argument, to retry these computers. Note that a log is created only when used in conjunction with the */ping* argument. |
| /verbose | Causes the script to display more detailed, step-by-step status messages. |
| /path:path | Specifies the path where the archive files will be saved. The script will create a subfolder for each targeted computer and will name individual files with the current date. The path specified must already exist. |

You can run this script with the */?* parameter to display the command's syntax.

# Under the Hood

This script uses a straightforward Windows Management Instrumentation (WMI) query to retrieve the Security event log, archive it, and clear it. Note that clearing takes place only when the archive was successful, helping to ensure events are not lost by accident. The following code does the work:

```
Set oWMIService = GetObject("winmgmts:{impersonationLevel=impersonate,(Security,
Backup)}!\\" & sName & "\root\cimv2")
Set cLogFiles = oWMIService.ExecQuery("Select * from Win32_NTEventLogFile where
LogFileName='Security'")
If Not IsObject(clogfiles) Then
    WScript.Echo "** Could not retrieve logs from " & sName
Else
    For Each oLogfile in cLogFiles
        sFolder = WScript.Arguments.Named("path")
            If Not oFSO.FolderExists(sfolder) Then
                WScript.Echo "** Folder " & sfolder & " must exist and does not."
                WScript.Quit
            End if
        If Not oFSO.FolderExists(oFSO.BuildPath(sfolder,sName)) Then
            Verbose " Creating folder for " & sName
            oFSO.CreateFolder oFSO.BuildPath(sfolder,sName)
        End If
        Verbose "  Backing up security log on " & sName
        errResult = oLogFile.BackupEventLog(oFSO.BuildPath(sfolder,sName & "\"
& FormatDateTime(2,Date) & ".evt"))
        If errBackupLog <> 0 Then
            Wscript.Echo "** Security log on " & sName & " could not be backed up."
        Else
            Verbose "  Clearing security log on " & sName
            oLogFile.ClearEventLog()
        End If
    Next
End If
```

Note that the script specifically requests both Security and Backup permissions; both are required to archive and clear the Security event log. If the user account used to run the script can't obtain these permissions, the script will return an error.

Note that the archived files are given the current date as determined by the computer on which the script is run; if you are archiving logs from computers located in different time zones, the log file names might not precisely match the events contained within the logs. Consider the file name to be just an indicator of when the log archive was created; it has no relation to the events within the file.

# Troubleshooting

As with most scripts, this script can run into a couple of common errors. First, one or more targeted computers might not be available, a condition the script can handle properly. You can reduce the script's execution time by including the */ping* argument, which tests connectivity prior to trying to execute the WMI query. The second possible error is that you won't have permission to view or clear the security log. This error is unusual if you're running the script as an administrator, but the script will detect this error, display a message, and continue running.

The script is not designed to be run more than once per day. Each archived security log is given the current date as its file name, such as 1-1-2005.evt. If the script is run twice in one day and used to target the same computer each time, the script will be successful the first time but will return an error the second time. This is the intended functionality so that it avoids overwriting any existing log files.

# To Learn More

- Find more event log management samples in Microsoft Visual Basic® Script (VBScript) at *http://www.microsoft.com/technet/scriptcenter/scripts/logs /eventlog/default.mspx.*

# Back Up Keys

> **Note**   This script is included with Windows Server 2003 when Certificate Services is installed.

| Operating System | Supported? | Prerequisites |
| --- | --- | --- |
| Microsoft® Windows® 2000 family | No | Certificate Services installed |
| Microsoft Windows XP Professional | No | |
| Microsoft Windows Server™ 2003 family | Yes | |

## Description

Essentially, the certificate (and associated public and private keys) for a Certificate Authority (CA) is its license to issue keys to users, computers, and other entities. Without the keys contained in its CA certificate, a CA is useless. If those keys become damaged or lost, every certificate ever issued by the CA becomes useless. It's therefore an excellent idea to create reliable backups of CA certificates (and to test those backups). The certificates don't change, so this isn't a task you need to perform frequently.

## Performing This Task Manually

The Certification Authority console provides a graphical means for backing up and restoring CA certificates; simply right-click the appropriate CA in the tree view and select the option to back up or restore the certificate for that CA.

## Example

The Certutil.exe command-line utility provides a scriptable means of backing up the certificates for multiple CAs, making it easier to get a complete set of backups for an entire PKI. The basic use of the command-line tool is as follows:

```
Certutil.exe -backupkey -config server\caname -p password path
```

Replace *server\caname* with the name of the server and CA to back up; replace *path* with the location for the backup files to be written. This command can be added to a batch file to target multiple computers simply by listing the command multiple times and changing each instance to target a different *server\caname*. Note that the *password* argument is the password that will be used to protect the backed-up keys. If you include this command in a batch file, be sure to remove the password after running the script so that the password cannot be discovered by reading the batch file.

# Syntax

This command has many command-line arguments. The most common are described in the following table.

| | |
|---|---|
| -backupkey | Specifies that certificates and private keys should be backed up. |
| -f | Specifies that existing backup files should be overwritten and replaced. |
| -gmt | Displays times in Greenwich Mean Time (GMT; also called Universal Time Constant or UTC). |
| -seconds | Displays times using seconds and milliseconds. |
| -v | Specifies verbose output for the command. |
| -config server\caname | Specifies the CA that will be targeted. |
| -p password | Specifies a password that will protect the exported (backed up) certificate. |
| Path | Specifies the location to which the backup files will be written. |

You can run this script with the /? parameter to display the script's syntax.

# Under the Hood

Windows Server 2003 Certificate Services runs in one of two modes: Standalone, meaning issued certificates are stored in the registry, and Enterprise, meaning certificates are stored in Active Directory. Enterprise mode is available only to CAs running on Active Directory domain controllers. Certutil.exe is designed to work with either mode; be aware that exporting keys (which includes backing up certificates) creates a copy of the keys that is often less protected than the copy of the keys in either the registry or Active Directory. After all, files can be moved around and copied more readily than data in Active Directory or in the registry. It is therefore important to assign a strong password to the backups, and to use NTFS permissions to secure the backups against unauthorized access.

The backup operation of Certutil.exe produces a PKCS #12 (.pfx) file, which is an industry-standard file format for storing certificates. For maximum safety, these files should be written to permanent backup media (such as a backup tape, a CD-R, or other media) for archiving, and the physical media should be stored in a safe and secured location such as a locked fire safe or secure off-site storage location.

# Troubleshooting

Certutil.exe assumes that the user account used to run the tool has permission to perform the desired operations within Certificate Services. Because Certificate Services represents such a critical portion of an organization's security, it is often secured in such a way that normal administrative accounts—such as the Domain Admins group—don't have administrative access. Instead, administrative access to the PKI is granted to another group, often reducing the number of individual users who have control over the PKI. Be sure you are running Certutil.exe using an appropriate user account. If necessary, execute the tool by using the Runas command to provide alternative user credentials.

# To Learn More

- Learn more about using the Certutil command at *http://www.microsoft.com /resources/documentation/WindowsServ/2003/standard/proddocs/en-us /Default.asp?url=/resources/documentation/WindowsServ/2003/standard /proddocs/en-us/sag_CS_CertUtil2.asp.*

- Read more about Certificate Services at *http://www.microsoft.com/resources /documentation/WindowsServ/2003/all/techref/en-us/Default.asp?url= /Resources/Documentation/windowsserv/2003/all/techref/en-us /w2k3tr_crtsv_what.asp.*

# Restore Keys

> **Note**   The script is included with Windows Server 2003 when Certificate Services is installed.

| Operating System | Supported? | Prerequisites |
|---|---|---|
| Windows 2000 family | No | Certificate Services installed |
| Windows XP Professional | No | |
| Windows Server 2003 family | Yes | |

## Description

The certificate (and associated public and private keys) for a Certificate Authority (CA) is essentially its license to issue keys to users, computers, and other entities. Without the keys contained in its CA certificate, a CA is useless. If those keys become damaged or lost, every certificate ever issued by the CA becomes useless. Provided you have a backup of the CA's certificate, you can restore that backup to restore a CA to functionality and prevent the keys it has issued from becoming useless.

## Performing This Task Manually

The Certification Authority console provides a graphical means for backing up and restoring CA certificates; simply right-click the appropriate CA in the tree view and select the option to back up or restore the certificate for that CA.

## Example

The Certutil.exe command-line utility provides a scriptable means of restoring the certificates for multiple CAs, making it easier to restore a complete set of backups for an entire PKI. You generally need to restore only a single CA at a given time, but during disaster recovery scenarios you might need to restore multiple CAs (for example, if you are performing disaster recovery at an off-site facility). Having a scriptable means of performing the restore will allow your CAs to be up and running more quickly. The basic use of the command-line tool is as follows:

```
Certutil.exe -restorekey -config -f server\caname -p password path
```

Replace *server\caname* with the name of the server and CA to back up; replace *path* with the location of the backup file (a .pfx file). This command can be added to a batch file to target multiple computers by listing the command multiple times and changing each instance to target a different *server\caname*. Note that the *password* argument is the password that will be used to open the backed-up keys; if you include this command in a batch file, be sure to remove the password after running the script so that the password cannot be discovered by reading the batch file.

## Syntax

This command has several command-line arguments, as listed in the following table.

| | |
|---|---|
| -restorekey | Specifies that certificates and private keys should be restored from backup. |
| -f | Specifies that existing backup files should be overwritten and replaced. |
| -gmt | Displays times in Greenwich Mean Time (GMT; also called Universal Time Constant or UTC). |
| -seconds | Displays times using seconds and milliseconds |
| -v | Specifies verbose output for the command. |
| -config server\caname | Specifies the CA that will be targeted. |
| -p password | Specifies the password that protects the exported (backed up) certificate. |
| Path | Specifies the location where the backup file (a .pfx file) is located. |

You can run this script with the /? parameter to display the script's syntax.

## Under the Hood

The restore functionality of Certutil.exe is designed to read a PKCS #12 file, an industry-standard format for storing certificates. Certificates can be read from any readable media, including CD-Rs. Note that the maximum password length is 32 characters.

Certutil.exe uses remote procedure calls (RPCs) to connect to CAs and restore certificates. Be sure that the CAs you target are reachable on RPC ports (a broad range of ports, making it difficult to perform this task across a firewall).

## Troubleshooting

Certutil.exe assumes that the user account used to run the tool has permission to perform the desired operations within Certificate Services. Because Certificate Services represents such a critical portion of an organization's security, it is often secured in such a way that normal administrative accounts—such as the Domain Admins group—don't have administrative access. Instead, administrative access to the PKI is granted to another group, often reducing the number of individual users who have control over the PKI. Be sure you are running Certutil.exe by using an appropriate user account; if necessary, execute the tool by using the Runas command to provide alternative user credentials.

# To Learn More

- Learn more about using the Certutil command at *http://www.microsoft.com /resources/documentation/WindowsServ/2003/standard/proddocs/en-us /Default.asp?url=/resources/documentation/WindowsServ/2003/standard /proddocs/en-us/sag_CS_CertUtil2.asp.*

- Read more about Certificate Services at *http://www.microsoft.com/resources /documentation/WindowsServ/2003/all/techref/en-us/Default.asp?url= /Resources/Documentation/windowsserv/2003/all/techref/en-us /w2k3tr_crtsv_what.asp.*

# Back Up a CA or the CA Database

> **Note** This script is included with Windows Server 2003 when Certificate Services is installed.

| Operating System | Supported? | Prerequisites |
|---|---|---|
| Windows 2000 family | No | Certificate Services installed |
| Windows XP Professional | No | |
| Windows Server 2003 family | Yes | |

## Description

The database used by Certificate Services contains configuration information, issued keys, and other critical data. Routinely backing this information up will help protect against a loss of data should the CA become damaged or corrupted. Backups can also be used to restore the CA to operation after a disaster, such as at an off-site disaster recovery facility.

## Performing This Task Manually

The Certification Authority console provides a graphical means for backing up and restoring the CA configuration and its certificates; simply right-click the appropriate CA in the tree view and select the option to back up or restore the CA. However, the command-line approach provides somewhat better diagnostic output in the event that a problem occurs, and the command-line approach can be automated (using the Task Scheduler) to ensure regular backups are conducted.

## Example

The Certutil.exe command-line utility provides a scriptable means of backing up the certificates for multiple CAs, making it easier to get a complete set of backups for an entire PKI. The basic use of the command-line tool is as follows:

```
Certutil.exe -backupdb -config server\caname
```

Replace *server\caname* with the name of the server and CA to back up; replace *path* with the location for the backup files to be written. This command can be added to a batch file to target multiple computers by listing the command multiple times and changing each instance to target a different *server\caname*. Note that the *password* argument is the password that will be used to protect the backed-up keys; if you include this command in a batch file, be sure to remove the password after running the script so that the password cannot be discovered by reading the batch file.

Specifying *–backup* rather than *–backupdb* will perform a more lengthy backup that includes the database, the CAs keys, and other components—essentially a complete backup of the entire CA.

## Syntax

This command has several command-line arguments, as listed in the following table.

| | |
|---|---|
| -backupdb | Specifies a backup operation for the database. Use *–backup* to specify a full backup of the entire CA. |
| -f | Specifies that existing backup files should be overwritten and replaced. |
| -gmt | Displays times in Greenwich Mean Time (GMT; also called Universal Time Constant or UTC). |
| -seconds | Displays times using seconds and milliseconds. |
| -v | Specifies verbose output for the command. |
| -config server\caname | Specifies the CA that will be targeted. |
| Path | Specifies the location to which the backup files will be written. |
| Incremental | Specifies an incremental backup, meaning you will need the last full backup and all incremental backups to perform a restore. |
| Keeplog | Does not delete the database log files. Without specifying this, the log files are consolidated into a single archive file, which is retained. |

You can run this script with the */?* parameter to display the script's syntax.

## Under the Hood

The full backup operation is generally the most desirable—even on a large CA that has issued many keys, the backup operation is relatively quick. An incremental backup can be faster, but it requires you to maintain a larger set of files (a full backup and all incremental backups made since the last full backup) to successfully restore the CA. I typically prefer a full backup, if for no other reason than to reduce the number of backup files that must be managed. If you do choose to use incremental backups, each backup must be made to an independent directory tree so that the backup files don't overwrite one another.

## Troubleshooting

Certutil.exe assumes that the user account used to run the tool has permission to perform the desired operations within Certificate Services. Because Certificate Services represents such a critical portion of an organization's security, it is often secured in such a way that normal administrative accounts—such as the Domain Admins group—don't have administrative access. Instead, administrative access to the PKI is granted to another group, often reducing the number of individual users who have control over the PKI. Be sure you are running Certutil.exe using appropriate user account; if necessary, execute the tool by using the Runas command to provide alternative user credentials.

## To Learn More

- Learn more about using the Certutil command at *http://www.microsoft.com /resources/documentation/WindowsServ/2003/standard/proddocs/en-us /Default.asp?url=/resources/documentation/WindowsServ/2003/standard /proddocs/en-us/sag_CS_CertUtil2.asp.*

- Read more about Certificate Services at *http://www.microsoft.com/resources /documentation/WindowsServ/2003/all/techref/en-us/Default.asp?url= /Resources/Documentation/windowsserv/2003/all/techref/en-us /w2k3tr_crtsv_what.asp.*

# Restore a CA or the CA Database

> **Note**   This script is included with Windows Server 2003 when Certificate Services is installed.

| Operating System | Supported? | Prerequisites |
|---|---|---|
| Windows 2000 family | No | Certificate Services installed |
| Windows XP Professional | No | |
| Windows Server 2003 family | Yes | |

## Description

Restoring a CA database (or, if necessary, the entire CA, including keys) provides a means for returning a nonfunctional CA to service without losing any information. This task is especially useful in disaster recovery scenarios, and because the Certutil.exe tool is scriptable, you can more easily restore multiple CAs in a short period of time—a good technique to use when, for example, you are bringing your business back online at an off-site disaster recovery facility.

## Performing This Task Manually

The Certification Authority console provides a graphical means for backing up and restoring the CA configuration and its certificates; simply right-click the appropriate CA in the tree view and select the option to back up or restore the CA. However, the command-line approach provides somewhat better diagnostic output in the event that a problem occurs, and the command-line approach can be automated (using the Task Scheduler) to restore multiple CAs at once.

## Example

The Certutil.exe command-line utility provides a scriptable means of backing up the certificates for multiple CAs, making it easier to restore multiple CAs at one time. The basic use of the command-line tool is as follows:

```
Certutil.exe -f -restoredb -config server\caname -p password path
```

Replace *server\caname* with the name of the server and CA to restore; replace *path* with the location of the backup files. Note that you might need to stop the Certificate Service service to perform any restore of the database. This command can be added to a batch file to target multiple computers by listing the command multiple times and changing each instance to target a different *server\caname*. Note that the *password* argument is the password that will be used to protect the backed-up keys. If you include this command in a batch file, be sure to remove the password after running the script so that the password cannot be discovered by reading the batch file.

# Syntax

This command has several command-line arguments, as listed in the following table.

| | |
|---|---|
| -restoredb | Specifies a restore operation for the database. Use *–restore* to specify a full restore of the entire CA. |
| -f | Specifies that the backup files should overwrite the database (often used with a full backup). |
| -gmt | Displays times in Greenwich Mean Time (GMT; also called Universal Time Constant or UTC). |
| -seconds | Displays times using seconds and milliseconds. |
| -v | Specifies verbose output for the command. |
| -config server\caname | Specifies the CA that will be targeted. |
| -p password | Specifies the password that protects the backup files. Maximum of 32 characters. |
| Path | Specifies the location to which the backup files will be written. |

You can run this script with the /? parameter to display the script's syntax.

# Under the Hood

To restore a full backup and subsequent incremental backups, restore the full backup first, and then repeat the restore operation with each incremental backup in chronological order. (In other words, the backups must be restored in the same order they were originally made.) Specify the *–f* argument only when restoring a full backup; this argument will essentially delete the CA database and replace it with the backup file. When restoring a full and multiple incremental backups, do not restart the server until all backups have been restored. Restarting the server automatically initiates database recovery, which assumes all files you intend to restore are in place.

# Troubleshooting

Certutil.exe assumes that the user account used to run the tool has permission to perform the desired operations within Certificate Services. Because Certificate Services represents such a critical portion of an organization's security, it is often secured in such a way that normal administrative accounts—such as the Domain Admins group—don't have administrative access. Instead, administrative access to the PKI is granted to another group, often reducing the number of individual users who have control over the PKI. Be sure you are running Certutil.exe using an appropriate user account; if necessary, execute the tool by using the Runas command to provide alternative user credentials.

## To Learn More

- Learn more about using the Certutil command at *http://www.microsoft.com /resources/documentation/WindowsServ/2003/standard/proddocs/en-us /Default.asp?url=/resources/documentation/WindowsServ/2003/standard /proddocs/en-us/sag_CS_CertUtil2.asp.*

- Read more about Certificate Services at *http://www.microsoft.com/resources /documentation/WindowsServ/2003/all/techref/en-us/Default.asp?url= /Resources/Documentation/windowsserv/2003/all/techref/en-us /w2k3tr_crtsv_what.asp.*

# Publish a CRL

> **Note**   This script is included with Windows Server 2003 when Certificate Services is installed.

| Operating System | Supported? | Prerequisites |
|---|---|---|
| Windows 2000 family | No | Certificate Services installed |
| Windows XP Professional | No | |
| Windows Server 2003 family | Yes | |

## Description

About Certificate Revocation List (CRL) is a list of certificates that have been revoked by a CA. Client computers and other security principals regularly download a CRL and use it to check the validity of any certificates presented to them. The CRL is basically a list of certificates that should not be accepted, even though they appear to be valid and are not expired.

## Performing This Task Manually

The Certification Authority console provides a graphical means for publishing a CRL: simply right-click the Revoked Certificates folder and select the option to publish a CRL. However, in environments with multiple CAs, each CA might maintain its own CRL, making the graphical means of publishing CRLs overly time-consuming.

## Example

Publishing a CRL using the Certutil.exe command is straightforward:

```
Certutil.exe -crl -config server\caname
```

Replace *server\caname* with the appropriate server and CA name. You can add this command to a batch file, specifying different servers, to publish a CRL from multiple stand-alone CAs at once.

## Syntax

This command has several command-line arguments, as listed in the following table.

| | |
|---|---|
| -crl | Specifies that a CRL should be published |
| -gmt | Displays times in Greenwich Mean Time (GMT; also called Universal Time Constant or UTC). |
| -seconds | Displays times with seconds and milliseconds |

| | |
|---|---|
| -v | Specifies verbose output for the command. |
| -config server\caname | Specifies the CA that will be targeted. |
| Delta | Specifies that a delta-CRL should be published. It will contain all CRL changes since the last CRL or delta-CRL was created. |
| DD:HH | Normally a CRL will contain all revoked certificates. Specify days and hours (in the form *DD:HH*) to have the CRL contain only those certificates that were revoked in the past *DD* days and *HH* hours. |

You can run this script with the /? parameter to display the script's syntax.

# Under the Hood

CAs can be configured to automatically publish CRLs on a regular basis; however, you might wish to force CRL publication after revoking particularly sensitive certificates. For example, if you discover that a code-signing certificate has been compromised and is being used to sign malicious code, you will want to revoke that certificate immediately and publish a CRL as quickly as possible. Note, however, that clients are typically configured to download CRLs on a periodic basis; publishing a CRL does not immediately ensure that all clients will receive it. This is a factor to consider when configuring clients. Certutil.exe can also be used to immediately retrieve the current CRL from the default CA:

```
Certutil -getcrl outfile
```

Note that *outfile* is the name of the file you want the CRL written to. This command can be included in a client logon script, which will at least execute the next time users log on to their computers.

# Troubleshooting

Certutil.exe assumes that the user account used to run the tool has permission to perform the desired operations within Certificate Services. Because Certificate Services represents such a critical portion of an organization's security, it is often secured in such a way that normal administrative accounts—such as the Domain Admins group—don't have administrative access. Instead, administrative access to the PKI is granted to another group, often reducing the number of individual users who have control over the PKI. Be sure you are running Certutil.exe using an appropriate user account; if necessary, execute the tool by using the Runas command to provide alternative user credentials.

## To Learn More

- Learn more about using the Certutil command at *http://www.microsoft.com /resources/documentation/WindowsServ/2003/standard/proddocs/en-us /Default.asp?url=/resources/documentation/WindowsServ/2003/standard /proddocs/en-us/sag_CS_CertUtil2.asp.*

- Read more about Certificate Services at *http://www.microsoft.com/resources /documentation/WindowsServ/2003/all/techref/en-us/Default.asp?url= /Resources/Documentation/windowsserv/2003/all/techref/en-us /w2k3tr_crtsv_what.asp.*

# Request Renewal CA Certificate

> **Note**   This script is included with Windows Server 2003 when Certificate Services is installed.

| Operating System | Supported? | Prerequisites |
|---|---|---|
| Windows 2000 family | No | Certificate Services installed |
| Windows XP Professional | No | |
| Windows Server 2003 family | Yes | |

## Description

When a CA's root certificate expires, the CA loses the ability to issue more certificates and jeopardizes all certificates already issued by the CA, which technically expire no later than the CA's own root certificate. Although CA expiration is infrequent—most organizations configure their CAs to be valid for at least two years, and many for as long as five—being able to renew them all with a single batch file can save time and improve consistency.

## Performing This Task Manually

The Certification Authority console provides a graphical means for renewing a CA. Generally, you right-click the CA certificate and select the Renew option. However, performing this task on multiple computers can be somewhat time-consuming.

## Example

The Certutil.exe command-line tool makes it easier to request a renewal certificate for a CA:

```
Certutil.exe –renewcert –config server\caname
```

Replace *server\caname* with the appropriate server and CA name. You can add this command to a batch file, specifying different servers, to renew multiple CAs at one time. Additional command-line arguments allow the command to be customized; in particular, you might use the *reusekeys* argument.

## Syntax

This command has several command-line arguments, as listed in the following table.

| | |
|---|---|
| -renewcert | Specifies that the targeted CA renew its certificate. |
| -gmt | Displays times in Greenwich Mean Time (GMT; also called Universal Time Constant or UTC). |

| | |
|---|---|
| `-seconds` | Displays times using seconds and milliseconds. |
| `-v` | Specifies verbose output for the command. |
| `-config server\caname` | Specifies the CA that will be targeted. |
| `Reusekeys` | Specifies that the CA's existing public and private keys be reused rather than new keys being issued. This is a decision your organization needs to make; see "Under the Hood" for more details. |

You can run this script with the */?* parameter to display the script's syntax.

## Under the Hood

A CA's certificate consists of a public and private key, often referred to as a *key pair*. The CA's *private key* is used to digitally sign all issued certificates; anyone wanting to validate the authenticity of a key can obtain the CA's *public certificate*, which can then be used to decrypt and validate the signature. By retaining the same keys (by using the *reusekeys* argument), you ensure that all previously issued certificates can be verified.

However, retaining the same keys for a long period of time increases the chances that they will be cryptographically broken and compromised, allowing unauthorized parties to duplicate the CA's private key and forge signatures. Omitting the *reusekeys* argument forces a new key pair to be generated in the renewal, reducing the likelihood of forged keys. This does mean that all previously issued certificates might be treated as invalid and will need to be reissued; however, common practice has all issued certificates expiring before the CA certificate expires anyway, so those certificates would expire on their own and need to be reissued.

The question of whether to reuse keys is one every organization should investigate on its own and decide on according to its own business needs.

## Troubleshooting

Certutil.exe assumes that the user account used to run the tool has permission to perform the desired operations within Certificate Services. Because Certificate Services represents such a critical portion of an organization's security, it is often secured in such a way that normal administrative accounts—such as the Domain Admins group—don't have administrative access. Instead, administrative access to the PKI is granted to another group, often reducing the number of individual users who have control over the PKI. Be sure you are running Certutil.exe using an appropriate user account; if necessary, execute the tool by using the Runas command to provide alternative user credentials.

# To Learn More

- Learn more about using the Certutil command at *http://www.microsoft.com /resources/documentation/WindowsServ/2003/standard/proddocs/en-us /Default.asp?url=/resources/documentation/WindowsServ/2003/standard /proddocs/en-us/sag_CS_CertUtil2.asp*.

- Read more about Certificate Services at *http://www.microsoft.com/resources /documentation/WindowsServ/2003/all/techref/en-us/Default.asp?url= /Resources/Documentation/windowsserv/2003/all/techref/en-us /w2k3tr_crtsv_what.asp*.

## Chapter 14

# Service Management Tasks

Services are perhaps one of the most overlooked aspects of the Microsoft® Windows® operating system when it comes to both manual and automated maintenance. Services just quietly sit in the background doing their jobs; it's easy to forget they're there. When you do need to manage services, doing so is difficult because Windows provides limited means for graphically changing service parameters, and no means for changing them on multiple computers.

Tasks automated in this chapter include:

- Changing the logon account used by a service
- Changing the logon password used by a service
- Changing a service's startup mode
- Listing all computers that use a particular service
- Listing all services that use a particular logon account
- Removing a service
- Stopping and disabling an unwanted service

# Change Service Logon Accounts

> **On the CD**   The sample script can be found on the CD that accompanies this book at \Chap14\ChangeServiceLogonAcct\ChangeServiceLogonAcct.wsf.

| Operating System | Supported? | Prerequisites |
|---|---|---|
| Microsoft Windows 2000 family | Yes | ■ Windows Script Host (WSH) 5.6 or later |
| Microsoft Windows XP Professional | Yes | ■ Windows Management Instrumentation (WMI) |
| Microsoft Windows Server™ 2003 family | Yes | ■ Administrative permission on targeted computers |
| | | ■ Network connectivity to each remote computer |

## Description

This script, ChangeServiceLogonAcct.wsf, is designed to modify the user account that a service uses to log on. You can specify either a local or a domain account, or a built-in account such as LocalService or LocalSystem. This script is an excellent way to change a service that has been using LocalSystem to a more manageable domain or local account, for example. Typically, you would also need to use the ChangeServiceLogonPassword.wsf script, discussed later in this chapter, to provide the service with the correct password for its new account. ChangeServiceLogonAcct.wsf does not perform both tasks because when changing to an account such as Local-System, no password is required.

## Performing This Task Manually

To manually modify a service's startup account or password, you will need to open the Computer Management console and navigate to the desired service. Right-click that service and select Properties to open its Properties dialog box. From there, you can enter a new user account or password as desired. The Computer Management console does provide the means to connect to remote computers, but using it to change multiple services on multiple computers can be error-prone and unnecessarily time-consuming.

## Example

This script allows you to target one computer or multiple computers. If you wanted to use it to target a single remote computer named ServerA, you would use this code:

```
ChangeServiceLogonAcct.wsf /computer:ServerA /service:MyService
/account:MYDOMAIN\MyAccount
```

Note the convention used to specify the new account: *domain\account*. Also note that the service name must be the service's registered internal name (the Service Name listed on the General tab of the service's Properties dialog box), such as Messenger; it does not refer to the service's executable name, nor does it refer to the service's *caption*, which is what you will find listed under the Services node of the Computer Management console.

You can also target a list of computers from a text file. The text file is expected to contain one computer name per line and no other information. Assuming the file is named C:\Computers.txt, you would use this syntax:

```
ChangeServiceLogonAcct.wsf /list:C:\Computers.txt /service:MyService
/account:MYDOMAIN\MyAccount
```

Finally, you can target an entire organizational unit of computer accounts. If your domain contains an OU named West, you would use the following syntax:

```
ChangeServiceLogonAcct.wsf /container:west /service:MyService
/account:MYDOMAIN\MyAccount
```

Note that the *container* argument will work against only the default domain of the computer running the script. In other words, the OU specified must exist within the same domain as that of the computer running the script. If the specified OU has nested OUs, you can include their computer accounts as well by specifying one additional argument:

```
ChangeServiceLogonAcct.wsf /container:west /recurse /service:MyService
/account:MYDOMAIN\MyAccount
```

## Syntax

This script can be executed as a command-line utility. Set CScript.exe to be your default script processor, as described in Chapter 3, "Working with VBScript."

| | |
|---|---|
| `/list:path`<br>`/computer:name`<br>`/container:name` | One and only one of these is required by the script. Use */list* to target a list of computers contained within a text file. Use */computer* to target a single computer. Use */container* to target an organizational unit within Microsoft Active Directory®. |
| `/recurse` | When used with */container*, also targets computers contained within nested OUs. |
| `/ping` | Verifies the connectivity to all targeted computers prior to attempting a connection. Using this argument will reduce the timeout wait when one or more computers cannot be reached on the network. |

| | |
|---|---|
| /log:path | Logs unreachable computer names to the specified file. This file can then be used later, along with the /list argument, to retry these computers. Note that a log is created only when used in conjunction with the /ping argument. |
| /verbose | Causes the script to display more detailed, step-by-step status messages. |
| /service:name | Specifies the service to change. |
| /account:domain\account | Specifies the account the service would use. To specify a built-in account, use something like "NT AUTHORITY\LocalSystem", enclosed in quotation marks because "NT AUTHORITY" contains a space. |

You can run this script with the /? parameter to display the command's syntax.

# Under the Hood

This script uses a straightforward Windows Management Instrumentation (WMI) query to retrieve the desired service instance (an instance of the *Win32_Service* class) and uses that instance's *Change()* method to modify the service's startup parameters:

```
Dim cServices, oService, errResult
Verbose "  Connecting to " & sName
Set cServices = QueryWMI(sName,"root\cimv2","Select * From Win32_Service WHERE Name
= '" & wscript.arguments.named("service") & "'","","")
If Not IsObject(cServices) Then
    WScript.Echo "  ** Couldn't get WMI from " & sName
Else
    For Each oService In cServices
    Verbose "  Changing " & sName
    errResult = oService.change(,,,,,,WScript.Arguments.Named("account"),"")
    Verbose "  Result for " & sName & ":" & errResult
  Next
End if
```

The *Change()* method provides a number of possibilities for changing a service; because only the logon account is being changed, the other parameters are left blank, as evidenced by the sequential commas in the *Change()* method's argument list.

# Troubleshooting

As with most scripts, this script can run into a couple of common errors. First, one or more targeted computers might not be available, a condition the script can handle properly. You can reduce the script's execution time by including the /ping argument, which tests connectivity prior to trying to execute the WMI query. The second possible error is that you won't have permission to perform the task. This situation is unusual if you're running the script as an administrator, but the script will detect this error, display a message or error code, and continue running.

The most common error, however, is specifying a service name that is incorrect or a user account that is improperly formatted. In the first case, the script will seem to do nothing, because it is unable to retrieve instances of a service that does not exist. In the second case, the script will display an error message because it will be unable to properly retrieve the user account specified.

## To Learn More

- Find more service management samples in Microsoft Visual Basic® Script (VBScript) at *http://www.microsoft.com/technet/scriptcenter/scripts/os/services /default.mspx.*

- Read more about Windows services management in Windows online Help and Support Center.

# Change Service Logon Passwords

> **On the CD**   The sample script can be found on the CD that accompanies this book at \Chap14\ChangeServiceLogonPassword\ChangeServiceLogonPassword.wsf.

| Operating System | Supported? | Prerequisites |
|---|---|---|
| Windows 2000 family | Yes | ■ WSH 5.6 or later |
| Windows XP Professional | Yes | ■ WMI |
| Windows Server 2003 family | Yes | ■ Administrative permission on targeted computers |
| | | ■ Network connectivity to each remote computer |

## Description

This script, ChangeServiceLogonPassword.wsf, is designed to modify the user account password that a service uses to log on. This is an excellent task to perform on a regular basis: change the account's password in your domain, and then update your services to use the new password.

## Performing This Task Manually

To manually modify a service's startup account or password, you will need to open the Computer Management console and navigate to the desired service. Right-click that service and select Properties to open its Properties dialog box. From there, you can enter a new user account or password as desired. The Computer Management console does provide the means to connect to remote computers, but using it to change multiple services on multiple computers can be error-prone and unnecessarily time-consuming.

## Example

This script allows you to target one computer or multiple computers. If you wanted to use it to target a single remote computer named ServerA, you would use this code:

```
ChangeServiceLogonPassword.wsf /computer:ServerA /service:MyService
/password:MyP@s5w0rD!
```

Note that the service name must be the service's registered internal name (the Service Name listed on the General tab of the service's Properties dialog box), such as Messenger; the service name does not refer to the service's executable name, nor does it refer to the service's *caption*, which is what you will find listed under the Services node of the Computer Management console.

You can also target a list of computers from a text file. The text file is expected to contain one computer name per line and no other information. Assuming the file is named C:\Computers.txt, you would use this syntax:

```
ChangeServiceLogonPassword.wsf /list:C:\Computers.txt /service:MyService
/password:MyP@s5w0rD!
```

Finally, you can target an entire organizational unit of computer accounts. If your domain contains an OU named West, you would use the following syntax:

```
ChangeServiceLogonPassword.wsf /container:west /service:MyService
/password:MyP@s5w0rD!
```

Note that the *container* argument will work against only the default domain of the computer running the script. In other words, the OU specified must exist within the same domain as that of the computer running the script. If the specified OU has nested OUs, you can include their computer accounts as well by specifying one additional argument:

```
ChangeServiceLogonPassword.wsf /container:west /recurse /service:MyService
/password:MyP@s5w0rD!
```

## Syntax

This script can be executed as a command-line utility. Set CScript.exe to be your default script processor, as described in Chapter 3.

| | |
|---|---|
| `/list:path`<br>`/computer:name`<br>`/container:name` | One and only one of these is required by the script. Use */list* to target a list of computers contained within a text file. Use */computer* to target a single computer. Use */container* to target an organizational unit within Active Directory. |
| `/recurse` | When used with */container*, also targets computers contained within nested OUs. |
| `/ping` | Verifies the connectivity to all targeted computers prior to attempting a connection. Using this argument will reduce the timeout wait when one or more computers cannot be reached on the network. |
| `/log:path` | Logs unreachable computer names to the specified file. This file can then be used later, along with the */list* argument, to retry these computers. Note that a log is created only when used in conjunction with the */ping* argument. |
| `/verbose` | Causes the script to display more detailed, step-by-step status messages. |
| `/service:name` | Specifies the service to change. |
| `/password:password` | Specifies the new password to use. |

You can run this script with the */?* parameter to display the command's syntax.

## Under the Hood

This script uses a straightforward Windows Management Instrumentation (WMI) query to retrieve the desired service instance (an instance of the *Win32_Service* class) and uses that instance's *Change()* method to modify the service's startup parameters:

```
Dim cServices, oService, errResult
Verbose "  Connecting to " & sName
Set cServices = QueryWMI(sName,"root\cimv2","Select * From Win32_Service
WHERE Name = '" & wscript.arguments.named("service") & "'","","")
If Not IsObject(cServices) Then
    WScript.Echo "  ** Couldn't get WMI from " & sName
Else
    For Each oService In cServices
    Verbose "  Changing " & sName
    errResult = oService.change(,,,,,,WScript.Arguments.Named("password"))
    Verbose "  Result for " & sName & ":" & errResult
    Next
End if
```

The *Change()* method provides a number of possibilities for changing a service; because only the logon password is being changed, the other parameters are left blank, as evidenced by the sequential commas in the *Change()* method's argument list.

Note that this script requires that you know which service you want to change; it does not allow you to target all services running under a particular user account. If you use a given account to run more than one service, a useful modification of the script might be to change the password for all services using the specified user account. A quick way to make this modification would be to specify the user account name in the */service* argument when running the script, and to modify the script as follows:

```
Set cServices = QueryWMI(sName,"root\cimv2","Select * From Win32_Service
WHERE StartName = '" & wscript.arguments.named("service") & "'","","")
```

This change retrieves all instances of the *Win32_Service* class for which the logon account is the one specified in the */service* argument. The password change is applied to each instance returned by the query.

## Troubleshooting

As with most scripts, this script can run into a couple of common errors. First, one or more targeted computers might not be available, a condition the script can handle properly. You can reduce the script's execution time by including the */ping* argument, which tests connectivity prior to trying to execute the WMI query. The second possible error is that you won't have permission to perform the task. This situation is unusual if you're running the script as an administrator, but the script will detect this error, display a message or error code, and continue running.

The most common error, however, is specifying a service name that is incorrect. In this case, the script will seem to do nothing, because it is unable to retrieve instances of a service that does not exist.

## To Learn More

- Find more service management samples in VBScript at *http:// www.microsoft.com/technet/scriptcenter/scripts/os/services/default.mspx.*

- Read more about Windows services management in Windows online Help and Support Center.

# Change Service Startup Mode

> **On the CD**   The sample script can be found on the CD that accompanies this book at \Chap14\ChangeServiceStartMode\ChangeServiceStartMode.wsf.

| Operating System | Supported? | Prerequisites |
|---|---|---|
| Windows 2000 family | Yes | ■  WSH 5.6 or later |
| Windows XP Professional | Yes | ■  WMI |
| Windows Server 2003 family | Yes | ■  Administrative permission on targeted computers |
| | | ■  Network connectivity to each remote computer |

## Description

This script, ChangeServiceStartMode.wsf, is designed to change a service's startup on multiple computers to Automatic, Manual, or Disabled. This is a useful way of temporarily disabling an unwanted service, setting a new service to have an appropriate startup mode, and so forth.

## Performing This Task Manually

To manually modify a service's startup mode, you will need to open the Computer Management console and navigate to the desired service. Right-click that service and select Properties to open its Properties dialog box. From there, you can select a new startup mode. The Computer Management console does provide the means to connect to remote computers, but using it to change multiple services on multiple computers can be error-prone and unnecessarily time-consuming.

## Example

This script allows you to target one computer or multiple computers. If you want to use it to target a single remote computer named ServerA, you would use this code:

```
ChangeServiceStartMode.wsf /computer:ServerA /service:MyService /mode:manual
```

Note that the service name must be the service's registered internal name (the Service Name listed on the General tab of the service's Properties dialog), such as Messenger. The service name does not refer to the service's executable name, nor does it refer to the service's *caption*, which is what you will find listed under the node section of the Computer Management console. Valid values for the */mode* argument include manual, automatic, and disabled.

You can also target a list of computers from a text file. The text file is expected to contain one computer name per line and no other information. Assuming the file is named C:\Computers.txt, you would use this syntax:

```
ChangeServiceStartMode.wsf /list:C:\Computers.txt /service:MyService /mode:manual
```

Finally, you can target an entire organizational unit of computer accounts. If your domain contains an OU named West, you would use the following syntax:

```
ChangeServiceStartMode.wsf /container:west /service:MyService /mode:manual
```

Note that the */container* argument will work against only the default domain of the computer running the script. In other words, the OU specified must exist within the same domain as that of the computer running the script. If the specified OU has nested OUs, you can include their computer accounts as well by specifying one additional argument:

```
ChangeServiceStartMode.wsf /container:west /recurse /service:MyService /mode:manual
```

## Syntax

This script can be executed as a command-line utility. Set CScript.exe to be your default script processor, as described in Chapter 3.

| | |
|---|---|
| /list:path<br>/computer:name<br>/container:name | One and only one of these is required by the script. Use */list* to target a list of computers contained within a text file. Use */computer* to target a single computer. Use */container* to target an organizational unit within Active Directory. |
| /recurse | When used with */container*, also targets computers contained within nested OUs. |
| /ping | Verifies the connectivity to all targeted computers prior to attempting a connection. Using this argument will reduce the timeout wait when one or more computers cannot be reached on the network. |
| /log:path | Logs unreachable computer names to the specified file. This file can then be used later, along with the */list* argument, to retry these computers. Note that a log is created only when used in conjunction with the */ping* argument. |
| /verbose | Causes the script to display more detailed, step-by-step status messages. |
| /service:name | Specifies the service to change. |
| /mode:[ manual \|<br>automatic \| disabled ] | Specifies the new startup mode for the account. |

You can run this script with the /? parameter to display the command's syntax.

# Under the Hood

This script uses a straightforward Windows Management Instrumentation (WMI) query to retrieve the desired service instance (an instance of the *Win32_Service* class) and uses that instance's *Change()* method to modify the service's startup parameters:

```
Dim cServices, oService, errResult
Verbose "  Connecting to " & sName
Set cServices = QueryWMI(sName,"root\cimv2","Select * From Win32_Service
WHERE Name = '" & wscript.arguments.named("service") & "'","","")
If Not IsObject(cServices) Then
    WScript.Echo "  ** Couldn't get WMI from " & sName
Else
    For Each oService In cServices
    Verbose "  Changing " & sName
    errResult = oService.change(,,,,WScript.Arguments.Named("mode"))
    Verbose "  Result for " & sName & ":" & errResult
    Next
End if
```

The *Change()* method provides a number of possibilities for changing a service. Because only the startup mode is being changed, the other parameters are left blank, as evidenced by the sequential commas in the *Change()* method's argument list.

# Troubleshooting

As with most scripts, this script can run into a couple of common errors. First, one or more targeted computers might not be available, a condition the script can handle properly. You can reduce the script's execution time by including the */ping* argument, which tests connectivity prior to trying to execute the WMI query. The second possible error is that you won't have permission to perform the task. This situation is unusual if you're running the script as an administrator, but the script will detect this error, display a message or error code, and continue running.

The most common error, however, is specifying a service name that is incorrect. In this case, the script will simply seem to do nothing because it is unable to retrieve instances of a service that does not exist.

# To Learn More

- Find more service management samples in VBScript at *http://www.microsoft.com/technet/scriptcenter/scripts/os/services/default.mspx*.

- Read more about Windows services management in Windows online Help and Support Center.

# Listing Computers That Use a Specified Service

> **On the CD**   The sample script can be found on the CD that accompanies this book at \Chap14\ListComputersUsingService\ListComputerUsingService.wsf.

| Operating System | Supported? | Prerequisites |
|---|---|---|
| Windows 2000 family | Yes | ■ WSH 5.6 or later |
| Windows XP Professional | Yes | ■ WMI |
| Windows Server 2003 family | Yes | ■ Administrative permission on targeted computers |
| | | ■ Network connectivity to each remote computer |

## Description

This script, ListComputerUsingService.wsf, is designed to target multiple computers and determine which ones are hosting a particular service. This is a useful task when performing a network inventory or audit, or for removing an unneeded service from all computers that are running it. For example, you could use this script to quickly determine which domain computers are running Microsoft Internet Information Services (IIS) to ensure that those computers receive the proper patches for IIS when they become available.

## Performing This Task Manually

You can use the Computer Management console to review the list of installed and running services. You can also run NET START from a command line to see a list of running (but not stopped or disabled) services. Using either of these techniques on multiple computers, however, can be time-consuming.

## Example

This script allows you to target one computer or multiple computers. If you want to use it to target a single remote computer named ServerA, you would use this code:

```
ListComputersUsingService.wsf /computer:ServerA /service:MyService
```

Note that the service name must be the service's registered internal name (the Service Name listed on the General tab of the service's Properties dialog box), such as Messenger; the service name does not refer to the service's executable name, nor does it refer to the service's *caption*, which is what you will find listed under the Services node of the Computer Management console. Used in the fashion shown, the script will output the list of computers to the command-line window.

You can also target a list of computers from a text file. The text file is expected to contain one computer name per line and no other information. Assuming the file is named C:\Computers.txt, you would use this syntax:

```
ListComputersUsingService.wsf /list:C:\Computers.txt /service:MyService
/output:C:\Usage.csv
```

Notice that this command writes the information to a file named C:\Usage.csv, as specified in the /output argument.

Finally, you can target an entire organizational unit of computer accounts. If your domain contains an OU named West, you would use the following syntax:

```
ListComputersUsingService.wsf /container:west /service:MyService
/output:C:\Usage.csv
```

Note that the /container argument will work against only the default domain of the computer running the script. In other words, the OU specified must exist within the same domain as that of the computer running the script. If the specified OU has nested OUs, you can include their computer accounts as well by specifying one additional argument:

```
ListComputersUsingService.wsf /container:west /recurse /service:MyService
/output:C:\Usage.csv
```

## Syntax

This script can be executed as a command-line utility. Set CScript.exe to be your default script processor, as described in Chapter 3.

| | |
|---|---|
| /list:path<br>/computer:name<br>/container:name | One and only one of these is required by the script. Use /list to target a list of computers contained within a text file. Use /computer to target a single computer. Use /container to target an organizational unit within Active Directory. |
| /recurse | When used with /container, also targets computers contained within nested OUs. |
| /ping | Verifies the connectivity to all targeted computers prior to attempting a connection. Using this argument will reduce the timeout wait when one or more computers cannot be reached on the network. |
| /log:path | Logs unreachable computer names to the specified file. This file can then be used later, along with the /list argument, to retry these computers. Note that a log is created only when used in conjunction with the /ping argument. |
| /verbose | Causes the script to display more detailed, step-by-step status messages. |

| | |
|---|---|
| /service:name | Specifies the service to look for. |
| /output:path | Specifies a file to which the list of computers should be written. |

You can run this script with the /? parameter to display the command's syntax.

# Under the Hood

This script uses a straightforward Windows Management Instrumentation (WMI) query to retrieve the desired service instance (an instance of the *Win32_Service* class). If any instances are returned by the query, the computer name is written to the command-line window or a file.

```
Dim cServices, oService, sOutput
Verbose " Connecting to WMI on " & sName
Set cServices = QueryWMI(sName,"root\cimv2","Select * From Win32_Service
WHERE Name = '" & wscript.arguments.named("service") & "'","","")
If Not IsObject(cServices) Then
    Verbose " ** Service not found, or couldn't connect to WMI, on " & sName
Else
    For Each oService In cServices
        sOutput = sName
        If WScript.Arguments.Named.Exists("output") Then
            LogFile WScript.Arguments.Named("output"),sOutput,False
        Else
            WScript.Echo sOutput
        End If
    Next
End If
```

One important issue with this script's function is that it cannot differentiate between targeted computers that are unreachable, computers for which you don't have permissions, and computers that do not contain the service specified. In all three cases, the WMI query returns an empty result set. You can specify the /ping and /log arguments to create a list of computers that could not be contacted, which allows you to more easily target only those computers again at a later time.

# Troubleshooting

As with most scripts, this script can run into a couple of common errors. First, one or more targeted computers might not be available, a condition the script can handle properly. You can reduce the script's execution time by including the /ping argument, which tests connectivity prior to trying to execute the WMI query. The second possible error is that you won't have permission to perform the task. This situation is unusual if you're running the script as an administrator, but the script will detect this error, display a message or error code, and continue running.

The most common error, however, is specifying a service name that is incorrect. In this case, the script will seem to do nothing, because it is unable to retrieve instances of a service that does not exist.

## To Learn More

- Find more service management samples in VBScript at *http://www.microsoft.com/technet/scriptcenter/scripts/os/services/default.mspx.*

- Read more about Windows services management in Windows online Help and Support Center.

# Listing Services That Use a Specified Account

> **On the CD**   The sample script can be found on the CD that accompanies this book at \Chap14\ListServicesUsingAcct\ListServicesUsingAccount.wsf.

| Operating System | Supported? | Prerequisites |
|---|---|---|
| Windows 2000 family | Yes | ■ WSH 5.6 or later |
| Windows XP Professional | Yes | ■ WMI |
| Windows Server 2003 family | Yes | ■ Administrative permission on targeted computers |
| | | ■ Network connectivity to each remote computer |

## Description

This script, ListServicesUsingAccount.wsf, is designed to list all services on all targeted computers that are using a specified user account to log on. This is a very useful task for a security audit and allows you to, for example, quickly identify all services that are using the powerful LocalSystem account or a specified domain user account.

## Performing This Task Manually

To manually review this information, you use the Computer Management console. You will need to navigate to each service, double-click it to open its Properties dialog box, and then review the logon settings. This is a cumbersome, time-consuming process for a single computer, not to mention for multiple computers.

## Example

This script allows you to target one computer or multiple computers. If you want to use it to target a single remote computer named ServerA, you would use this code:

```
ListServicesUsingAccount.wsf /computer:ServerA /account:MYDOMAIN\MyAccount
```

Note the convention used to specify the new account: *domain\account*. If you are targeting a local account such as LocalSystem, you would exclude the domain name in the argument. This particular command will display the list of computers and services at the command line.

You can also target a list of computers from a text file. The text file is expected to contain one computer name per line and no other information. Assuming the file is named C:\Computers.txt, you would use this syntax:

```
ListServicesUsingAccount.wsf /list:C:\Computers.txt /output:C:\Usage.csv
/account:MYDOMAIN\MyAccount
```

Notice that this command writes the information to a file named C:\Usage.csv, as specified by the */output* argument.

Finally, you can target an entire organizational unit of computer accounts. If your domain contains an OU named West, you would use the following syntax:

```
ListServicesUsingAccount.wsf /container:west /output:C:\Usage.csv
/account:MYDOMAIN\MyAccount
```

Note that the */container* argument will work against only the default domain of the computer running the script. In other words, the OU specified must exist within the same domain as that of the computer running the script. If the specified OU has nested OUs, you can include their computer accounts as well by specifying one additional argument:

```
ListServicesUsingAccount.wsf /container:west /recurse /output:C:\Usage.csv
/account:MYDOMAIN\MyAccount
```

## Syntax

This script can be executed as a command-line utility. Set CScript.exe to be your default script processor, as described in Chapter 3.

| | |
|---|---|
| `/list:path`<br>`/computer:name`<br>`/container:name` | One and only one of these is required by the script. Use */list* to target a list of computers contained within a text file. Use */computer* to target a single computer. Use */container* to target an organizational unit within Active Directory. |
| `/recurse` | When used with */container*, also targets computers contained within nested OUs. |
| `/ping` | Verifies the connectivity to all targeted computers prior to attempting a connection. Using this argument will reduce the timeout wait when one or more computers cannot be reached on the network. |
| `/log:path` | Logs unreachable computer names to the specified file. This file can then be used later, along with the */list* argument, to retry these computers. Note that a log is created only when used in conjunction with the */ping* argument. |
| `/verbose` | Causes the script to display more detailed, step-by-step status messages. |
| `/output:path` | Specifies a text file to which the script's output will be written. |
| `/account:domain\account` | Specifies the account to look for. |

You can run this script with the */?* parameter to display the command's syntax.

## Under the Hood

This script uses a straightforward Windows Management Instrumentation (WMI) query to retrieve the desired service instance (an instance of the *Win32_Service* class), based on the services' *StartName* property:

```
Dim cServices, oService, sOutput
Verbose " Connecting to WMI on " & sName
Set cServices = QueryWMI(sName,"root\cimv2","Select * From Win32_Service WHERE
StartName = '" & wscript.arguments.named("account") & "'","","")
If Not IsObject(cServices) Then
    Verbose " ** Account not in use, or couldn't connect to WMI, on " & sName
Else
    For Each oService In cServices
        sOutput = sName & "," & oService.Name
        If WScript.Arguments.Named.Exists("output") Then
            LogFile WScript.Arguments.Named("output"),sOutput,False
        Else
            WScript.Echo sOutput
        End If
    Next
End If
```

One important issue about this script's function is that it cannot differentiate between targeted computers that are unreachable, computers for which you don't have permissions, and computers that do not contain a service using the account you specified. In all three cases, the WMI query returns an empty result set. You can specify the */ping* and */log* arguments to create a list of computers that could not be contacted, which allows you to more easily target only those computers again at a later time.

## Troubleshooting

As with most scripts, this script can run into a couple of common errors. First, one or more targeted computers might not be available, a condition the script can handle properly. You can reduce the script's execution time by including the */ping* argument, which tests connectivity prior to trying to execute the WMI query. The second possible error is that you won't have permission to perform the task. This situation is unusual if you're running the script as an administrator, but the script will detect this error, display a message or error code, and continue running.

The most common error, however, is specifying a user account that is improperly formatted. In that case, the script will display an error message because it will be unable to properly retrieve the user account specified.

## To Learn More

- Find more service management samples in VBScript at *http://www.microsoft.com/technet/scriptcenter/scripts/os/services/default.mspx.*

- Read more about Windows services management in Windows online Help and Support Center.

# Remove Services

> **On the CD**   The sample script can be found on the CD that accompanies this book at \Chap14\RemoveService\RemoveService.wsf.

| Operating System | Supported? | Prerequisites |
|---|---|---|
| Windows 2000 family | Yes | ■ WSH 5.6 or later |
| Windows XP Professional | Yes | ■ WMI |
| Windows Server 2003 family | Yes | ■ Administrative permission on targeted computers |
| | | ■ Network connectivity to each remote computer |

## Description

This script, RemoveService.wsf, removes a designated service from all targeted computers that contain that service. This script provides an excellent way to clean up older services that are no longer in use. Although stopping and disabling the unneeded service is a good first step, doing so does not ensure that the service will not be re-enabled; for maximum security, unused services should be removed from the computer.

## Performing This Task Manually

Windows does not provide a means of directly removing services other than editing the registry.

## Example

This script allows you to target one computer or multiple computers. If you want to use it to target a single remote computer named ServerA, you would use this code:

```
RemoveService.wsf /computer:ServerA /service:MyService
```

Note that the service name must be the service's registered internal name (the Service Name listed on the General tab of the service's Properties dialog box), such as Messenger; the service name does not refer to the service's executable name, nor does it refer to the service's *caption*, which is what you will find listed under the Services node of the Computer Management console.

You can also target a list of computers from a text file. The text file is expected to contain one computer name per line and no other information. Assuming the file is named C:\Computers.txt, you would use this syntax:

```
RemoveService.wsf /list:C:\Computers.txt /service:MyService
```

Finally, you can target an entire organizational unit of computer accounts. If your domain contains an OU named West, you would use the following syntax:

```
RemoveService.wsf /container:west /service:MyService
```

Note that the *container* argument will work against only the default domain of the computer running the script. In other words, the OU specified must exist within the same domain as that of the computer running the script. If the specified OU has nested OUs, you can include their computer accounts as well by specifying one additional argument:

```
RemoveService.wsf /container:west /recurse /service:MyService
```

## Syntax

This script can be executed as a command-line utility. Set CScript.exe to be your default script processor, as described in Chapter 3.

| | |
|---|---|
| /list:path<br>/computer:name<br>/container:name | One and only one of these is required by the script. Use */list* to target a list of computers contained within a text file. Use */computer* to target a single computer. Use */container* to target an organizational unit within Active Directory. |
| /recurse | When used with */container*, also targets computers contained within nested OUs. |
| /ping | Verifies the connectivity to all targeted computers prior to attempting a connection. Using this argument will reduce the timeout wait when one or more computers cannot be reached on the network. |
| /log:path | Logs unreachable computer names to the specified file. This file can then be used later, along with the */list* argument, to retry these computers. Note that a log is created only when used in conjunction with the */ping* argument. |
| /verbose | Causes the script to display more detailed, step-by-step status messages. |
| /service:name | Specifies the service to remove. |

You can run this script with the /? parameter to display the command's syntax.

## Under the Hood

This script uses a straightforward Windows Management Instrumentation (WMI) query to retrieve the desired service instance (an instance of the *Win32_Service* class) and uses that instance's *Delete()* method to modify the service's startup parameters:

```
Dim cServices, oService, errResult
Verbose "  Connecting to " & sName
Set cServices = QueryWMI(sName,"root\cimv2","Select * From Win32_Service WHERE
```

```
Name = '" & wscript.arguments.named("service") & "'","","")
If Not IsObject(cServices) Then
    WScript.Echo "  ** Couldn't get WMI from " & sname
Else
    For Each oService In cServices
    Verbose "  Changing " & sName
    errResult = oService.change(,,,,"Disabled")
    Verbose "  Result for " & sName & ":" & errResult
    Verbose "  Stopping on " & sName
    On Error Resume Next
    oService.stopservice()
    If Err <> 0 Then
        Verbose "  Stopped On " & sName
    Else
        WScript.Echo "  ** Error stopping on " & sName
    End if
    Verbose "  Removing from " & sName
    oService.Delete()
    If Err <> 0 Then
        Verbose "  Removed from " & sName
    Else
        WScript.Echo "  ** Error removing from " & sName
    End If
End If
```

In order to help avoid errors, the script first tries to stop the service, along with its dependent services, so that Windows will permit the service to be removed. The service might remain visible in the Services console until after a reboot, and if clicked, it might report that it has been marked for deletion.

Neither Windows nor this script provides any means of restoring the service once it has been removed; you will need to reinstall the service's software or manually reconstruct the service's registry entries. Because undoing the results of this script can be so complex, I recommend using the next script, StopDisableService.wsf, to first stop and disable any service you think is a candidate for removal. This will allow you to operate for several weeks with the service turned off, to see if any problems arise. Re-enabling a service is much easier than reinstalling it! If no problems arise and the disabled service is still a candidate for removal, you can use this script to automate the task.

# Troubleshooting

As with most scripts, this script can run into a couple of common errors. First, one or more targeted computers might not be available, a condition the script can handle properly. You can reduce the script's execution time by including the */ping* argument, which tests connectivity prior to trying to execute the WMI query. The second possible error is that you won't have permission to perform the task. This situation is unusual if you're running the script as an administrator, but the script will detect this error, display a message or error code, and continue running.

The most common error, however, is simply specifying a service name that is incorrect. In this case, the script will simply seem to do nothing, because it is unable to retrieve instances of a service that does not exist.

## To Learn More

- Find more service management samples in VBScript at *http://www.microsoft.com/technet/scriptcenter/scripts/os/services/default.mspx*.

- Read more about Windows services management in the Windows online Help and Support Center.

# Stopping and Disabling Services

> **On the CD**   The sample script can be found on the CD that accompanies this book at \Chap14\StopDisableService\StopDisableService.wsf.

| Operating System | Supported? | Prerequisites |
|---|---|---|
| Windows 2000 family | Yes | ■  WSH 5.6 or later |
| Windows XP Professional | Yes | ■  WMI |
| Windows Server 2003 family | Yes | ■  Administrative permission on targeted computers |
| | | ■  Network connectivity to each remote computer |

## Description

This script, StopDisableService.wsf, is designed to stop a service (and any dependent services it may have) and set the service's startup type to Disabled. This is a good first step to take in removing an unnecessary service, because it allows you to quickly return the service to operation if it turns out the service is necessary after all.

## Performing This Task Manually

To manually modify a service's startup mode or to stop it, you will need to open the Computer Management console and navigate to the desired service. Right-click that service and select Properties to open its Properties dialog box; from there, you can change the startup mode. The Computer Management console does provide the means to connect to remote computers, but using it to change multiple services on multiple computers can be error-prone and unnecessarily time-consuming.

## Example

This script allows you to target one computer or multiple computers. If you want to use it to target a single remote computer named ServerA, you would use this code:

```
StopDisableService.wsf /computer:ServerA /service:MyService
```

Note that the service name must be the service's registered internal name (the Service Name listed on the General tab of the service's Properties dialog box), such as Messenger; it does not refer to the service's executable name, nor does it refer to the service's *caption*, which is what you will find listed under the Services node of the Computer Management console.

You can also target a list of computers from a text file. The text file is expected to contain one computer name per line and no other information. Assuming the file is named C:\Computers.txt, you would use this syntax:

```
StopDisableService.wsf /list:C:\Computers.txt /service:MyService
```

Finally, you can target an entire organizational unit of computer accounts. If your domain contains an OU named West, you would use the following syntax:

```
StopDisableService.wsf /container:west /service:MyService
```

Note that the *container* argument will work against only the default domain of the computer running the script. In other words, the OU specified must exist within the same domain as that of the computer running the script. If the specified OU has nested OUs, you can include their computer accounts as well by specifying one additional argument:

```
StopDisableService.wsf /container:west /recurse /service:MyService
```

## Syntax

This script can be executed as a command-line utility. Set CScript.exe to be your default script processor, as described in Chapter 3.

| | |
|---|---|
| /list:path<br>/computer:name<br>/container:name | One and only one of these is required by the script. Use */list* to target a list of computers contained within a text file. Use */computer* to target a single computer. Use */container* to target an organizational unit within Active Directory. |
| /recurse | When used with */container*, also targets computers contained within nested OUs. |
| /ping | Verifies the connectivity to all targeted computers prior to attempting a connection. Using this argument will reduce the timeout wait when one or more computers cannot be reached on the network. |
| /log:path | Logs unreachable computer names to the specified file. This file can then be used later, along with the */list* argument, to retry these computers. Note that a log is created only when used in conjunction with the */ping* argument. |
| /verbose | Causes the script to display more detailed, step-by-step status messages. |
| /service:name | Specifies the service to change. |

You can run this script with the */?* parameter to display the command's syntax.

# Under the Hood

This script uses a straightforward Windows Management Instrumentation (WMI) query to retrieve the desired service instance (an instance of the *Win32_Service* class) and uses that instance's *Change()* method to stop the service and modify its startup parameters:

```
Dim cServices, oService, errResult
Verbose "  Connecting to " & sName
Set cServices = QueryWMI(sName,"root\cimv2","Select * From Win32_Service WHERE
Name = '" & wscript.arguments.named("service") &" '","","")
If Not IsObject(cServices) Then
    WScript.Echo "  ** Couldn't get WMI from " & sName
Else
    For Each oService In cServices
    Verbose "  Changing " & sName
    errResult = oService.change(,,,,"Disabled")
    Verbose "  Result for " & sName & ":" & errResult
    Verbose "  Stopping on " & sName
    On Error Resume Next
    oService.stopservice()
    If Err <> 0 Then
        Verbose "  Stopped On " & sName
    Else
        WScript.Echo "  ** Error stopping on " & sName
    End if
    Next
End if
```

The *Change()* method provides a number of possibilities for changing a service. Because only the service startup type is being changed, the other parameters are left blank, as evidenced by the sequential commas in the *Change()* method's argument list. The *StopService()* method is designed to not only stop the designated service but also stop any dependent services that might rely on it.

# Troubleshooting

As with most scripts, this script can run into a couple of common errors. First, one or more targeted computers might not be available, a condition the script can handle properly. You can reduce the script's execution time by including the */ping* argument, which tests connectivity prior to trying to execute the WMI query. The second possible error is that you won't have permission to perform the task. This situation is unusual if you're running the script as an administrator, but the script will detect this error, display a message or error code, and continue running.

The most common error, however, is simply specifying a service name that is incorrect. In this case, the script will seem to do nothing because it is unable to retrieve instances of a service that does not exist. You might also run into an instance where the specified service cannot be stopped; the script will in those cases display an error message and continue processing.

## To Learn More

- Find more service management samples in VBScript at *http://www.microsoft.com/technet/scriptcenter/scripts/os/services/default.mspx*.

- Read more about Windows services management in Windows online Help and Support Center.

Chapter 15

# User Account Management Tasks

User account management encompasses some of the most commonly performed management tasks in a Microsoft® Windows® environment. Unfortunately, many of these tasks are also dull and repetitive to complete manually, so automation is a perfect solution. Note that the tasks automated in this chapter are intended for a Microsoft Active Directory® domain, and are not suitable for management of local user accounts on domain member or stand-alone computers.

Tasks automated in this chapter include:

- Creating multiple user accounts simultaneously
- Creating multiple contacts simultaneously
- Changing an attribute's value for all users
- Disabling unused user accounts

- Clearing published certificates for a user
- Expiring passwords
- Expiring user accounts
- Listing users with old passwords
- Unlocking locked user accounts

# Add Users from a Database

> **On the CD**   The sample script can be found on the CD that accompanies this book at \Chap15\AddUsers\AddUsers.wsf.

| Operating System | Supported? | Prerequisites |
|---|---|---|
| Microsoft Windows 2000 family | Yes | ■ Windows Script Host (WSH) 5.6 or later |
| Microsoft Windows XP Professional | Yes | ■ Active Directory |
| Microsoft Windows Server™ 2003 family | Yes | ■ Administrative permissions within Active Directory |

## Description

This script, AddUsers.wsf, is designed to read user account information from a Microsoft Excel spreadsheet or a Microsoft Access database and create new user accounts based on that information. New accounts can be created in a specified organizational unit (OU), and you can set a wide variety of attributes for the new accounts.

> **Tip**   If you have user account information in a different format, such as a Microsoft SQL Server™ database, export the information to a comma-separated values (CSV) file, which can be opened by using Excel. Save the file again as a native Excel spreadsheet to use it with this script.

## Performing This Task Manually

The Active Directory Users and Computers console provides a graphical means of creating new user accounts. Just open the console, right-click an OU, and select New, then User to create a new user. This is a straightforward process when creating single new users; however, manually creating multiple new users at one time can be unnecessarily time-consuming. Many organizations might, for example, have a human resources database that already contains information about the new users; exporting that information for use by this script will reduce redundant data entry and administrative overhead.

## Example

This script has three required arguments, which are used as follows:

```
AddUsers.wsf /file:Sample.xls /type:Excel /table:"[Sheet1$]"
```

The *file:/* argument specifies the file to be read (a sample Excel file is included on the CD). The *type:/* argument must be either Excel or Access, indicating the file being opened. The */table:* argument specifies the Access table name or Excel sheet name containing your data. In the case of Excel, note the special formatting for the sheet name: enclosed in square brackets ([]) and followed by a dollar sign ($). Excel spreadsheets must have column names as the first row of the sheet.

At a minimum, your table must include a column named *sAMAccountName*, which specifies the new user name, and a column named *Password*, which is the new user's password. You can include other columns named after Active Directory single-valued attributes. Examples include:

- *givenName*
- *initials*
- *displayName*
- *description*
- *mail*
- *wWWHomePage*
- *streetAddress*
- *postalCode*
- *st* (state or province)
- *l* (lowercase letter L; stands for *locality* and is used for the city name)
- *profilePath*
- *scriptPath*
- *homeDirectory*
- *homePhone*
- *pager*
- *mobile*
- *fascimileTelephoneNumber*
- *iPPhone*
- *info*
- *title*
- *department*
- *company*

By default, new accounts are created in the root of the domain. To specify a specific container or OU, include the */ou:* argument:

```
AddUsers.wsf /file:Sample.xls /type:Excel /table:"[Sheet1$]" /ou:"ou=west"
```

This creates the accounts in an OU named West.

To provide better security, all new accounts are disabled when created. You will need to enable the accounts when they are ready to be used.

## Syntax

This script can be executed as a command-line utility. Set CScript.exe to be your default script processor, as described in Chapter 3.

| | |
|---|---|
| `/file:path` | Specifies the path and file name of a Microsoft Excel or Microsoft Access file. |
| `/type:[ Excel | Access ]` | Specifies either Excel or Access to define the type of file specified in the *file:/* argument. |
| `/table:name` | Specifies the name of the table containing the data to be added to the domain. For Access, a simple table name such as *Data* is acceptable. For Excel, specify the sheet name in square brackets with a dollar sign: *[Sheet1$]*. |
| `/verbose` | Specifies that the script display detailed status messages as the script executes. |
| `/ou:name` | Optional. Specifies the name of a container or an organizational unit (OU) in which to create the new objects. If omitted, objects are created in the domain root container. Example: /ou:"ou=west" |

You can run this script with the */?* parameter to display the command's syntax.

## Under the Hood

This script uses Microsoft ActiveX® Data Objects (ADO) to read the data file and Microsoft Active Directory Services Interface (ADSI) to create the new objects in the domain. The following code creates an OLE DB connection string for ADO and opens the connection to the specified data file:

```
'build connection String
Dim sConn
Select Case lcase(WScript.Arguments.named("type"))
    Case "access"
        sConn = "Provider=Microsoft.Jet.OLEDB.4.0;Data Source="
& WScript.Arguments.Named("file") & ";"
    Case "excel"
        sConn = "Provider=Microsoft.Jet.OLEDB.4.0;Data Source="
& WScript.Arguments.Named("file") & ";Extended Properties=Excel 8.0;"
```

```
        Case Else
            WScript.Echo "** Unknown file type specified"
            wscript.quit
    End Select

    'open connection
    On Error Resume Next
    Dim oCN
    Verbose "Opening connection to data file..."
    Set oCN = CreateObject("ADODB.Connection")
    oCN.Open sConn
    If Err <> 0 Then
        WScript.Echo "** Error opening file"
        WScript.Echo Err.Description
        WScript.Quit
    End If
    On Error goto 0
```

The following code creates the connection to the domain or the specified OU:

```
    'create ADSI connection
    On Error Resume Next
    Dim oOU, oRoot
    Verbose "Connecting to domain..."
    Set oRoot = GetObject("LDAP://rootDSE")
    If Err <> 0 Then
        WScript.Echo "** Error connecting to domain"
        WScript.Echo Err.Description
        WScript.Quit
    End If
    If Not WScript.Arguments.Named.exists("ou") Then
        Verbose "Connecting to default container..."
        Set oOU = GetObject("LDAP://" & oRoot.Get("defaultNamingContext"))
        If Err <> 0 Then
            WScript.Echo "** Error connecting to default container"
            WScript.Echo Err.Description
            WScript.Quit
        End if
    Else
        Verbose "Connecting to OU..."
        Set oOU = GetObject("LDAP://" & WScript.Arguments.Named("ou") & ","
    & oRoot.Get("defaultNamingContext"))
        If Err <> 0 Then
            WScript.Echo "** Error connecting to OU"
            WScript.Echo Err.Description
            WScript.Quit
        End If
    End If
```

Notice that the end result of this code is a variable named *oOU*, which represents the connected object (the domain or a specific OU). A subsequent line of code utilizes this variable to create the new object:

```
    Set oUser = oOU.Create("user", "cn=" & sName)
```

The resulting variable, *oUser*, is used to set the specified properties for the new account.

# Troubleshooting

A number of errors can occur during the execution of this script. First and foremost, you must have permission to create new objects of this type within the domain or specified OU. You must also take care to provide the proper table name, and in the case of an Excel spreadsheet, ensure that the first row contains the appropriate column names. The script attempts to check all of these things and displays an appropriate error message if necessary.

It's also possible for you to specify an invalid value for one or more object properties. If you do, the script will generally display a generic error indicating that the property could not be properly set. You might also specify an invalid property name (a common mistake is to use "*city*" instead of "*l*"); in this case, the script will display the same generic error message for this condition. In the event that an error is displayed when setting a property, first verify that you have permission to write the property in question, that the property name is correctly spelled, and that the value you provided is valid for that property.

Incorrect permissions can cause a number of errors, especially if you allow the script to create accounts in the root of the domain. I recommend always selecting a destination OU and specifying it by using the */ou* argument, rather than create accounts in the root of the domain.

# To Learn More

- Read more about ADO on the Microsoft Data Access home page at *http:// msdn.microsoft.com/data/Default.aspx*.

- Read more about ADSI at *http://www.microsoft.com/windows2000/techinfo/ howitworks/activedirectory/adsilinks.asp*.

# Add Contacts from a Database

> **On the CD**   The sample script can be found on the CD that accompanies this book at \Chap15\AddContacts\AddContacts.wsf.

| Operating System | Supported? | Prerequisites |
|---|---|---|
| Windows 2000 family | Yes | ■  WSH 5.6 or later |
| Windows XP Professional | Yes | ■  Active Directory |
| Windows Server 2003 family | Yes | ■  Administrative permissions within Active Directory |

## Description

This script, AddContacts.wsf, is designed to read contact account information from an Excel spreadsheet or an Access database and create new contact accounts based on that information. New accounts can be created in a specified organizational unit (OU), and you can set a wide variety of attributes for the new contacts.

> **Tip**   If you have user account information in a different format, such as a SQL Server database, export the information to a comma-separated values (CSV) file, which can be opened by Excel. Save the file again as a native Excel spreadsheet to use it with this script.

## Performing This Task Manually

The Active Directory Users and Computers console provides a graphical means of creating new contacts. Just open the console, right-click an OU, and select New, then Contact to create a new contact. This is a straightforward process when creating single new contacts; however, manually creating multiple new contacts at one time can be unnecessarily time-consuming. Many organizations might, for example, have a database that already contains information about the necessary contacts; exporting that information for use by this script will reduce redundant data entry and administrative overhead.

## Example

This script has three required arguments, which are used as follows:

```
AddContacts.wsf /file:Sample.xls /type:Excel /table:"[Sheet1$]"
```

The *file:/* argument specifies the file to be read (a sample Excel file is included on the CD). The *type:/* argument must be either Excel or Access, indicating the file being opened. The */table:* argument specifies the Access table name or Excel sheet name containing your data. In the case of Excel, note the special formatting for the sheet name: enclosed in square brackets and followed by a dollar sign. The first sheet of an Excel spreadsheet must have column names.

At a minimum, your table must include a column named *sAMAccountName*, which specifies the new contact name. You can include other columns named after Active Directory single-valued attributes. Examples include:

- *givenName*
- *initials*
- *displayName*
- *description*
- *mail*
- *wWWHomePage*
- *streetAddress*
- *postalCode*
- *st* (state or province)
- *l* (lowercase letter L; stands for *locality* and is used for the city name)
- *homePhone*
- *pager*
- *mobile*
- *fascimileTelephoneNumber*
- *iPPhone*
- *info*
- *title*
- *department*
- *company*

By default, new contact accounts are created in the root of the domain. To specify a specific container or OU, include the */ou:* argument:

```
AddContacts.wsf /file:Sample.xls /type:Excel /table:"[Sheet1$]" /ou:"ou=west"
```

This creates the accounts in an OU named West.

# Syntax

This script can be executed as a command-line utility. Set CScript.exe to be your default script processor, as described in Chapter 3, "Working with VBScript."

| | |
|---|---|
| /file:path | The path and file name of a Microsoft Excel or Microsoft Access file. |
| /type:[ Excel \| Access ] | Specifies either Excel or Access to define the type of file specified in the *file:/* argument. |
| /table:name | The name of the table containing the data to be added to the domain. For Access, a simple table name such as *Data* is acceptable. For Excel, specifies the sheet name in square brackets with a dollar sign: *[Sheet1$]*. |
| /verbose | Displays detailed status messages as the script executes. |
| /ou:name | Optional. Specifies the name of a container or an organizational unit (OU) in which to create the new objects. If omitted, objects are created in the domain root container. Example: /ou:"ou=West" |

You can run this script with the /? parameter to display the command's syntax.

# Under the Hood

This script uses ActiveX Data Objects (ADO) to read the data file and Active Directory Services Interface (ADSI) to create the new objects in the domain. The following code creates an OLE DB connection string for ADO and opens the connection to the specified data file:

```
'build connection string
Dim sConn
Select Case lcase(WScript.Arguments.named("type"))
   Case "access"
        sConn = "Provider=Microsoft.Jet.OLEDB.4.0;Data Source="
& WScript.Arguments.Named("file") & ";"
   Case "excel"
        sConn = "Provider=Microsoft.Jet.OLEDB.4.0;Data Source="
& WScript.Arguments.Named("file") & ";Extended Properties=Excel 8.0;"
   Case Else
        WScript.Echo "** Unknown file type specified"
        wscript.quit
End Select

'open connection
On Error Resume Next
Dim oCN
Verbose "Opening connection to data file..."
Set oCN = CreateObject("ADODB.Connection")
oCN.Open sConn
If Err <> 0 Then
   WScript.Echo "** Error opening file"
   WScript.Echo Err.Description
```

```
        WScript.Quit
End If
On Error goto 0
```

The following code creates the connection to the domain or the specified OU:

```
'create ADSI connection
On Error Resume Next
Dim oOU, oRoot
Verbose "Connecting to domain..."
Set oRoot = GetObject("LDAP://rootDSE")
If Err <> 0 Then
    WScript.Echo "** Error connecting to domain"
    WScript.Echo Err.Description
    WScript.Quit
End If
If Not WScript.Arguments.Named.exists("ou") Then
    Verbose "Connecting to default container..."
    Set oOU = GetObject("LDAP://" & oRoot.Get("defaultNamingContext"))
    If Err <> 0 Then
        WScript.Echo "** Error connecting to default container"
        WScript.Echo Err.Description
        WScript.Quit
    End if
Else
    Verbose "Connecting to OU..."
    Set oOU = GetObject("LDAP://" & WScript.Arguments.Named("ou") & ","
& oRoot.Get("defaultNamingContext"))
    If Err <> 0 Then
        WScript.Echo "** Error connecting to OU"
        WScript.Echo Err.Description
        WScript.Quit
    End If
End If
```

Notice that the end result of this code is a variable named *oOU*, which represents the connected object (the domain or a specific OU). A subsequent line of code utilizes this variable to create the new object:

```
Set oContact = oOU.Create("contact", "cn=" & sName)
```

The resulting variable, *oContact*, is used to set the specified properties for the new account.

## Troubleshooting

A number of errors can occur during the execution of this script. First and foremost, you must have permission to create new objects of this type within the domain or specified OU. You must also take care to provide the proper table name, and in the case of an Excel spreadsheet, ensure that the first row contains the appropriate column names. The script attempts to check all these things and displays an appropriate error message if necessary.

It's also possible for you to specify an invalid value for one or more object properties. If you do, the script will generally display a generic error message indicating that the property could not be properly set. You might also specify an invalid property name (a common mistake is to use "city" instead of "l"); the script will display the same generic error message for this condition. In the event that an error is displayed for setting a property, first verify that you have permission to write the property in question, that the property name is correctly spelled, and that the value you provided is valid for that property.

## To Learn More

- Read more about ADO on the Microsoft Data Access home page at *http:// msdn.microsoft.com/data/Default.aspx*.

- Read more about ADSI at *http://www.microsoft.com/windows2000/techinfo /howitworks/activedirectory/adsilinks.asp*.

# Change an Attribute for Multiple Users

> **On the CD**   The sample script can be found on the CD that accompanies this book at \Chap15\ChangeAttrib\ChangeAttrib.wsf.

| Operating System | Supported? | Prerequisites |
|---|---|---|
| Windows 2000 family | Yes | ■  WSH 5.6 or later |
| Windows XP Professional | Yes | ■  Active Directory |
| Windows Server 2003 family | Yes | ■  Administrative permissions within Active Directory |

## Description

This script, ChangeAttrib.wsf, is designed to change a single Active Directory user attribute for a group of users. For example, if an organizational unit (OU) full of users moves to a new office, you might use this script to quickly change their mailing address information within Active Directory.

## Performing This Task Manually

The Active Directory Users and Computers console provides a graphical means of editing user accounts. Just open the console, click an OU, and double-click a user account to display its Properties dialog box. Most attributes can be modified from the various tabs of the Properties dialog box, but manually changing multiple users is unnecessarily time-consuming and error-prone.

## Example

This script has two required arguments, which are used as follows:

```
ChangeAttrib.wsf /attrib:"l" /value:"Las Vegas"
```

This will change the "*l*" attribute (which stands for *locality*) to "*Las Vegas*" for all domain users. The script can also be targeted to a specific OU:

```
ChangeAttrib.wsf /attrib:"l" /value:"Las Vegas" /ou:"ou=West"
```

This will change the "*l*" attribute for all users in the West OU. Note that the script automatically includes child OUs and all users within those child OUs to an infinite level. The script does not provide a way to target a single OU and ignore any child OUs it might have.

Attribute names must be exactly as defined within Active Directory; you can use the Active Directory Schema console to explore available attributes. Examples include:

- *givenName*
- *initials*
- *displayName*
- *description*
- *mail*
- *wWWHomePage*
- *streetAddress*
- *postalCode*
- *st* (state or province)
- *l* (lowercase letter L; stands for *locality* and is used for the city name)
- *homePhone*
- *pager*
- *mobile*
- *fascimileTelephoneNumber*
- *iPPhone*
- *info*
- *title*
- *department*
- *company*

# Syntax

This script can be executed as a command-line utility. Set CScript.exe to be your default script processor, as described in Chapter 3.

| | |
|---|---|
| `/ou:ou` | Optional. Specifies an OU that the script should target. Must take the form *ou:"ou=West"*. |
| `/attrib:attribute` | Specifies the attribute to change. |
| `/value:newvalue` | Specifies the new value for the attribute. Values that contain spaces must be contained within double quotation marks. |
| `/verbose` | Displays detailed status messages as the script executes. |

You can run this script with the */?* parameter to display the command's syntax.

# Under the Hood

This script uses Active Directory Services Interface (ADSI) to connect to Active Directory and make the change. Here's the main portion of the script:

```
On Error Resume Next
oADObject.Put WScript.Arguments.Named("attrib"),WScript.Arguments.Named("value")
oADObject.SetInfo
If Err <> 0 Then
    WScript.Echo "** Error setting attribute for " & oADObject.Name
End if
```

The remainder of the script's code handles the initial connection to Active Directory (either at the root of the domain or in a specific OU) and the process of iterating through the available users and any child OUs.

# Troubleshooting

The most common error this script can encounter is a lack of permissions to make the appropriate changes in Active Directory. It's also possible for Active Directory to refuse to change the attribute. This can generally occur for newly created user accounts that have not completely replicated throughout the domain, and it can also occur in certain rare conditions when the Active Directory database is in an inconsistent state. In all cases, the script will display an error message and continue. You can try the operation again later, if necessary, after account replication is completed or any Active Directory problems are corrected.

If you experience a condition in which the script is unable to change attributes for any user, and it displays an error message for each user attempted, the problem is either related to permissions or to the condition of the Active Directory database. Ensure that you can make changes to the attribute in question by using the graphical user interface, because doing so eliminates permissions as a potential problem.

# To Learn More

- Read more about ADSI at *http://www.microsoft.com/windows2000/techinfo/howitworks/activedirectory/adsilinks.asp*.
- Find more Microsoft Visual Basic® Script (VBScript) samples related to user management at *http://www.microsoft.com/technet/scriptcenter/scripts/ad/users/default.mspx*.

# Disable Old User Accounts

> **On the CD**   The sample script can be found on the CD that accompanies this book at \Chap15\DisableOldUsers\DisableOldUsers.wsf.

| Operating System | Supported? | Prerequisites |
|---|---|---|
| Windows 2000 family | Yes | ■ WSH 5.6 or later |
| Windows XP Professional | Yes | ■ Active Directory |
| Windows Server 2003 family | Yes | ■ Administrative permissions within Active Directory |

## Description

This script, DisableOldUsers.wsf, will disable all user accounts that have not been used in a specified number of days. This is a useful script to run on a regular basis to disable unused security accounts. It allows you to easily review those accounts to determine whether they can be removed from the domain.

> **Warning**   This script relies on an Active Directory attribute that is replicated properly only in a Windows Server 2003 Active Directory domain, which has only Windows Server 2003 domain controllers. Earlier versions of Active Directory set this attribute on a per-domain controller basis rather than replicate it, which results in this script incorrectly disabling active user accounts.

## Performing This Task Manually

The Active Directory Users and Computers console allows you to disable a user account by right-clicking it and selecting Disable Account. However, the console does not provide an easy way to determine the last date on which an account was used. This script reads that information from Active Directory and automatically disables accounts for you.

## Example

This script has only one required argument, which is used as follows:

```
DisableOldUsers.wsf /age:90
```

This example will disable all user accounts that have not been used in 90 days. You can limit the script to the users contained within a single organizational unit (OU) and its child OUs by specifying the OU name:

```
DisableOldUsers.wsf /age:90 / ou:"ou=West"
```

You can also have the script create a file that lists the user accounts that were disabled:

```
DisableOldUsers.wsf /age:90 /output:C:\OldUsers.txt
```

Finally, you can have the script run in a report-only mode. In this mode, the script creates the same output of users whose accounts have not been used in the specified number of days, but the script will not disable any accounts. The syntax for this option is:

```
DisableOldUsers.wsf /age:90 /checkonly
```

I recommend using the */checkonly* argument the first time you run the script to see how many user accounts would be disabled. Doing so allows you to provide a common-sense check of the script's results to ensure that accounts aren't disabled unnecessarily.

## Syntax

This script can be executed as a command-line utility. Set CScript.exe to be your default script processor, as described in Chapter 3.

| | |
|---|---|
| `/ou:ou` | Optional. Specifies an OU that the script should target. Must take the form *ou:"ou=West"*. |
| `/checkonly` | Optional. Forces the script to check user accounts but not disable any. |
| `/age:days` | Required. Specifies the minimum number of inactive days a user account must have to be considered old. |
| `/verbose` | Specifies that the script display detailed status messages as the script executes. |
| `/output:file` | Optional. Specifies that the script's output be written to the specified file. |

You can run this script with the */?* parameter to display the command's syntax.

## Under the Hood

This script uses Active Directory Services Interface (ADSI) to connect to Active Directory and make the change. Here's the main portion of the script:

```
Verbose "Checking " & oADObject.Get("sAMAccountName")
dLast = oADObject.LastLogin
If Err <> 0 Then
    Verbose " (never logged in)"
    Output oADObject.Get("sAMAccountName") & " never logged in"
    if not wscript.Arguments.Named.Exists("checkonly") Then
        oADObject.Put "userAccountControl", oADObject.Get("userAccountControl") Or 2
    End If
```

```
Else
    Verbose " - " & dLast
    If DateDiff("d",dLast,Date) > CInt(WScript.Arguments.named("age")) Then
        Output oADObject.Get("sAMAccountName") & " last logged in on " & dLast & " ("
& DateDiff("d",dLast,Date) & " days ago)"
        if not wscript.Arguments.Named.Exists("checkonly") Then
            oADObject.Put "userAccountControl",
oADObject.Get("userAccountControl") Or 2
        End If
    End If
End If
```

The script uses the Active Directory *LastLogin* property. All domain controllers—even as far back as Microsoft Windows NT®—populated this attribute with the current date each time a user logged on, but prior to Windows Server 2003, this attribute was not replicated across domain controllers. In other words, the only domain controller with the correct *LastLogin* property was the domain controller that most recently authenticated the user. In Windows Server 2003, domain controllers replicate this attribute along with most other attributes so that each domain controller (after replication completes) has the correct *LastLogin* information.

Note that the script is designed to target organizational units only; containers—such as the built-in Users and Computers containers—are not supported.

## Troubleshooting

As always, permissions represent a potential problem for this script. You must have permission to query the Active Directory information as well as disable the user account (unless */checkonly* is specified).

The most likely problem is that the domain controller the script uses (which is determined by the computer running the script) does not have the correct *LastLogin* information for all user accounts. In a Windows Server 2003 Active Directory with only Windows Server 2003 domain controllers, this indicates a replication failure; prior to Windows Server 2003, this condition is by design and cannot be avoided. In any case, always run the script with */checkonly* first so that you can verify a few known accounts to make sure they are not targeted for disabling. Then you can run the script without */checkonly* to actually disable old accounts.

## To Learn More

- Read more about ADSI at *http://www.microsoft.com/windows2000/techinfo/ howitworks/activedirectory/adsilinks.asp*.

- Find more VBScript samples related to user management at *http:// www.microsoft.com/technet/scriptcenter/scripts/ad/users/default.mspx*.

# Delete Published User Certificates

 **On the CD**   The sample script can be found on the CD that accompanies this book at \Chap15\DeletePubCerts\DeletePubCerts.wsf.

| Operating System | Supported? | Prerequisites |
|---|---|---|
| Windows 2000 family | Yes | ■ WSH 5.6 or later |
| Windows XP Professional | Yes | ■ Active Directory |
| Windows Server 2003 family | Yes | ■ Administrative permissions within Active Directory |

## Description

This script, DeletePubCerts.wsf, will delete all certificates that have been published in Active Directory for users. You might use this script to quickly remove certificates that have been incorrectly published, or use it in a test environment to delete all certificates so that you can conduct additional issuing tests.

## Performing This Task Manually

The Active Directory Users and Computers console, the main interface through which user accounts are managed, does not provide a manual way to delete published certificates for a batch of user accounts.

## Example

This script has no required arguments. The script can be used as follows:

```
DeletePubCerts.wsf
```

Running this code deletes all published certificates for all users. You can limit the effect of the script to a single organizational unit (OU) and its nested OUs by specifying an additional argument naming the OU:

```
DeletePubCerts.wsf /ou:"ou=West"
```

The script will automatically iterate through any nested OUs.

## Syntax

This script can be executed as a command-line utility. Set CScript.exe to be your default script processor, as described in Chapter 3.

| /ou:ou | Optional. Specifies an OU that the script should target. Must take the form *ou:"ou=West"*. |
| /verbose | Specifies that the script display detailed status messages as the script executes. |

You can run this script with the */?* parameter to display the command's syntax.

## Under the Hood

This script uses Active Directory Services Interface (ADSI) to connect to Active Directory and make the change. Here's the main portion of the script:

```
Verbose "Clearing " & oADObject.Get("sAMAccountName")
oADObject.PutEx 1, "userCertificate", 0
oADObject.SetInfo
```

The *userCertificate* attribute contains published certificates; it is a multi-valued attribute, meaning it can contain information about multiple certificates. The *PutEx* method used in the preceding code clears the attribute, and then the *SetInfo* method saves this information back to Active Directory.

## Troubleshooting

Lack of permissions will cause the script to display an error message and stop running. An inconsistent or corrupt Active Directory database can also cause the same problem, although this is rare. In the event of any error, an error message will provide a clue as to the source of the problem. Try to correct the source of the problem before running the script again.

## To Learn More

- Read more about ADSI at *http://www.microsoft.com/windows2000/techinfo/ howitworks/activedirectory/adsilinks.asp*.

- Find more VBScript samples related to user management at *http:// www.microsoft.com/technet/scriptcenter/scripts/ad/users/default.mspx*.

# Expire Passwords

**On the CD**   The sample script can be found on the CD that accompanies this book at \Chap15\ExpirePasswords\ExpirePasswords.wsf.

| Operating System | Supported? | Prerequisites |
|---|---|---|
| Windows 2000 family | Yes | ■  WSH 5.6 or later |
| Windows XP Professional | Yes | ■  Active Directory |
| Windows Server 2003 family | Yes | ■  Administrative permissions within Active Directory |

## Description

This script, ExpirePasswords.wsf, will set all targeted user account passwords to expired (except accounts that are configured to have passwords that never expire). This script can be used to quickly force all users to change their passwords the next time they log on.

## Performing This Task Manually

To perform this task manually for a single user, follow these steps:

1.  Open the Active Directory Users and Computers console.

2.  Right-click the user account and select Properties. The Properties dialog box will be displayed.

3.  On the Account tab, select the User Must Change Password At Next Logon check box.

4.  Click OK.

On a Windows Server 2003 domain controller, you can perform this task for multiple users within the same organizational unit (OU)—simply select multiple users instead of a single user. However, there is no way to simultaneously target all users in the domain or users in any nested OUs.

## Example

This script has no required arguments and can be run as follows:

```
ExpirePasswords.wsf
```

You can limit the effects of the script to a single OU and its child OUs by specifying the */ou:* argument:

```
ExpirePasswords.wsf /ou:"ou=West"
```

All nested OUs will be automatically included.

# Syntax

This script can be executed as a command-line utility. Set CScript.exe to be your default script processor, as described in Chapter 3.

| | |
|---|---|
| /ou:ou | Optional. Specifies an OU that the script should target. Must take the form *ou:"ou=West"*. |
| /verbose | Specifies that the script display detailed status messages as the script executes. |

You can run this script with the */?* parameter to display the command's syntax.

# Under the Hood

This script uses Active Directory Services Interface (ADSI) to connect to Active Directory and make the change. Here's the entire script:

```
'connect to the root of AD
Dim rootDSE, domainObject
Set rootDSE=GetObject("LDAP://RootDSE")
If WScript.Arguments.Named.Exists("ou") Then
    Verbose "Connecting to OU " & WScript.Arguments.Named("ou")
    Set oDomain = GetObject("LDAP://" & wscript.Arguments.Named("ou") & ","
& rootDSE.Get("defaultNamingContext"))
Else
    Verbose "Connecting to root of domain"
    Set oDomain = GetObject("LDAP://" & rootDSE.Get("defaultNamingContext"))
End If

'start with the root container
WorkWithObject(oDomain)

Sub WorkWithObject(oContainer)
 Dim oADObject
 For Each oADObject in oContainer
  Select Case oADObject.Class
   Case "user"
    Verbose oADObject.Name
    oADObject.Put "pwdLastSet",0
    oADObject.SetInfo
   Case "organizationalUnit" , "container"
    'oADObject is an OU or container...
    'go through its objects
    WorkWithObject(oADObject)
```

```
   End Select
 Next
End Sub


Sub Verbose(sMsg)
    If WScript.Arguments.Named.Exists("verbose") Then
        WScript.Echo " " & sMsg
    End If
End Sub
```

This script connects to the root of the domain or, if specified, a specific OU, and iterates through each user account and OU contained within it.

## Troubleshooting

This script's most likely problem is insufficient permissions to query the information from Active Directory or to set the necessary attributes in Active Directory. Should this occur, the script will display an error message and stop running.

## To Learn More

- Read more about ADSI at *http://www.microsoft.com/windows2000/techinfo/ howitworks/activedirectory/adsilinks.asp.*

- Find more VBScript samples related to user management at *http:// www.microsoft.com/technet/scriptcenter/scripts/ad/users/default.mspx.*

# Expire User Accounts

> **On the CD**   The sample script can be found on the CD that accompanies this book at \Chap15\ExpireUsers\ExpireUsers.wsf.

| Operating System | Supported? | Prerequisites |
|---|---|---|
| Windows 2000 family | Yes | ■ WSH 5.6 or later |
| Windows XP Professional | Yes | ■ Active Directory |
| Windows Server 2003 family | Yes | ■ Administrative permissions within Active Directory |

## Description

This script, ExpireUsers.wsf, will set all targeted user accounts to expired. This script can be used to quickly expire all accounts within a specified organizational unit (OU), such as contractor accounts within an OU after that contract has ended.

Note that this script will not immediately stop the targeted user accounts from working. Account expiration takes place at the end of the current day, and takes effect only after the specified accounts have logged off.

## Performing This Task Manually

To perform this task manually for a single user, follow these steps:

1. Open the Active Directory Users and Computers console.
2. Right-click the user account and select Properties. The Properties dialog box will be displayed.
3. On the Account tab, select the End Of option and provide the current date.
4. Click OK.

On a Windows Server 2003 domain controller, you can perform this task for multiple users within the same organizational unit (OU): just select multiple users instead of a single user. However, there is no way to simultaneously target all users in the domain or users in any nested OUs.

## Example

This script has no required arguments and can be run as follows:

```
ExpireUsers.wsf
```

You can limit the effects of the script to a single OU and its nested OUs by specifying the /*ou*: argument:

```
ExpireUsers.wsf /ou:"ou=West"
```

All child OUs will be automatically included.

## Syntax

This script can be executed as a command-line utility. Set CScript.exe to be your default script processor, as described in Chapter 3.

| | |
|---|---|
| /ou:ou | Optional. Specifies an OU that the script should target. Must take the form *ou:"ou=West"*. |
| /verbose | Specifies that the script display detailed status messages as the script executes. |

You can run this script with the /? parameter to display the command's syntax.

## Under the Hood

This script uses Active Directory Services Interface (ADSI) to connect to Active Directory and make the change. Here's the entire script:

```
'connect to the root of AD
Dim rootDSE, domainObject
Set rootDSE=GetObject("LDAP://RootDSE")
If WScript.Arguments.Named.Exists("ou") Then
    Verbose "Connecting to OU " & WScript.Arguments.Named("ou")
    Set oDomain = GetObject("LDAP:// " & wscript.Arguments.Named("ou") & ","
& rootDSE.Get("defaultNamingContext"))
Else
    Verbose "Connecting to root of domain"
    Set oDomain = GetObject("LDAP:// " & rootDSE.Get("defaultNamingContext"))
End If

'start with the root container
WorkWithObject(oDomain)

Sub WorkWithObject(oContainer)
 Dim oADObject
 For Each oADObject in oContainer
  Select Case oADObject.Class
   Case "user"
    Verbose oADObject.Name
    oADObject.Put "accountExpirationDate", Now
    oADObject.SetInfo
   Case "organizationalUnit" , "container"
    'oADObject is an OU or container...
    'go through its objects
    WorkWithObject(oADObject)
```

```
      End Select
   Next
End Sub


Sub Verbose(sMsg)
   If WScript.Arguments.Named.Exists("verbose") Then
      WScript.Echo " " & sMsg
   End If
End Sub
```

This script connects to the root of the domain or, if specified, to a specific OU, and iterates through each user account and OU contained within it.

## Troubleshooting

This script's most likely problem is insufficient permissions to query the information from Active Directory or to set the necessary attributes in Active Directory. Should this occur, the script will display an error message and stop running.

## To Learn More

- Read more about ADSI at *http://www.microsoft.com/windows2000/techinfo/ howitworks/activedirectory/adsilinks.asp*.

- Find more VBScript samples related to user management at *http:// www.microsoft.com/technet/scriptcenter/scripts/ad/users/default.mspx*.

# List Accounts with Old Passwords

> **On the CD**   The sample script can be found on the CD that accompanies this book at \Chap15\OldPasswords\OldPasswords.wsf.

| Operating System | Supported? | Prerequisites |
|---|---|---|
| Windows 2000 family | Yes | ■  WSH 5.6 or later |
| Windows XP Professional | Yes | ■  Active Directory |
| Windows Server 2003 family | Yes | ■  Administrative permissions within Active Directory |

## Description

This script, OldPasswords.wsf, will list all user accounts that have not changed their passwords in a specified number of days. This script can be useful as a security auditing tool, and also as a preliminary check before changing domain password policy on maximum password age. For example, if you are considering a change to make the maximum password age 45 days rather than 90, this script will tell you how many users will be immediately affected.

## Performing This Task Manually

Windows does not provide a means of manually determining password age on a per-account basis.

## Example

This script has one required argument, which is used as follows:

```
OldPasswords.wsf /age:90
```

This lists all user accounts whose passwords are older than 90 days. You can also target a specific organizational unit (OU):

```
OldPasswords.wsf /age:90 /ou:"ou=West"
```

Targeting an OU will also target all nested OUs.

## Syntax

This script can be executed as a command-line utility. Set CScript.exe to be your default script processor, as described in Chapter 3.

| | |
|---|---|
| /ou:ou | Optional. Specifies an OU that the script should target. Must take the form *ou:"ou=West"*. |
| /age:days | Required. Specifies the maximum password age, causing the script to list user accounts with a password age greater than this figure. |
| /verbose | Specifies that the script display detailed status messages as the script executes. |

You can run this script with the */?* parameter to display the command's syntax.

## Under the Hood

This script uses Active Directory Services Interface (ADSI) to connect to Active Directory and make the change. Here's the main portion of the script:

```
Verbose "Checking " & oADObject.Get("sAMAccountName")
Verbose " - Last changed on " & oADObject.PasswordLastChanged & " ("
& DateDiff("d",oADObject.PasswordLastChanged,Date) & " days)"
If Err <> 0 Then
    Verbose " (never changed)"
    Output oADObject.Get("sAMAccountName") & " password never changed"
Else
    If DateDiff("d",oADObject.PasswordLastChanged,Date) > CInt(WScript.Arguments
.named("age")) Then
        Output oADObject.Get("sAMAccountName") & " last changed On "
& oADObject.PasswordLastChanged & " ("
& DateDiff("d",oADObject.PasswordLastChanged,Date) & " days old)"
    End If
End if
```

The script checks the *PasswordLastChanged* attribute to determine the date on which the password was last changed, and then calculates the password's age in days based on the current system date.

## Troubleshooting

This script has only one opportunity for a problem: when you do not have permissions in Active Directory to query the necessary attributes. If you have permissions, this script should not run into any problems.

## To Learn More

- Read more about ADSI at *http://www.microsoft.com/windows2000/techinfo/ howitworks/activedirectory/adsilinks.asp*.

- Find more VBScript samples related to user management at *http:// www.microsoft.com/technet/scriptcenter/scripts/ad/users/default.mspx*.

# Unlock Locked Users

> **On the CD** The sample script can be found on the CD that accompanies this book at \Chap15\UnlockLockedUsers\UnlockLockedUsers.wsf.

| Operating System | Supported? | Prerequisites |
|---|---|---|
| Windows 2000 family | Yes | ■ WSH 5.6 or later |
| Windows XP Professional | Yes | ■ Active Directory |
| Windows Server 2003 family | Yes | ■ Administrative permissions within Active Directory |

## Description

This script, UnlockLockedUsers.wsf, will unlock all targeted user accounts. This can be useful when a large number of accounts were locked by accident, or when a large number of accounts were locked because of some failure.

## Performing This Task Manually

To perform this task manually for a single user, follow these steps:

1. Open the Active Directory Users and Computers console.
2. Right-click the user account and select Properties. The Properties dialog box will be displayed.
3. On the Account tab, clear the Account Is Locked Out check box.
4. Click OK.

## Example

This script has no required arguments and can be run as follows:

```
UnlockLockedUsers.wsf
```

To target a specific OU, specify the /ou: argument:

```
UnlockLockedUsers.wsf /ou:"ou=West"
```

All child OUs of the specified OU will also be targeted.

## Syntax

This script can be executed as a command-line utility. Set CScript.exe to be your default script processor, as described in Chapter 3.

| | |
|---|---|
| /ou:ou | Optional. Specifies an OU that the script should target. Must take the form */ou:"ou=West"*. |
| /verbose | Specifies that the script display detailed status messages as the script executes. |

You can run this script with the */?* parameter to display the command's syntax.

## Under the Hood

This script uses Active Directory Services Interface (ADSI) to connect to Active Directory and make the change. Here's the main portion of the script:

```
If oADObject.IsAccountLocked = True Then
    Verbose oADObject.Name
    oADObject.IsAccountLocked = False
End If
```

The script simply reverses the *IsAccountLocked* attribute whenever that attribute is set to True. You should carefully review the script's output to ensure no accounts were unlocked that should be locked.

## Troubleshooting

This script has only one opportunity for a problem: when you do not have permissions in Active Directory to query the necessary attributes. If you have permissions, this script should not run into any problems.

## To Learn More

- Read more about ADSI at *http://www.microsoft.com/windows2000/techinfo/howitworks/activedirectory/adsilinks.asp*.

- Find more VBScript samples related to user management at *http://www.microsoft.com/technet/scriptcenter/scripts/ad/users/default.mspx*.

# Chapter 16
# Login Script Tasks

This chapter is a bit different from others in this book. In this chapter, I assume that you're writing your own logon scripts in Microsoft® Visual Basic® Script (VBScript), and that you're looking for shortcuts so that you can perform common logon-related tasks. Even though many common tasks are easily accomplished using some of the Microsoft Windows® Script Host's built-in objects, I provide you with easy-to-use subroutines and functions that you can paste into your logon scripts and start using.

Tasks included in this chapter:

- Checking to see whether a user is a member of a group
- Writing events to the local event log
- Pausing the script
- Displaying a message
- Retrieving user information
- Mapping a drive
- Mapping a printer
- Setting the default printer

# Check Group Membership

> **On the CD**   The sample script can be found on the CD that accompanies this book at \Chap16\CheckGroupMembership.vbs.

| Operating System | Supported? | Prerequisites |
|---|---|---|
| Microsoft Windows 2000 family | Yes | ■ Windows Script Host (WSH) 5.6 or later |
| Microsoft Windows XP Professional | Yes | |
| Microsoft Windows Server™ 2003 family | Yes | ■ Active Directory |

## Description

This script, CheckGroupMembership.vbs, contains a single function that checks to see whether a given user is a member of a specified group. The function returns a True or False value, allowing your logon script to execute tasks—such as mapping drives—based on the user's membership in a particular group.

## Example

Use this script as follows:

```
If IsMember("cn=DonJ,ou=West,dc=company,dc=com","SalesUsers") Then
 'the user is a member - do something appropriate
Else
 'the user is not a member - do something appropriate
End If
```

Note that the user must be identified using a complete, fully qualified Lightweight Directory Access Protocol (LDAP) reference.

## Syntax

This script is intended to be included in, and called from, a larger VBScript-based logon script. This script's syntax is as follows:

```
IsMember(sUser,sGroup)
```

sUser            Specifies the user to check. Must be a fully qualified LDAP reference.

sGroup           Specifies the name of the group to check.

## Under the Hood

This script uses Microsoft Active Directory® Services Interface (ADSI) to retrieve the groups that the specified user belongs to, and then checks each group for a match with the group you specify. The script code is as follows:

```
Function IsMember(sUser,sGroup)
    'sUser must be a complete LDAP string:
    ' cn=DonJ,ou=West,dc=company,dc=com
    '

    On Error Resume Next
    Const PROPERTY_NOT_FOUND  = &h8000500D

    Set oUser = GetObject(sUser)
    If Not IsObject(oUser) Then
        IsMember = False
        Exit Function
    End If

    arrMemberOf = oUser.GetEx("memberOf")
    If Err.Number = PROPERTY_NOT_FOUND Then
        IsMember = False
        Exit Function
    Else
        For Each Group in arrMemberOf
            If Group = sGroup Then
                IsMember = True
                Exit Function
            End If
        Next
    End If

    IsMember = False
End Function
```

## Troubleshooting

Provided you use a fully qualified LDAP reference for the user, you shouldn't have any problems using this script. Although the script will run under the user's security context (as do all logon scripts), users have permission to query their own group membership information from the domain.

# Write an Event Log Entry

> **On the CD**    The sample script can be found on the CD that accompanies this book at \Chap16\WriteEvent.vbs.

| Operating System | Supported? | Prerequisites |
|---|---|---|
| Windows 2000 family | Yes | WSH 5.6 or later |
| Windows XP Professional | Yes | |
| Windows Server 2003 family | Yes | |

## Description

This script, WriteEvent.vbs, contains a single subroutine that writes an event log entry to the local Application event log.

## Example

Use this script as follows:

```
WriteEvent("My Event Text",0)
```

The second argument specifies the type of event to be written, such as an error or a warning. See the next "Syntax" section for a list of possible values.

## Syntax

This script is intended to be included in, and called from, a larger VBScript-based logon script. This script's syntax is as follows:

```
WriteEvent sText, iType
```

sText           Specifies the text of the event to be written

iType           Specifies a number indicating the type of event:

- 0   Success
- 1   Error
- 2   Warning
- 4   Informational
- 8   Audit success
- 16   Audit failure

## Under the Hood

This script uses the Windows Script Host *Shell* object to write an event log entry. The script code is as follows:

```
Sub WriteEvent(sText, iType)
  ' iType can be:
  ' 0 = Success
  ' 1 = Error
  ' 2 = Warning
  ' 4 = Informational
  ' 8 = Audit success
  ' 16 = Audit failure
  Dim oShell
  Set oShell = WScript.CreateObject("WScript.Shell")
  oShell.LogEvent iType,sText
End Sub
```

## Troubleshooting

Provided the user running the logon script has permission to log events (which she does by default), this script should not encounter any problems.

# Pause the Script

> **On the CD**   The sample script can be found on the CD that accompanies this book at \Chap16\Pause.vbs.

| Operating System | Supported? | Prerequisites |
|---|---|---|
| Windows 2000 family | Yes | WSH 5.6 or later |
| Windows XP Professional | Yes | |
| Windows Server 2003 family | Yes | |

## Description

This script, Pause.vbs, pauses the script for a specified period of time. You might use this to cause the logon script to wait for a few seconds while other events are processing.

## Example

Use this script as follows:

```
Pause 10
```

The script accepts one argument, which is the number of seconds you want the script to pause.

## Syntax

This script is intended to be included in, and called from, a larger VBScript-based logon script. This script's syntax is as follows:

```
Pause iSeconds
```

iSeconds                Specifies the number of seconds to pause.

## Under the Hood

This script uses the built-in *WScript* object's *Sleep* method, which pauses a script for a given number of milliseconds. The script code is as follows:

```
Sub Pause(iSeconds)
 WScript.Sleep(iSeconds * 1000)
End Sub
```

The script multiplies your specified number of seconds by 1,000 to achieve the correct delay period in milliseconds.

## Troubleshooting

This script is unlikely to encounter any problems. If you encounter an error when using a large value for *iSeconds*, try using a smaller value and calling the subroutine multiple times (each time using that smaller value) to achieve the desired pause duration.

# Display a Message

**On the CD**   The sample script can be found on the CD that accompanies this book at \Chap16\ShowMessage.vbs.

| Operating System | Supported? | Prerequisites |
|---|---|---|
| Windows 2000 family | Yes | WSH 5.6 or later |
| Windows XP Professional | Yes | |
| Windows Server 2003 family | Yes | |

## Description

This script, ShowMessage.vbs, utilizes the Windows Script Host's built-in ability to show pop-up messages. These messages can be simple dialog boxes with an OK button, or they can be more complex and offer the user a choice of buttons to click. The messages can also be timed to disappear automatically, making them ideal for use as a logon script welcome message.

## Example

Use this script as follows:

```
iVar = ShowMessage("Welcome","Welcome to the domain",0,0+64)
```

The last argument controls the icon and buttons displayed in the message box. See the following section titled "Syntax" for details about possible values. *iVar* will contain a value indicating which button the user clicked:

- **−1** No button was clicked. The dialog box was automatically cancelled after the number of seconds specified.

- **1** OK was clicked.

- **2** Cancel was clicked.

- **3** Abort was clicked.

- **4** Retry was clicked.

- **5** Ignore was clicked.

- **6** Yes was clicked.

- **7** No was clicked.

# Syntax

This script is intended to be included in, and called from, a larger VBScript-based logon script. This script's syntax is as follows:

```
ShowMessage(sTitle, sMessage, iSeconds, iFeatures)
```

| | |
|---|---|
| sTitle | Specifies the title of the message box. |
| sMessage | Specifies the main text to be displayed. |
| iSeconds | Specifies the number of seconds to display the message before automatically removing it. Set this to zero to require a response from the user. |
| iFeatures | Specifies the icon and buttons to display. Start by selecting a value for the buttons: |

- 0   OK button
- 1   OK and cancel buttons
- 2   Abort, Retry, and Ignore buttons
- 3   Yes, Cancel, and No buttons
- 4   Yes and No buttons
- 5   Retry and Cancel buttons

Then add one of the following values to select an icon:

- 0   No icon
- 16   Stop icon
- 32   Question icon
- 48   Exclamation icon
- 64   Information icon

# Under the Hood

This script uses the Windows Script Host's *Shell* object to display the message box. The script code is as follows:

```
Function ShowMessage(sTitle, sMessage, iSeconds, iFeatures)
    Dim oShell
    Set oShell = CreateObject("WScript.Shell")
    ShowMessage = oShell.Popup(sMessage,iSeconds,sTitle,iFeatures)
End Function
```

# Troubleshooting

Remember that the function will return -1 if you specify a number of seconds and the user does not click a button before the message box is automatically cancelled.

# Retrieve User Information

**On the CD**   The sample script can be found on the CD that accompanies this book at \Chap16\GetUserInfo.vbs.

| Operating System | Supported? | Prerequisites |
|---|---|---|
| Windows 2000 family | Yes | WSH 5.6 or later |
| Windows XP Professional | Yes | |
| Windows Server 2003 family | Yes | |

## Description

This script, GetUserInfo.vbs, contains three functions that can be used to retrieve the currently logged-on user's name, the logon domain, and the name of the local computer.

## Example

Use this script as follows:

```
sUsername = GetUserName()
sDomain = GetUserDomain()
sComputer = GetComputerName()
```

## Syntax

This script is intended to be included in, and called from, a larger VBScript-based logon script. This script's three functions have no required or optional arguments; simply assign the result of these functions to a variable to populate the variable with the desired information.

## Under the Hood

This script is actually a collection of three functions that each uses the Windows Script Host's *Network* object to retrieve user information. The script code is as follows:

```
Function GetUserName()
 Dim oNetwork
 Set oNetwork = CreateObject("WScript.Network")
 GetUserName = oNetwork.UserName
End Function

Function GetUserDomain()
 Dim oNetwork
 Set oNetwork = CreateObject("WScript.Network")
```

```
 GetUserDomain = oNetwork.UserDomain
End Function

Function GetComputerName()
 Dim oNetwork
 Set oNetwork = CreateObject("WScript.Network")
 GetComputerName = oNetwork.ComputerName
End Function
```

## Troubleshooting

The *Network* object will not function properly unless run on a computer that is a member of a Windows domain (Windows NT® or Active Directory). Using this script on client computers that log on to only a NetWare directory tree, for example, will result in error messages.

# Map a Drive

**On the CD**   The sample script can be found on the CD that accompanies this book at \Chap16\MapDrive.vbs.

| Operating System | Supported? | Prerequisites |
|---|---|---|
| Windows 2000 family | Yes | WSH 5.6 or later |
| Windows XP Professional | Yes | |
| Windows Server 2003 family | Yes | |

## Description

This script, MapDrive.vbs, contains a single subroutine that maps a network drive to a specified Universal Naming Convention (UNC) path.

## Example

Use this script as follows:

```
MapDrive "Z:","\\Server\share"
```

Note that the drive letter must be one that is not currently in use; if it is, an error will occur.

## Syntax

This script is intended to be included in, and called from, a larger VBScript-based logon script. This script's syntax is as follows:

```
MapDrive sLetter, sUNC
```

| | |
|---|---|
| sLetter | Specifies the drive letter to use. |
| sUNC | Specifies the UNC path to map the drive letter to. |

## Under the Hood

This script uses the Windows Script Host's *Network* object to map a drive. The script code is as follows:

```
Sub MapDrive(sLetter,sUNC)
 Dim oNetwork
 Set oNetwork = WScript.CreateObject("WScript.Network")
 oNetwork.MapNetworkDrive sLetter,sUNC
End Sub
```

# Troubleshooting

An error will occur when the user does not have permission to the destination UNC, when the user's client computer does not contain a redirector capable of connecting to the destination UNC, or when the destination UNC is unreachable at the time.

# Map a Printer

> **On the CD**   The sample script can be found on the CD that accompanies this book at \Chap16\MapPrinter.vbs.

| Operating System | Supported? | Prerequisites |
| --- | --- | --- |
| Windows 2000 family | Yes | WSH 5.6 or later |
| Windows XP Professional | Yes | |
| Windows Server 2003 family | Yes | |

## Description

This script, MapPrinter.vbs, contains a single subroutine that adds a Windows printer connection to a specified printer. On computers running Windows 2000 and later, the printer driver does not need to be installed on the client computer; the client is capable of downloading the driver from the print server, provided the print server is also running Windows 2000 or later. This script is not intended to add printer connections to printers that are not hosted on print servers running Windows 2000 (or later).

## Example

Use this script as follows:

```
MapPrinter "\\Server\PrinterShare", "Generic Printer"
```

Note that the second argument should contain the full name of the printer to be added.

## Syntax

This script is intended to be included in, and called from, a larger VBScript-based logon script. This script's syntax is as follows:

```
MapPrinter sUNC, sName
```

sUNC              Specifies the Universal Naming Convention (UNC) path of the printer share.

sName             Specifies the complete name of the printer driver associated with the printer being mapped.

## Under the Hood

This script uses the Windows Script Host's *Network* object to add the printer connection. The script code is as follows:

```
Sub MapPrinter(sUNC,sName)
    Dim oNetwork
    Set oNetwork = CreateObject("WScript.Network")
    oNetwork.AddWindowsPrinterConnection sUNC,sName
End Sub
```

## Troubleshooting

The user must have permission to use the printer mapped; if it does not, an error will occur. Errors will also occur when the UNC specified is not reachable at the time or the printer driver name is incorrect.

# Set the Default Printer

> **On the CD**    The sample script can be found on the CD that accompanies this book at \Chap16\SetDefaultPrinter.vbs.

| Operating System | Supported? | Prerequisites |
|---|---|---|
| Windows 2000 family | Yes | WSH 5.6 or later |
| Windows XP Professional | Yes | |
| Windows Server 2003 family | Yes | |

## Description

This script, SetDefaultPrinter.vbs, contains a single subroutine that sets a specified printer—which must already be connected—to be the system's default printer.

## Example

Use this script as follows:

```
SetDefaultPrinter "Network Printer 1"
```

The single argument must be the name of the printer as defined on the computer where the script is running. You can see an example of this name by looking in the computer's Printers and Faxes folder.

## Syntax

This script is intended to be included in, and called from, a larger VBScript-based logon script. This script's syntax is as follows:

```
SetDefaultPrinter sName
```

sName                    Specifies the name of the printer that will be made the default.

## Under the Hood

This script uses the Windows Script Host's *Network* object to set the default printer. The script code is as follows:

```
Sub SetDefaultPrinter(sName)
    Dim oNetwork
    Set oNetwork = CreateObject("WScript.Network")
    oNetwork.SetDefaultPrinter sName
End Sub
```

## Troubleshooting

An error will occur when the specified printer is not already mapped or connected on the computer.

# Part V
# IIS 6.0 Tasks

Chapter 17

# IIS Web Site Management Tasks

This chapter covers automation of Web site administration in Microsoft® Windows Server™ 2003 using Microsoft Internet Information Services (IIS) 6.0. Many of the tasks in this chapter can target multiple computers as they are; other tasks can target multiple computers when they are used in conjunction with the Iismultiany.vbs script presented in Chapter 19, "General IIS Management Tasks."

Tasks discussed in this chapter include the following:

- Creating Web sites
- Creating Web virtual directories
- Modifying Web site settings
- Replicating Web site content
- Copying Web site settings
- Listing Web virtual directories that have Script or Execute permissions

# Create Web Sites

The discussed scripts are included with Windows Server 2003, running IIS 6.0, and can be found at C:\Windows\System32\Iisweb.vbs and Iisftp.vbs.

| Operating System | Supported? | Prerequisites |
|---|---|---|
| Microsoft Windows® 2000 family | No | ■ Microsoft Windows Script Host (WSH) 5.6 or later |
| Microsoft Windows XP Professional | No | ■ IIS 6.0 |
| Windows Server 2003 family | Yes | |

## Description

This script, Iisweb.vbs, is included with IIS 6.0 and performs a number of Web-related administration tasks. Its simpler functions include starting, stopping, and pausing the Web services within IIS. It can also be used to create new Web sites. If you need to target multiple servers at one time, use the script Iismultiany.wsf in Chapter 19 instead of Iisweb.vbs.

## Example

The following example creates a new Web site that uses C:\Inetpub\Wwwroot as its root path, 80 as its TCP port, and all unassigned IP addresses:

```
Iisweb /create c:\inetput\wwwroot "Web Site" /b 80
```

Note that this script is intended to be run from the CScript host. From a command line, you can make CScript the default by running **CScript //h:Cscript**.

## Syntax

This script's syntax for creating a new FTP site is as follows:

```
Iisftp /create path sitename /b port /I address
```

| | |
|---|---|
| Path | Required. Specifies the root path for the new FTP site. |
| Sitename | Required. Specifies the name of the new FTP site as it appears in the Internet Information Services console. |
| /b port<br>/I address | You must specify /b, /i, or some combination of these. The /b argument specifies the TCP port the new FTP site will use; the default is 80. The /i argument specifies the IP address the new FTP site will use; the default is to use all unassigned IP addresses. Each FTP site you create must have a unique port/address combination. |

| `/s servername` | Specifies a remote IIS server to target. |
| `/u username`<br>`/p password` | Specifies alternate credentials to use when connecting to a remote IIS server. |
| `/dontstart` | Creates the new FTP site but doesn't start it. This allows you to create the site and then set up your desired security permissions before making the site active. |

## Under the Hood

Iisweb.vbs is a Microsoft Visual Basic® Script (VBScript) file, supplied by Microsoft, that uses Windows Management Instrumentation (WMI) to modify the IIS 6.0 metabase. IIS automatically detects the metabase modification, rereads the metabase, and then puts the new configuration—containing your new Web site—into effect immediately.

## Troubleshooting

To ensure this script doesn't run into any major errors, either have the permissions necessary to perform the script's task or provide alternate credentials that have the appropriate permissions. One common mistake is to specify as new a site name that already exists, or to specify a *port/address/hostname* combination that is already in use by another Web site. Both of these scenarios will result in an error, and you'll need to rerun the script with different values for the appropriate arguments.

# Create FTP Virtual Directories

The discussed script is included with Windows Server 2003, running IIS 6.0, and can be found at C:\Windows\System32\Iisvdir.vbs

| Operating System | Supported? | Prerequisites |
|---|---|---|
| Windows 2000 family | No | ■  WSH 5.6 or later |
| Windows XP Professional | No | ■  IIS 6.0 |
| Windows Server 2003 family | Yes | |

## Description

This script, Iisvdir.vbs, is included with IIS 6.0 and performs a number of administration tasks related to Web virtual directories. If you need to target multiple servers at one time, use the script Iismultiany.wsf in Chapter 19 instead of Iisvdir.vbs. Before you can work with Web virtual directories, you must first create a Web site (see the previous script for a way to automate that task).

> **Note**   Iisvdir.vbs will create a single virtual directory; if you need to create a batch of virtual directories, include Iisvdir.vbs in a normal batch (.bat) file.

## Example

The following example creates a new Web virtual directory in a Web site named "Web Site." The virtual directory points to the physical path C:\inetpub\ftpuploads, and the virtual directory alias will be \Downloads.

```
Iisvdir /create "Default Web Site" Downloads C:\Inetpub\downloads
```

Note that the physical path C:\Inetpub\downloads will be created by this script if the path does not already exist.

If you already have a virtual path named \Uploads\Users, and you want to add a new virtual directory named Private to the end of this path—for a path of \Uploads\Users\Private—you would use the following:

```
Iisvdir /create "Default Web Site"/Uploads/Users Private C:\Inetpub\Privateroot
```

This new virtual directory would have the physical path C:\Inetpub\Privateroot.

# Syntax

This script's syntax for creating a new Web virtual directory is as follows:

```
Iisvdir /create site/alias_path alias physical_Path
```

| | |
|---|---|
| Site | Required. Specifies the name of the Web site to target. |
| Alias_path | Specifies the virtual path, which must exist, of the new virtual directory. For example, *"Web Site"/Users/Public* specifies the site *"Web Site"* and */Users/Public* is the virtual path. |
| Alias | Required. Specifies the alias of the new virtual directory. |
| Physical_Path | Required. Specifies the physical path, which will be created if it doesn't exist, of the new virtual directory. |
| /s servername | Specifies a remote IIS server to target. |
| /u username /p password | Specifies alternate credentials to use when connecting to a remote IIS server. |

# Under the Hood

Iisvdir.vbs is a VBScript file, supplied by Microsoft, that uses Windows Management Instrumentation (WMI) to modify the IIS 6.0 metabase. IIS automatically detects the metabase modification, rereads the metabase, and then puts the new configuration—containing your new Web virtual directory—into effect immediately.

# Troubleshooting

To ensure this script doesn't run into any major errors, either have the permissions necessary to perform the script's task or provide alternate credentials that have the appropriate permissions. One common mistake is to specify a site name that doesn't exist or a virtual path that doesn't exist. Both the site name and virtual path must exist for the command to complete.

# Modify Web Site Settings

**On the CD**   The sample script can be found on the CD that accompanies this book at \Chap17\ModWeb.wsf.

| Operating System | Supported? | Prerequisites |
| --- | --- | --- |
| Windows 2000 family | No | ■  WSH 5.6 or later |
| Windows XP Professional | No | ■  IIS 6.0 is required |
| Windows Server 2003 family | Yes | |

## Description

This script, ModWeb.wsf, will change properties for a Web virtual server (also called a Web site). The script will also list available Web virtual servers, and can target multiple computers. This script is a good way to reconfigure multiple servers to have a consistent configuration.

## Example

Use this script as follows:

```
ModWeb.wsf /computer:server2 /listsites
```

This will list all Web sites on Server2. You will need a service instance name in order to make any modifications to the service:

```
ModWeb.wsf /computer:server2 /site:W3SVC /prop:AllowKeepAlive /val:False
```

This modifies the service named Service1 on the server Server2, setting its *AllowKeepAlive* property to False. Available properties are:

- *AllowKeepAlive*
- *ConnectionTimeout*
- *DontLog*
- *ServerComment*
- *MaxConnections*
- *MaxBandwidth*
- *ContentIndexed*

**Tip**   You can learn about these properties and their purposes, as well as the valid range of values for them, in the MSDN® Library. Look for "IisWebServiceSetting" in the Index.

This script can also be used to target multiple servers listed in a file or an entire organizational unit (OU) of servers. To target servers listed in a file:

```
ModWeb.wsf /list:C:\list.txt /site:Service1 /prop:AuthAnonymous /val:False
```

To target an OU named West in Microsoft Active Directory®:

```
ModWeb.wsf /ou:West /site:Service1 /prop:AuthAnonymous /val:False
```

You can also include nested OUs:

```
ModWeb.wsf /ou:West /recurse /site:Service1 /prop:AuthAnonymous /val:False
```

# Syntax

This script's syntax is as follows:

| | |
|---|---|
| /list:path<br>/computer:name<br>/container:name | One and only one of these is required by the script. Use */list* to target a list of computers contained within a text file. Use */computer* to target a single computer. Use */container* to target an organizational unit within Active Directory. |
| /recurse | When used with */container*, also targets computers contained within nested OUs. |
| /ping | Verifies the connectivity to all targeted computers prior to attempting a connection. Using this argument will reduce the timeout wait when one or more computers cannot be reached on the network. |
| /log:path | Logs unreachable computer names to the specified file. This file can then be used later, along with the */list* argument, to retry these computers. Note that a log is created only when used in conjunction with the */ping* argument. |
| /verbose | Causes the script to display more detailed, step-by-step status messages. |
| /listsites | Lists all Web services on the targeted computers so that you can determine the names of the available services. |
| /site:service<br>/prop:property<br>/val:new_value | These arguments must be used together. Specifies the name of the Web service to target (*/svc*), the property to change (*/prop*), and the new value for the property (*/val*). |

# Under the Hood

This script uses Windows Management Instrumentation to modify instances of the *IIsWebServiceSetting* class. As you can see in the following code, the script is designed to work only with a subset of the available class properties—those that are most likely to be modified in an enterprise environment. However, you can modify the script to work with almost any of the class's properties just by adding *Case* statements for each desired property:

```
Dim oWMI, oSvcs, oItem
On Error Resume Next
```

```
            Verbose "  Getting WMI on " & sName
            Set oWMI = GetObject("winmgmts:{authenticationLevel=pktPrivacy}\\" & sName &
        "\root\MicrosoftIISv2")
        If Err <> 0 Then
            WScript.Echo "  ** Couldn't get WMI on " & sName
            LogBadConnect(sName)
        Else
            Verbose "  Getting SMTP on " & sName
            Set oSvcs = oWMI.ExecQuery("SELECT * FROM IIsWebServiceSetting")
            If Not IsObject(oSvcs) Then
                WScript.Echo "  ** Couldn't get Web on " & sName
                LogBadConnect(sName)
            Else
                For Each oItem In oSvcs
                    If WScript.Arguments.Named.Exists("listsites") Then
                        WScript.Echo oItem.Name
                    Else
                        If oItem.Name = WScript.Arguments.Named("site) Then
                            Select Case lcase(WScript.Arguments.Named("prop"))
                                Case "allowkeepalive"
                                    oItem.allowkeepalive = WScript.Arguments.Named("val")
                                Case "connectiontimeout"
                                    oItem.connectiontimeout = WScript.Arguments.Named("val")
                                Case "dontlog"
                                    oItem.dontlog = WScript.Arguments.Named("val")
                                Case "servercomment"
                                    oItem.servercomment = WScript.Arguments.Named("val")
                                Case "maxbandwidth"
                                    oItem.maxbandwidth = WScript.Arguments.Named("val")
                                Case "maxconnections"
                                    oItem.maxconnections = WScript.Arguments.Named("val")
                                Case "contentindexed"
                                    oItem.contentindexed = WScript.Arguments.Named("val")
                            End select
                            oItem.Put_
                            If Err <> 0 Then
                                WScript.Echo "  ** Error setting property on " & sName
                            End If
                        End if
                    End If
                Next
            End If
        End if
```

# Troubleshooting

Other than the obvious problems that can arise if you try to use this script without
having the necessary permissions, or if you run the script against a server that doesn't
have IIS 6.0 installed and a Web virtual server configured, only one scenario can cause
a major problem in this script: specifying an invalid value for a property. Many properties, such as *ContentIndexed*, accept only a Boolean (True or False) value. Specifying
a string or an integer might result in an error or in unexpected behavior.

# Replicate Web Site Content

Robocopy.exe is included with Microsoft Windows Server 2003 Resource Kit Tools, downloadable from *http://www.microsoft.com/downloads/details.aspx?FamilyID=9d467a69-57ff-4ae7-96ee-b18c4790cffd&displaylang=en.*

| Operating System | Supported? | Prerequisites |
|---|---|---|
| Windows 2000 family | Yes | None |
| Windows XP Professional | Yes | |
| Windows Server 2003 family | Yes | |

## Description

Robocopy.exe is a command-line utility that provides robust file copy capabilities. It can be used to replicate Web content from one Web server to multiple destination servers. Creating a batch file that runs Robocopy against multiple destinations provides single-command replication to an entire Web farm. The batch file can also be scheduled to ensure content is replicated on a regular basis, if desired.

Robocopy differs significantly from the built-in Windows Xcopy command in that Robocopy is better built for over-the-network copying. Robocopy ensures that files are copied, and it does not recopy a file if the source and destination files' timestamps are the same. Also, in general, it takes additional steps to confirm that a file is correctly copied when using Robocopy.

## Example

A simple Robocopy command is as follows:

```
Robocopy.exe c:\inetpub\wwwroot \\server2\c$\inetpub\wwwroot *.* /S /Z /COPY:DATSOU
```

This command copies all files and subfolders from the local path C:\inetpub\wwwroot to the remote path \\server2\c$\inetpub\wwwroot. Files are copied in a restartable mode, allowing Robocopy to restart the copy if it fails. All file attributes, including security, ownership, and auditing attributes, are copied; this will work only when the security attributes on a file are assigned only to domain or built-in user accounts (such as Administrator).

## Syntax

This command's basic syntax is as follows:

```
Robocopy sourcepath destinationpath filespec
```

| | |
|---|---|
| Sourcepath | Required. Identifies the path from which to copy. |
| Destinationpath | Required. Identifies the path to which copies should be made. |
| Filespec | Required. Specifies the files to copy. May include wildcards, such as *.*, which represent all files. |

| /S | Copies subfolders unless they are empty. |
|---|---|
| /E | Copies subfolders, even if they are empty. |
| /LEV:level | Copies only top levels of subfolders. For example, */LEV:2* copies two levels of subfolders. |
| /Z | Uses restartable mode. |
| /B | Uses backup (nonrestartable) mode. This switch helps if source files will be opened by another process at the same time. |
| /ZB | Uses restartable mode if possible. Otherwise, uses backup mode. |
| /COPY:options | Specifies what to copy. Options include a nondelimited list (DAT is the default) using the following options:<br>■ *D* File data<br>■ *A* File attributes<br>■ *T* Timestamp<br>■ *S* Security attributes<br>■ *O* File ownership<br>■ *U* File auditing attributes |
| /MON:changes | Monitors the source files for changes. If more changes occur during the copy operation than are specified in the *changes* parameter, restart it. |
| /XF:filespec | Excludes the specified files from the copy. |

## Under the Hood

Robocopy.exe is a robust command-line tool written to use native Windows Application Programming Interface (API) calls. You cannot make changes to the way Robocopy operates, except as provided for in its command-line arguments. For more information about additional command-line arguments, see *http://www.microsoft.com/resources/ documentation/WindowsServ/2003/all/techref/en-us/Default.asp?url=/Resources/ Documentation/windowsserv/2003/all/techref/en-us/robocopy_syntax.asp*.

## Troubleshooting

Robocopy will provide detailed error messages if any errors occur. Typically, the most common problem is copying security, ownership, or auditing attributes out of their context. In other words, do not copy these attributes unless all files and folders have only security permissions assigned to domain or local built-in user and group accounts.

# Copy Web Site Settings

The discussed script is included with Windows Server 2003, running IIS 6.0, and can be found at C:\Windows\System32\Iiscnfg.vbs.

| Operating System | Supported? | Prerequisites |
|---|---|---|
| Windows 2000 family | No | ■   WSH 5.6 or later |
| Windows XP Professional | No | ■   IIS 6.0 |
| Windows Server 2003 family | Yes | |

## Description

This script, Iiscnfg.vbs, is included with IIS 6.0 and performs a number of IIS-related administration tasks. One of its functions can copy a local IIS server's configuration to other IIS servers.

## Example

The following example copies a local IIS configuration to a server named Server2:

```
Iiscnfg.vbs /copy /ts Server2 /tu Administrator /tp Password
```

## Syntax

This script's basic syntax for copying settings is as follows:

```
Iiscnfg /copy /ts server /tu user /tp password
```

| | |
|---|---|
| /s servername | Specifies a remote IIS server to target as the configuration source. |
| /u username<br>/p password | Specifies alternate credentials to use when connecting to a remote IIS server (using the /s argument). |
| /ts target_server | Specifies the target server where the configuration information will be copied. |
| /tu username<br>/tp password | Specifies the target server user name and password. |

## Under the Hood

Iiscnfg.vbs is a VBScript file, supplied by Microsoft, that uses Windows Management Instrumentation (WMI) to modify the IIS 6.0 metabase. IIS automatically detects the metabase modification, rereads the metabase, and then puts the new configuration into effect immediately.

# Troubleshooting

To ensure this script doesn't run into any major errors, either have the permissions necessary to perform the script's task or provide alternate credentials that have the appropriate permissions. One common mistake is to copy the IIS configuration to a server that can't support it. For example, copying the entire IIS configuration from a server that hosts FTP and Web sites to a server that does not have FTP installed will result in an impartial configuration on the destination server. Similarly, copying an IIS configuration does not include copying content: If the source server's Web site uses C:\Inetpub\wwwroot as its root path, this path must already exist on the destination server or a misconfiguration will result.

# List Virtual Directories with Execute or Script Permissions

**On the CD**   The sample script can be found on the CD that accompanies this book at \Chap17\VDirCheck.wsf.

| Operating System | Supported? | Prerequisites |
|---|---|---|
| Windows 2000 family | No | ■  WSH 5.6 or later |
| Windows XP Professional | No | ■  IIS 6.0 |
| Windows Server 2003 family | Yes | |

## Description

This script, VDirCheck.wsf, will list all Web virtual directories that have Script or Execute permissions assigned. These virtual directories represent potential security risks. The script will call special attention to virtual directories that also have Write permissions, which could potentially allow users or attackers to upload and execute malicious scripts or executables.

## Example

Use this script as follows:

```
VDirCheck.wsf /computer:server2
```

This will list all virtual directories having Script or Execute permissions on Server2. This script can also be used to target multiple servers listed in a file or an entire organizational unit (OU) of servers. To target servers listed in a file:

```
VDirCheck.wsf /list:c:\list.txt
```

To target an OU named West in Active Directory:

```
VDirCheck.wsf /ou:West
```

You can also include nested OUs:

```
VDirCheck.wsf /ou:West /recurse
```

## Syntax

This script's syntax is as follows:

| | |
|---|---|
| `/list:path`<br>`/computer:name`<br>`/container:name` | One and only one of these is required by the script. Use */list* to target a list of computers contained within a text file. Use */computer* to target a single computer. Use */container* to target an organizational unit within Active Directory. |

| | |
|---|---|
| /recurse | When used with /container, also targets computers contained within nested OUs. |
| /ping | Verifies the connectivity to all targeted computers prior to attempting a connection. Using this argument will reduce the timeout wait when one or more computers cannot be reached on the network. |
| /log:path | Logs unreachable computer names to the specified file. This file can then be used later, along with the /list argument, to retry these computers. Note that a log is created only when used in conjunction with the /ping argument. |
| /verbose | Causes the script to display more detailed, step-by-step status messages. |

## Under the Hood

This script uses Windows Management Instrumentation to modify instances of the *IIsWebVirtualDirSetting* class and check for Execute, Write, and Script permissions. The main portion of the code is as follows:

```
Dim oWMI, oSvcs, oItem
On Error Resume Next
Verbose "  Getting WMI on " & sName
Set oWMI = GetObject("winmgmts:{authenticationLevel=pktPrivacy}\\" & sName &
"\root\MicrosoftIISv2")
If Err <> 0 Then
   WScript.Echo "** Couldn't get WMI on " & sName
   LogBadConnect(sName)
Else
   Verbose "  Getting SMTP on " & sName
   Set oSvcs = oWMI.ExecQuery("SELECT * FROM IIsWebVirtualDirSetting")
   If Not IsObject(oSvcs) Then
        WScript.Echo "    ** Couldn't get VDir on " & sName
        LogBadConnect(sName)
   Else
        For Each oItem In oSvcs
             If oItem.AccessExecute Or oItem.AccessScript Then
                 If oItem.accesswrite Then
                      WScript.Echo "  *** WRITE+SCRIPT/
EXECUTE ACCESS APPLIED TO: "
                 End If
                 WScript.Echo oItem.Name & " (" & oItem.path & ")"
             End If
        Next
   End If
End if
```

## Troubleshooting

Other than the obvious problems that can arise if you try to use this script without having the necessary permissions, or if you run the script against a server that doesn't have IIS 6.0 installed and at least one Web virtual directory configured, this script shouldn't run into any problems.

Chapter 18

# FTP and SMTP Site Management Tasks

This chapter covers the automation of administration for the File Transfer Protocol (FTP) and Simple Mail Transport Protocol (SMTP) features of Microsoft® Internet Information Services (IIS) 6.0. Automating administration tasks is important when you have more than one server configured identically (such as in a server farm), when you need to deploy new servers quickly, or when you need to simplify the management of remote servers.

Most of the scripts in this chapter are provided by Microsoft and are included with Microsoft Windows Server™ 2003 when IIS 6.0 is installed. For more information about using these scripts for other administrative tasks (most of them have quite a bit of functionality built in), consult the Help and Support Center in Windows Server 2003.

Tasks included in this chapter are as follows:

- Creating FTP sites
- Batch-creating FTP virtual directories
- Modifying SMTP domain settings

# Create FTP Sites

The discussed script is included with Windows Server 2003, running IIS 6.0, and can be found at C:\Windows\System32\Iisftp.vbs.

| Operating System | Supported? | Prerequisites |
|---|---|---|
| Microsoft Windows® 2000 family | No | ■  Windows Script Host (WSH) 5.6 or later |
| Microsoft Windows XP Professional | No | |
| Windows Server 2003 family | Yes | ■  IIS 6.0 |

## Description

This script, Iisftp.vbs, is included with IIS 6.0 and performs a number of FTP-related administration tasks. Its simpler functions include starting, stopping, and pausing the FTP services within IIS, and it can also be used to create new FTP sites. If you need to target multiple servers at one time, use the script Iismultiany.vbs in Chapter 19, "General IIS Management Tasks," instead of Iisweb.vbs.

## Example

The following example creates a new FTP site that uses C:\Inetpub\Ftproot as its root path, 21 as its TCP port, and all unassigned IP addresses:

```
Iisftp /create c:\inetput\ftproot "FTP Site" /b 21
```

## Syntax

This script's syntax for creating a new FTP site is as follows:

```
Iisftp /create root name /b port
```

| | |
|---|---|
| Root | Required. Specifies the root path for the new FTP site. |
| Name | Required. Specifies the name of the new FTP site as it appears in the Internet Information Services console. |
| /b port<br>/i address | You must specify either /b, /i, or both. The /b argument specifies the TCP port the new FTP site will use; the default is 21. The /i argument specifies the IP address the new FTP site will use; the default is to use all unassigned IP addresses. Each FTP site you create must have a unique port/address combination. |
| /s servername | Specifies a remote IIS server to target. |
| /u username<br>/p password | Specifies alternate credentials to use when connecting to a remote IIS server. |

| `/dontstart` | Creates the new FTP site but doesn't start it. This allows you to create the site and then set up your desired security permissions before making the site active. |
| `/isolation Local \| AD` | Sets the new site's isolation mode to either *Local* or *AD* (Active Directory). |
| `/ADAdmin username` `/ADPass password` | When specifying */isolation AD*, specifies the Microsoft Active Directory® user name and password. |

## Under the Hood

Iisftp.vbs is a Microsoft Visual Basic® Script (VBScript) file, supplied by Microsoft, that uses Windows Management Instrumentation (WMI) to modify the IIS 6.0 metabase. IIS automatically detects the metabase modification, rereads the metabase, and then puts the new configuration—containing your new FTP site—into effect immediately.

## Troubleshooting

To ensure that this script doesn't run into any major errors, have the permissions necessary to perform the script's task or provide alternate credentials that have the appropriate permissions. One common mistake is to specify as a new site name a site that already exists or to specify a *port/address* combination that is already used by another FTP site. Both of these scenarios will result in an error, in which case you'll need to rerun the script with different values for the appropriate arguments.

# Create FTP Virtual Directories

The discussed script is included with Windows Server 2003, running IIS 6.0, and can be found at C:\Windows\System32\Iisftpdr.vbs.

| Operating System | Supported? | Prerequisites |
|---|---|---|
| Windows 2000 family | No | ■   WSH 5.6 or later |
| Windows XP Professional | No | ■   IIS 6.0 |
| Windows Server 2003 family | Yes | |

## Description

This script, Iisftpdr.vbs, is included with IIS 6.0 and performs a number of administration tasks related to FTP virtual directories. If you need to target multiple servers at one time, use the script Iismultiany.vbs in Chapter 19 instead of Iisftpdr.vbs. Before you can work with FTP virtual directories, you must first create an FTP site. (See the previous script for a way to automate that task.)

> **Note**    Iisftpdr.vbs will create a single virtual directory. If you need to create a batch of virtual directories, include Iisftpdr.vbs in a normal batch (.bat) file.

## Example

The following example creates a new FTP virtual directory in an FTP site named "*FTP Site*". The virtual directory points to the physical path C:\Inetpub\Ftpuploads, and the virtual directory alias is \Uploads.

```
Iisftpdr /create "FTP Site" Uploads C:\Inetpub\Ftpuploads
```

Note that the physical path will be created by this script if the path does not already exist.

If you already have a virtual path named \Uploads\Users, and you want to add a new virtual directory named Private to the end of this path—for a path of \Uploads\Users\Private—you would use the following code:

```
Iisftpdr /create "FTP Site"/Uploads/Users Private C:\Inetpub\Privateroot
```

This new virtual directory would have the physical path C:\Inetpub\Privateroot.

# Syntax

This script's syntax for creating a new FTP site is as follows:

```
Iisftpdr /create site/alias_path alias physical_Path
```

| | |
|---|---|
| Ftpsite | Required. Specifies the name of the FTP site to target. |
| Path | Specifies the virtual path, which must exist, of the new virtual direc-tory. For example, *"FTP Site"/Users/Public* specifies the site as*"FTP Site"* and /Users/Public as the virtual path. |
| Alias | Required. Specifies the alias of the new virtual directory. |
| Root | Required. Specifies the physical path, which will be created if it doesn't exist, of the new virtual directory. |
| /s servername | Specifies a remote IIS server to target. |
| /u username /p password | Specifies alternate credentials to use when connecting to a remote IIS server. |

# Under the Hood

Iisftpdr.vbs is a VBScript file, supplied by Microsoft, that uses Windows Management Instrumentation (WMI) to modify the IIS 6.0 metabase. IIS automatically detects the metabase modification, rereads the metabase, and the puts the new configuration–containing your new FTP virtual directory–into effect immediately.

# Troubleshooting

To ensure that this script doesn't run into any major errors, have the permissions necessary to perform the script's task or provide alternate credentials that have the appropriate permissions. One common mistake is to specify a site name that doesn't exist or a virtual path that doesn't exist. Both the site name and virtual path must exist for the command to complete.

# Modify SMTP Domain Settings

> **On the CD**   The sample script can be found on the CD that accompanies this book
> at \Chap18\ModSMTP.wsf.

| Operating System | Supported? | Prerequisites |
|---|---|---|
| Windows 2000 family | No | ■  WSH 5.6 or later |
| Windows XP Professional | No | ■  IIS 6.0 |
| Windows Server 2003 family | Yes | |

## Description

This script, ModSMTP.wsf, will change properties for an SMTP virtual server. The
script will also list available SMTP virtual servers and can target multiple computers.
This script is a good way to reconfigure multiple servers to have a consistent
configuration.

## Example

Use this script as follows:

```
ModSMTP.wsf /computer:server2 /listsvc
```

This code will list all SMTP service instances on Server2. You will need a service
instance name to make any modifications to the service:

```
ModSMTP.wsf /computer:server2 /svc:SmtpSvc /prop:AuthAnonymous /val:False
```

Note that the service name is case-sensitive. This code modifies the service named
Service1 on the server Server2, setting its *AuthAnonymous* property to False. Available
properties are:

- *AuthAnonymous*
- *AuthBasic*
- *AuthMD5*
- *AuthNTLM*
- *AuthPassport*
- *ConnectionTimeout*
- *DefaultLogonDomain*
- *MaxBandwidth*

- *MaxConnections*

- *MaxEndpointConnections*

- *ServerAutoStart*

- *SmtpLocalDelayExpireMinutes*

- *EnableReverseDNSLookup*

- *HopCount*

- *MasqueradeDomain*

- *SmartHost*

- *SmartHostType*

> **Tip**    You can learn about these properties and their purposes, as well as the valid range of values for them, in the Microsoft MSDN® Library. Look for "IisSmtpServiceSetting" in the index.

This script can also be used to target multiple servers listed in a file or an entire organizational unit (OU) of servers. To target servers listed in a file, use this code:

```
ModSMTP.wsf /list:C:\list.txt /svc:Service1 /prop:AuthAnonymous /val:False
```

To target an OU named West in Active Directory, use the following code:

```
ModSMTP.wsf /ou:West /svc:Service1 /prop:AuthAnonymous /val:False
```

You can also include nested OUs:

```
ModSMTP.wsf /ou:West /recurse /svc:Service1 /prop:AuthAnonymous /val:False
```

# Syntax

This script's syntax is as follows:

| | |
|---|---|
| /list:path<br>/computer:name<br>/container:name | One and only one of these is required by the script. Use */list* to target a list of computers contained within a text file. Use */computer* to target a single computer. Use */container* to target an organizational unit within Active Directory. |
| /recurse | When used with */container*, also targets computers contained within nested OUs. |
| /ping | Verifies the connectivity to all targeted computers prior to attempting a connection. Using this argument will reduce the timeout wait when one or more computers cannot be reached on the network. |

| | |
|---|---|
| /log:path | Logs unreachable computer names to the specified file. This file can then be used later, along with the */list* argument, to retry these computers. Note that a log is created only when used in conjunction with the */ping* argument. |
| /verbose | Causes the script to display more detailed, step-by-step status messages. |
| /listsvc | Lists all SMTP services on the targeted computers so that you can determine the names of the available services. |
| /svc:service /prop:property /val:new_value | These arguments must be used together. Specifies the name of the SMTP service to target (*/svc*), the property to change (*/prop*), and the new value for the property (*/val*). |

# Under the Hood

This script uses Windows Management Instrumentation to modify instances of the *IIsSmtpServiceSetting* class. As you can see in the following code, the script is designed to work only with a subset of the available class properties, that is, those that are most likely to be modified in an enterprise environment. However, you can modify the script to work with almost any of the class's properties just by adding additional *Case* statements for each desired property.

```
Dim oWMI, oSvcs, oItem
On Error Resume Next
Verbose "  Getting WMI on " & sName
Set oWMI = GetObject("winmgmts:{authenticationLevel=pktPrivacy}\\" & sName &
"\root\MicrosoftIISv2")
If Err <> 0 Then
    WScript.Echo "  ** Couldn't get WMI on " & sName
    LogBadConnect(sName)
Else
    Verbose "  Getting SMTP on " & sName
    Set oSvcs = oWMI.ExecQuery("SELECT * FROM IIsSmtpServiceSetting")
    If Not IsObject(oSvcs) Then
        WScript.Echo "  ** Couldn't get SMTP on " & sname
        LogBadConnect(sName)
    Else
        For Each oItem In oSvcs
            If WScript.Arguments.Named.Exists("listsvc") Then
                WScript.Echo oItem.Name
            Else
                If oItem.Name = WScript.Arguments.Named("svc") Then
                  Select Case lcase(WScript.Arguments.Named("prop"))
                    Case "authanonymous"
                        oItem.AuthAnonymous = WScript.Arguments.Named("val")
                    Case "authbasic"
                        oItem.AuthAnonymous = WScript.Arguments.Named("val")
                    Case "authmd5"
                        oItem.AuthMD5 = WScript.Arguments.Named("val")
                    Case "authntlm"
                        oItem.AuthNTLM = WScript.Arguments.Named("val")
```

```
             Case "authpassport"
                  oItem.AuthPassport = WScript.Arguments.Named("val")
             Case "connectiontimeout"
                  oItem.ConnectionTimeout = WScript.Arguments.Named("val")
             Case "defaultlogondomain"
                  oItem.DefaultLogonDomain = WScript.Arguments.Named("val")
             Case "maxbandwidth"
                  oItem.MaxBandwidth = WScript.Arguments.Named("val")
             Case "maxconnections"
                  oItem.MaxConnections = WScript.Arguments.Named("val")
             Case "maxendpointconnections"
                  oItem.MaxEndpointConnections = WScript.Arguments.Named("val")
             Case "serverautostart"
                  oItem.ServerAutoStart = WScript.Arguments.Named("val")
             Case "smtplocaldelayexpireminutes"
                 oItem.SMTPLocalDelayExpireMinutes = WScript.Arguments.Named("val")
             Case "enablereversednslookup"
                  oItem.EnableResverDNSLookup = WScript.Arguments.Named("val")
             Case "hopcount"
                  oItem.HopCount = WScript.Arguments.Named("val")
             Case "masqueradedomain"
                  oItem.MasqueradeDomain = WScript.Arguments.Named("val")
             Case "smarthost"
                  oItem.SmartHost = WScript.Arguments.Named("val")
             Case "smarthosttype"
                  oItem.SmartHystType = WScript.Arguments.Named("val")
        End Select
             oItem.Put_
             If Err <> 0 Then
                 WScript.Echo " ** Error setting property on " & sName
             End If
        End if
    End If
  Next
End If
End if
```

# Troubleshooting

Other than the obvious problems that can arise if you try to use this script without having the necessary permissions, or if you run the script against a server that doesn't have IIS 6.0 installed and an SMTP virtual server configured, you can create a problem for this script in only one major way—by specifying an invalid value for a property. Many properties, such as *AuthAnonymous*, accept only a Boolean (True or False) value. Specifying a string or integer might result in an error or in unexpected behavior.

Chapter 19

# General IIS Management Tasks

This chapter shows you how to automate general Microsoft® Internet Information Services (IIS) management tasks, particularly across multiple computers. In fact, the first task I'll cover in this chapter is how to run almost any IIS task—such as those presented in Chapter 17, "IIS Web Site Management Tasks," and Chapter 18, "FTP and SMTP Site Management Tasks"—against multiple IIS computers that are listed by name in a text file.

Tasks included in this chapter are as follows:

- Running IIS commands against multiple servers
- Backing up the IIS metabase
- Pausing the script
- Batch-creating POP3 Service mailboxes

# Run IIS Commands Against Multiple Servers

> **On the CD**   The sample script can be found on the CD that accompanies this book at \Chap19\Iismultiany.vbs.

| Operating System | Supported? | Prerequisites |
|---|---|---|
| Microsoft Windows® 2000 family | No | ■  Windows Script Host (WSH) |
| Microsoft Windows XP Professional · | No | 5.6 or later |
| Microsoft Windows Server™ 2003 family | Yes | ■  IIS 6.0 or later |

## Description

This script, Iismultiany.vbs, is designed to run one of the main IIS 6.0 command-line tools against multiple computers, making it easier to provision, configure, and manage multiple IIS servers that have identical settings (such as those in a Web farm). This script requires you to modify two elements before running it. This script is designed to be run on computers running Windows Server 2003, with IIS 6.0 installed.

This script is designed to work with the following Windows Server 2003 IIS management commands:

- Iisback
- Iiscnfg
- Iisext
- Iisftp
- Iisftpdr
- Iisvdir
- Iisweb

This script will not function with the Iisapp command.

## Example

Use this script by opening it in a text editor and modifying the information that appears in boldface here:

```
Dim sCommand
sCommand = "INSERT IIS COMMAND HERE"

Dim sFile
sFile = "c:\ListOfIISservers.txt"
```

The variable *sCommand* should be populated with an IIS command-line instruction, such as Iisweb. (I covered many of these instructions in Chapters 17 and 18.) Do not include the */s* argument in your command because the script will add it automatically. The variable *sFile* must point to a text file that lists one IIS server name per line; the command you specify in *sCommand* will be executed against each server listed in the file.

You can include the string *%name%* in your command syntax. This will be replaced with the name of the currently targeted server. For example, suppose you want to run a backup operation using the following command:

```
Iisback /backup %name%Backup /overwrite
```

Simply insert this string into the script. When the script is used to target a server named Server1, for example, the actual command executed will be:

```
Iisback /backup Server1Backup /overwrite /s Server1
```

This allows the backup name to be customized to match the server name.

## Syntax

This script has no command-line syntax. It is intended to be modified as just described and then executed as is.

## Under the Hood

This script reads server names from the specified file. It uses the Windows Script Host *Shell* object—specifically, that object's *Exec* method—to execute the command you specify. The *Replace()* function is used to substitute the current server name for the string *%name%* in your command. The exit code of the command you specify—which can indicate an error if one occurs while executing the command—is returned to this script and displayed on the command line. The script code is as follows:

```
Dim sCommand
sCommand = "INSERT IIS COMMAND HERE"

Dim sFile
sFile = "c:\ListOfIISservers.txt"

Dim oFSO, oTS
Set oFSO = CreateObject("Scripting.FileSystemObject")
On Error Resume Next
Set oTS = oFSO.OpenTextFile(sFile)
If Err <> 0 Then
    WScript.Echo Err.Description
    WScript.Echo "** Couldn't open " & sFile
    WScript.Quit
End If
```

```
Dim sServer, oShell, oExex, sCmd
Set oShell = CreateObject("WScript.Shell")
Do Until oTS.AtEndOfStream
    sServer = oTS.ReadLine
    sCmd = Replace(sComman,"%name%",sServer)
    WScript.Echo "Running against " & sServer
    Set oExec = oShell.Exec(sCmd & " /s " & sServer)
    Do While oExec.Status = 0
        WScript.Sleep 100
    Loop
    WScript.Echo "  Completed with exit code " & oExec.ExitCode
Loop
oTS.Close
WScript.Echo "Completed."
```

# Troubleshooting

Be sure to test independently each command you intend to use before including it in this script, because any errors this script encounters will be errors resulting from the command you specify.

# Back Up the IIS Metabase

The discussed script is included with Windows Server 2003, running IIS 6.0, and can be found at C:\Windows\System32\Iisback.vbs.

| Operating System | Supported? | Prerequisites |
|---|---|---|
| Windows 2000 family | No | ■  WSH 5.6 or later |
| Windows XP Professional | No | ■  IIS 6.0 or later |
| Windows Server 2003 family | Yes | |

## Description

This script, Iisback.vbs, is designed to back up the IIS metabase. The metabase contains all the configuration settings of IIS. Backing up the metabase allows you to more quickly restore a failed IIS server by recreating your Web sites, FTP sites, and other configuration items.

Iisback.vbs can be used with the first script in this chapter to back up the metabase on multiple IIS computers.

## Example

Use this script as follows:

```
Iisback /backup backupname
```

You can specify a number of optional arguments (detailed in the next "Syntax" section) to customize the script's behavior.

## Syntax

This script's syntax is as follows:

| | |
|---|---|
| /backup | Required. Specifies a backup operation. |
| /s server | Specifies the name of a remote server on which to perform the backup. |
| /u username<br>/p password | Specifies an alternate user name and password to be used when connecting to a remote computer. |
| /b backupname | Optional. Specifies the name of the backup; otherwise, one is automatically generated. |
| /v version | Specifies a version number to be assigned to the backup. Can be an integer, or *NEXT_VERSION* to provide a version number one higher than the last used. If this argument is not specified, */v NEXT_VERSION* is assumed. |
| /e backuppassword | Specifies a password with which to protect the backup. |
| /overwrite | Specifies that an existing backup of the same name should be overwritten. The default is off. |

## Under the Hood

This script—which was written by Microsoft and is included with Windows Server 2003 when IIS 6.0 is installed—uses Windows Management Instrumentation to back up the IIS metabase.

## Troubleshooting

Provided the user running the logon script has permission to back up IIS, or that alternate credentials with those permissions are specified, this script should not encounter any problems.

# Pause the Script

> **On the CD**   The sample script can be found on the CD that accompanies this book at \Chap19\Pause.vbs.

| Operating System | Supported? | Prerequisites |
|---|---|---|
| Windows 2000 family | Yes | WSH 5.6 or later |
| Windows XP Professional | Yes | |
| Windows Server 2003 family | Yes | |

## Description

This script, Pause.vbs, pauses the script for a specified period of time. You might use this script to cause a logon or other administrative script to wait for a few seconds while other events are processing.

## Example

Use this script as follows:

```
Pause 10
```

The script accepts one argument, which is the number of seconds you want it to pause.

## Syntax

This script is intended to be included in, and called from, a larger script based on Microsoft Visual Basic® Script (VBScript). This script's syntax is as follows:

```
Pause iSeconds
```

| | |
|---|---|
| iSeconds | Number of seconds to pause |

## Under the Hood

This script uses the built-in *WScript* object's *Sleep* method, which pauses a script for a given number of milliseconds. The script code is as follows:

```
Sub Pause(iSeconds)
 WScript.Sleep(iSeconds * 1000)
End Sub
```

The script multiplies your specified number of seconds by 1,000 to achieve the correct delay period in milliseconds.

# Troubleshooting

This script is unlikely to encounter any problems. If you encounter an error when using a large value for *iSeconds*, try using a smaller value and calling the subroutine multiple times (each time with that smaller value) to achieve the desired pause duration.

# Batch-Create POP3 Service Mailboxes

> **On the CD**   The sample script can be found on the CD that accompanies this book at \Chap19\BatchPOP.wsf.

| Operating System | Supported? | Prerequisites |
|---|---|---|
| Windows 2000 family | No | ■  WSH 5.6 or later |
| Windows XP Professional | No | ■  IIS 6.0 or later |
| Windows Server 2003 family | Yes | ■  Windows Server 2003 POP3 Service |

## Description

This script, BatchPOP.wsf, uses the Windows Server 2003 command-line tool Winpop to batch-create new POP3 Service mailbox accounts. This script can be used with a POP3 service that uses integrated (Microsoft Active Directory® or local) accounts as well as services that use nonintegrated accounts (in which passwords are stored in an encrypted file). In the latter case, you must specify a new password that will be used for all batch-created accounts.

## Example

Use this script as follows:

```
BatchPOP /file:C:\mailboxes.txt
```

This reads new mailbox names, which must be in the format *user@domain*, from a file named C:\mailboxes.txt. To create nonintegrated accounts, specify a password:

```
BatchPOP /file:C:\mailboxes.txt /password:Pa55wOrD!
```

## Syntax

This script's syntax is as follows:

| | |
|---|---|
| `/file:filename` | Required. Specifies the file containing the new user names. This file must have one user name per line, and names must be in the format *user@domain*. |
| `/password:password` | Optional. Forces the creation of nonintegrated accounts and assigns the specified password to all new accounts. |

# Under the Hood

This script uses the Windows Script Host's *Shell* object to execute the Winpop command:

```
'check for required arg
If not WScript.Arguments.Named.Exists("file") Then
    WScript.Echo "Must specify filename."
    WScript.Arguments.ShowUsage
    WScript.Quit
End If

'open file
Dim oFSO, oTS, sName
Set oFSO = CreateObject("Scripting.FileSystemObject")
On Error Resume Next
Set oTS = oFSO.OpenTextFile(WScript.Arguments.Named("file"))
If Err <> 0 Then
    WScript.Echo "** Error opening file."
    WScript.Quit
End If

Dim oShell, oExec
Set oShell = CreateObject("WScript.Shell")
Do Until oTS.AtEndOfStream

    sName = oTS.ReadLine
    If WScript.Arguments.Named.Exists("password") then
        Set oExec = oShell.Exec("winpop add " & sName & "
/createuser " & WScript.Arguments.Named("password"))
    Else
        Set oExec = oShell.Exec("winpop add " & sName)
    End If
    Do While oexec.Status <> 0
         WScript.Echo "Creating sName: Status is " & oExec.ExitCode
    Loop
Loop
oTS.Close
WScript.Echo "Command completed."
```

# Troubleshooting

If you experience problems, try running the Winpop command manually to create one new mailbox. You must resolve any problems that occur before this script will function. Any errors you do find will most likely be an error returned by the Winpop command, such as those stating that the user specified a password that does not meet minimum requirements or specified a new mailbox name that already exists. The script will display this error information when available and continue executing.

# Part VI
# Advanced Scripting Tools

Chapter 20
# User Interface and Databases

In this chapter, rather than show you how to automate entire administrative tasks, I provide you with some functions that you can use to write more advanced scripts of your own. The functions and subroutines in this chapter are designed to be pasted into your own scripts, giving your scripts some advanced capabilities without you needing to write complex scripts yourself.

Tasks included in this chapter are as follows:

- Displaying an HTML-formatted message
- Connecting to a database
- Querying information from a database
- Changing information in a database
- Adding information to a database

# Display HTML Messages

**On the CD**   The sample script can be found on the CD that accompanies this book at \Chap20\DisplayHTMLMessage.vbs.

| Operating System | Supported? | Prerequisites |
|---|---|---|
| Microsoft® Windows® 2000 family | Yes | ■ Windows Script Host (WSH) 5.6 or later |
| Microsoft Windows XP Professional | Yes | |
| Microsoft Windows Server™ 2003 family | Yes | ■ Microsoft Internet Explorer 5.5 or later |

## Description

This script, DisplayHTMLMessage.vbs, contains a single function that displays an HTML-formatted message for a specified number of seconds. The function uses Internet Explorer to render and display the HTML, and it programmatically controls Internet Explorer to give you a good deal of control over the message's appearance and behavior.

## Example

Use this script as follows:

```
HTMLMsgBox("<font color=red><center>PLEASE WAIT</center></font>", 10, 15, 200, 150, 10)
```

This code will display a message box containing the phrase "PLEASE WAIT," which will be displayed in red, centered text. The message box will be displayed 10 pixels below the top of the screen and 15 pixels from the left side of the screen, and will be 200 pixels wide and 150 pixels high. The message will be displayed for 10 seconds.

Note that the script cannot contain <BODY></BODY> or <HEAD></HEAD> tags; if you're copying HTML code from FrontPage®, only copy what appears *between* the <BODY> and </BODY> tags.

## Syntax

This script is intended to be included in, and called from within, a larger script. This script's syntax is as follows:

```
HTMLMsgBox(sHTML, iTop, iLeft, iWidth, iHeight, iSeconds)
```

| | |
|---|---|
| sHTML | Specifies the HTML to display. You can use an HTML editor such as Microsoft FrontPage to create the HTML for your message. |
| iTop | Specifies the position, in pixels, of the top edge of the window in relation to the top edge of the screen. |

| | |
|---|---|
| `iLeft` | Specifies the position, in pixels, of the left edge of the window in relation to the left edge of the screen. |
| `iWidth` | Specifies the width of the window in pixels. |
| `iHeight` | Specifies the height of the window in pixels. |
| `iSeconds` | Specifies the number of seconds the message will display. |

## Under the Hood

This script uses Internet Explorer's COM-based application programming interface to programmatically display, size, and position an Internet Explorer window and insert the specified HTML. Internet Explorer automatically renders the HTML. The function code is as follows:

```
Sub HTMLMsgBox(sHTML, iTop, iLeft, iWidth, iHeight, iSeconds)
    Dim oIE
    Set oIE = CreateObject("InternetExplorer.Application")
    oIE.AddressBar = False
    oIE.Height = iHeight
    oIE.Width = iWidth
    oIE.Top = iTop
    oIE.Left = iLeft
    oIE.ToolBar = False
    oIE.Navigate "about:blank"
    oIE.Document.body.innerhtml = sHTML
    Do While oIE.Busy
        WScript.Sleep 100
    Loop
    oIE.Visible = True
    WScript.Sleep iSeconds * 1000
    oIE.Quit
End Sub
```

The Internet Explorer toolbar and Address Bar are automatically hidden so that the window's appearance has the same style as a dialog box.

## Troubleshooting

This script will only work if Internet Explorer has not been removed or permanently disabled; any error messages relating to problems with the Internet Explorer installation will be associated with line 2 of the subroutine. These errors can be corrected by properly installing or enabling Internet Explorer.

**Note**   Using the Set Program Access and Defaults utility to disable access to Internet Explorer will not remove Internet Explorer and will not prevent this script from running. Internet Explorer does not need to be your default Web browser for this script to function properly. However, this script works only with Internet Explorer and will not substitute an alternate Web browser, even if you have specified one as your default Web browser.

# Connect to a Database

> **On the CD**   The sample script can be found on the CD that accompanies this book at \Chap20\ConnectDB.vbs.

| Operating System | Supported? | Prerequisites |
|---|---|---|
| Windows 2000 family | Yes | WSH 5.6 or later |
| Windows XP Professional | Yes | |
| Windows Server 2003 family | Yes | |

## Description

This script, ConnectDB.vbs, contains a single subroutine that connects to a Microsoft Excel, Microsoft Access, or Microsoft SQL Server™ database. This script is intended to be used in conjunction with QueryDB.vbs, ChangeDB.vbs, and InsertDB.vbs, which are covered later in this chapter.

## Example

Use this script as follows:

```
ConnectDB "sql","don-laptop", mydatabase","sqluser","password"
```

The first argument specifies a SQL Server database (as opposed to an Excel or Access database); the second argument indicates the SQL Server name. The third argument specifies the database to connect to, and the fourth and fifth specify the user credentials to utilize. The last three arguments are used only when connecting to a SQL Server database; Excel and Access require only the first two arguments.

## Syntax

This script is intended to be included in, and called from within, a larger script. This script's syntax is as follows:

```
ConnectDB(sType, sFile, sDatabase, sUser, sPwd)
```

| | |
|---|---|
| sType | Specifies the database type. Valid values include *sql*, *access*, and *excel*. |
| sFile | For an Access or Excel database, specifies the file name to open. For a SQL Server database, specifies the server name to connect to. |
| sDatabase | Used only for SQL Server connections (pass an empty string for Access or Excel); specifies the database name to open. |

| sUser | Used only for SQL Server connections (pass an empty string for Access or Excel); specifies the user name to use for the connection. |
| sPwd | Used only for SQL Server connections (pass an empty string for Access or Excel); specifies the password to use for the connection. |

# Under the Hood

This script's real value is to automatically select the proper Microsoft ActiveX® Data Objects (ADO) connection string based on the database type:

```
Sub ConnectDB(sType, sFile, sDatabase, sUser, sPwd)

    'build connection String
    Dim sConn
    Select Case lcase(sType)
        Case "access"
            sConn = "Provider=Microsoft.Jet.OLEDB.4.0;Data Source=" & sFile & ";"
        Case "excel"
            sConn = "Provider=Microsoft.Jet.OLEDB.4.0;Data Source=" & sFile & ";
Extended Properties=Excel 8.0;"
        Case "sql"
            sConn = "Provider=sqloledb;server=" & sFile & ";database=" & sDatabase
& ";uid=" & sUser & ";pwd=" & sPwd & ";"
        Case Else
            Err.Raise 0000001,"ConnectDB","Unknown database type"
            Exit Sub
    End Select

    Set oConnection = CreateObject("ADODB.Connection")
    oConnection.Open sConn

End Sub
```

Because of the way Microsoft Visual Basic® Script (VBScript) handles object references, such as the ADO *Connection* object, you must first declare the variable *oConnection* and set it equal to the *ADODB.Connection* COM object ID. Then you can call the *ConnectDB* subroutine. The following code demonstrates proper use of this subroutine:

```
Dim oConnection
Set oConnection = CreateObject("ADODB.Connection")
ConnectDB "sql","server", "database","user","password"
```

> **On the CD**   You'll find an additional script, Chap20\DatabaseExample.vbs, on the CD that accompanies this book. That script demonstrates the use of the *ConnectDB* subroutine in conjunction with the *QueryDB* subroutine to form a complete script for accessing a database.

# Troubleshooting

Connecting to Excel or Access databases will rarely result in a problem as long as the file you specify exists and is accessible to the script. Connecting to a SQL Server database can be more complex; this script is designed to work when the user name and password are defined as local logons on the SQL Server. Other conditions might work—for example, to use Windows Integrated authentication with SQL Server, you might be able to pass empty strings for the user name and password. If you encounter errors when using the *ConnectDB* subroutine, contact your SQL Server system administrator for more information about accessing the server from within a script.

# Query a Database

> **On the CD**    The sample script can be found on the CD that accompanies this book
> at \Chap20\QueryDB.vbs.

| Operating System | Supported? | Prerequisites |
|---|---|---|
| Windows 2000 family | Yes | WSH 5.6 or later |
| Windows XP Professional | Yes | |
| Windows Server 2003 family | Yes | |

## Description

This script, QueryDB.vbs, queries information from a database. You must first establish a connection to the database, which can be done using the ConnectDB.vbs script
described earlier in this chapter.

## Example

Use this script as follows:

```
Dim oRecordset
Set oRecordset = CreateObject("ADODB.Recordset")
QueryDB oConnection, "Titles", "*", ""
```

This example queries all columns and all records from the Titles table (or Excel
sheet), using a previously opened connection referenced in variable *oConnection*.

The following example (which is included on the CD that accompanies this book in
Chap20\DatabaseExample.vbs) shows how *QueryDB* can be used in conjunction
with *ConnectDB* to list all columns and all rows from a specified SQL Server database
table:

```
' **************************************************************
' Using ConnectDB to connect to the database
' **************************************************************
Dim oConnection
Set oConnection = CreateObject("ADODB.Connection")
ConnectDB "sql","don-laptop", "mydatabase","sqluser","password"


' **************************************************************
' Using QueryDB to query the database
' **************************************************************
Dim oRecordset
Set oRecordset = CreateObject("ADODB.Recordset")
QueryDB oConnection, "Titles", "*", ""
```

```
' list what's in the database
Do Until oRecordset.EOF
    For Each oField In oRecordset.Fields
        WScript.Echo oField.Name & ": " & oField.Value
    Next
    WScript.Echo ""
    oRecordset.Movenext
Loop



' ********************************************************************
' The functions and subroutines - no need to modify these
' ********************************************************************

Function QueryDB(oConn, sTable, sColumns, sCondition)

    Dim sQuery
    sQuery = "SELECT " & sColumns & " FROM " & sTable
    If sCondition <> "" Then
        sQuery = sQuery & "WHERE " & sCondition
    End If

    oRecordset.Open sQuery, oConn
End Function

Sub ConnectDB(sType, sFile, sDatabase, sUser, sPwd)

    'build connection String
    Dim sConn
    Select Case lcase(sType)
        Case "access"
            sConn = "Provider=Microsoft.Jet.OLEDB.4.0;Data Source=" & sFile & ";"
        Case "excel"
            sConn = "Provider=Microsoft.Jet.OLEDB.4.0;Data Source=" & sFile & ";
Extended Properties=Excel 8.0;"
        Case "sql"
            sConn = "Provider=sqloledb;server=" & sFile & ";database=" & sDatabase
& ";uid=" & sUser & ";pwd=" & sPwd & ";"
        Case Else
            Err.Raise 0000001,"ConnectDB","Unknown database type"
            Exit Sub
    End Select

    Set oConnection = CreateObject("ADODB.Connection")
    oConnection.Open sConn

End Sub
```

Note that both the *ConnectDB* and *QueryDB* subroutines have been copied and pasted into this example script.

# Syntax

This script is intended to be included in, and called from within, a larger script. This script's syntax is as follows:

```
QueryDB(oConn, sTable, sColumns, sCondition)
```

| | |
|---|---|
| oConn | Specifies an *ADODB.Connection* object that has already been declared and opened. |
| sTable | Specifies the database table name, or Excel sheet name, to be queried. |
| sColumns | Specifies a comma-delimited list of columns to be queried. Specify * to query all columns. |
| sCondition | Specifies a single comparison condition to limit the records queried from the database. For example, "Name='Don'" will query only records whose *Name* column contains the value *Don*. This is an optional argument. Pass an empty string to query all records. |

# Under the Hood

This subroutine builds a SQL query string based on the information you provide in the subroutine's arguments and then executes the subroutine:

```
Sub QueryDB(oConn, sTable, sColumns, sCondition)

    Dim sQuery
    sQuery = "SELECT " & sColumns & " FROM " & sTable
    If sCondition <> "" Then
        sQuery = sQuery & "WHERE " & sCondition
    End If

    oRecordset.Open sQuery, oConn
End Sub
```

Because of the way VBScript handles object reference variables, you must declare variable *oRecordset* and set it equal to the *ADODB.Recordset* COM object ID prior to calling *QueryDB*.

# Troubleshooting

Used properly, this script should not run into any problems. If you encounter errors, ensure that you're specifying valid table or sheet names (Excel sheet names must often be specified as *"[name$]"* to work properly), valid column names (in Excel, the column name is specified in the first row of the spreadsheet), and valid comparison conditions. Typically, error messages are specific about what needs to be changed, if anything goes wrong.

# Change Information in a Database

**On the CD**   The sample script can be found on the CD that accompanies this book at \Chap20\ChangeDB.vbs.

| Operating System | Supported? | Prerequisites |
| --- | --- | --- |
| Windows 2000 family | Yes | WSH 5.6 or later |
| Windows XP Professional | Yes | |
| Windows Server 2003 family | Yes | |

## Description

This script, ChangeDB.vbs, changes information in a database. You must first establish a connection to the database, which can be done using the ConnectDB.vbs script described earlier in this chapter.

## Example

Use this script as follows:

```
ChangeDB(oConnection, "MyTable", "ZIP=89123", "ZIP=89122")
```

This example changes the table *MyTable*, updating a column named *ZIP* to have the value *89123*. This change occurs for all database rows where the *ZIP* column contains *89122*. Variable *oConnection* is a previously declared and opened *ADODB.Connection* object.

## Syntax

This script is intended to be included in, and called from within, a larger script. This script's syntax is as follows:

```
ChangeDB(oConn, sTable, sChange, sCondition)
```

| | |
| --- | --- |
| oConn | Specifies an *ADODB.Connection* object that has already been declared and opened. |
| sTable | Specifies the database table name, or Excel sheet name, to be queried. |
| sChange | Specifies a comma-delimited list of changes in the format *column=newvalue*. For example, "ZIP=89123,State=NV" would update both the *ZIP* and *State* columns. |
| sCondition | Specifies a single comparison condition to limit the records queried from the database. For example, "Name='Don'" will update only records whose *Name* column contains the value *Don*. This is an optional argument. Pass an empty string to update all records. |

# Under the Hood

This subroutine builds a SQL query string based on the information you provide in the subroutine's arguments and then executes the subroutine:

```
' assumes connection object is opened
' use Sub ConnectDB to do this if necessary

Sub ChangeDB(oConn, sTable, sChange, sCondition)

    Dim sQuery
    sQuery = "UPDATE " sTable & " SET " & sChange
    If sCondition <> "" Then
        sQuery = sQuery & "WHERE " & sCondition
    End If

    oConn.Execute sQuery
End Sub
```

# Troubleshooting

Used properly, this script should not run into any problems. If you encounter errors, ensure that you're specifying valid table or sheet names (Excel sheet names must often be specified as *"[name$]"* to work properly), valid column names (in Excel, the column name is specified in the first row of the spreadsheet), and valid comparison conditions. Typically, error messages are specific about what needs to be changed if anything goes wrong.

# Add Information to a Database

**On the CD** The sample script can be found on the CD that accompanies this book at \Chap20\InsertDB.vbs.

| Operating System | Supported? | Prerequisites |
| --- | --- | --- |
| Windows 2000 family | Yes | WSH 5.6 or later |
| Windows XP Professional | Yes | |
| Windows Server 2003 family | Yes | |

## Description

This script, InsertDB.vbs, adds information to a database. You must first establish a connection to the database, which can be done using the ConnectDB.vbs script described earlier in this chapter.

## Example

Use this script as follows:

```
InsertDB(oConn, "MyTable", "Name,ZIP,State", "'Don','89123','NV'")
```

This example adds a new row to the table *MyTable*, setting the *Name* column to be *Don*, the *ZIP* column to be *89123*, and the *State* column to be *NV*. Note that string values must be included within single quotation marks, and that all values must be comma-delimited.

## Syntax

This script is intended to be included in, and called from within, a larger script. This script's syntax is as follows:

```
InsertDB(oConn, sTable, sColumns, sValues)
```

| | |
| --- | --- |
| oConn | An *ADODB.Connection* object that has already been declared and opened. |
| sTable | Specifies the database table name, or Excel sheet name, to be queried. |
| sColumns | Specifies a comma-delimited list of columns to be inserted. You must specify all columns for which the database requires a value. |
| sValues | Specifies a comma-delimited list of values. The order of the values must match the order of the columns specified in *sColumns*. String values must be included in single quotation marks. |

## Under the Hood

This subroutine builds a SQL query string based on the information you provide in the subroutine's arguments and then executes the subroutine:

```
' assumes connection object is opened
' use Sub ConnectDB to do this if necessary

Sub InsertDB(oConn, sTable, sColumns, sValues)

    Dim sQuery
    sQuery = "INSERT INTO " sTable & " (" & sColumns & ") VALUES (" & sValues & ")"
    oConn.Execute sQuery

End Sub
```

## Troubleshooting

Used properly, this script should not run into any problems. If you encounter errors, ensure that you're specifying valid table or sheet names (Excel sheet names must often be specified as *"[name$]"* to work properly), valid column names (in Excel, the column name is specified in the first row of the spreadsheet), and valid comparison conditions. Typically, error messages are specific about what needs to be changed, if anything goes wrong.

The most common mistake when inserting data into a database is to leave out one or more columns for which a value is required; the database will not accept the new row of data unless every required (called *non-Nullable*) column has a value. Another common mistake is to provide data of an incorrect type. If the database is expecting a numeric value for a column, for example, specifying a string value will result in an error.

# Chapter 21
# Wrapper Script

Most of the scripts presented in this book were written from a script template, or *wrapper*, which provides a consistent set of functionality across these scripts. In this chapter, I'll show you how to use that wrapper script to write your own scripts, helping save time and energy.

**On the CD**   You'll find the wrapper script on the CD that accompanies this book in \Chap21\wrapper.wsf.

**Warning**   The wrapper script does nothing as is. It is intended as a template, to which you can add your own script code to automate various Microsoft® Windows® administration tasks.

The wrapper has a number of built-in functions that you can take advantage of:

- It can query and target all computer names from a specified organizational unit (OU) in Microsoft Active Directory®. Use the */container:* argument to specify the target OU.

- When you instruct the script to target an OU, you can include child OUs in it as well. Include the */recurse* argument to have it do so.

- The script can target all computers listed in a file. Use the */list:* argument to specify the file name containing the computer names to target.

- The script can target a single computer by using the */computer:* argument to specify the computer name.

- The script can attempt to ping all targeted computers before attempting to connect to them. This improves script execution time when one or more computers are unreachable. Use the */ping* argument to activate this feature.

- In conjunction with the */ping* argument, the script can log unreachable computers to a file, and then can be used (along with the */list:* argument) to retry those computers later. Use the */log:* argument to activate this feature and specify a log file name. Within the script, you can log a bad connection using the *LogBadConnect* subroutine.

- The script supports verbose output. Run it with the */verbose* argument to activate this feature, and use the *Verbose* subroutine within the script to output verbose text.

- The script includes built-in functions named *QueryWMI()* and *QueryADSI()* that can be used to query Windows Management Instrumentation (WMI) or Active Directory Services Interface (ADSI).

- The script includes built-in functionality for writing information to a text log file. This functionality is provided by the *LogFile* subroutine.

# Overview

Here is the wrapper script in its entirety (only the Microsoft Visual Basic® Script, or VBScript, portion). The XML formatting associated with the WSF file format has been left out of this listing:

## Sample wrapper.wsf

```
'make sure we're running from CScript, not WScript
If LCase(Right(WScript.FullName,11)) <> "cscript.exe" Then
    If MsgBox("This script is designed to work with CScript, but you are running
it under WScript. " & _
        "This script may produce a large number of dialog boxes when running under
WScript, which you may " & _
        "find to be inefficient. Do you want to continue anyway?",4+256+32,"Script
host warning") = 7 Then
        WScript.Echo "Tip: Run ""Cscript //h:cscript"" from a command-line to make
CScript the default scripting host."
        WScript.Quit
    End If
End If


'count arguments
Dim iArgs
If WScript.Arguments.Named.exists("computer") Then iArgs = iArgs + 1
If WScript.Arguments.Named.exists("container") Then iArgs = iArgs + 1
If WScript.Arguments.Named.exists("list") Then iArgs = iArgs + 1
If iArgs <> 1 Then
    WScript.Echo "Must specify either /computer, /container, or /list arguments."
    WScript.Echo "May not specify more than one of these arguments."
    WScript.Echo "Run command again with /? argument for assistance."
    WScript.Quit
End If


'if ping requested, make sure we're on XP or later
Dim bPingAvailable, oLocalWMI, cWindows, oWindows
bPingAvailable = False
Set oLocalWMI = GetObject("winmgmts:\\.\root\cimv2")
Set cWindows = oLocalWMI.ExecQuery("Select BuildNumber from
Win32_OperatingSystem",,48)
For Each oWindows In cWindows
    If oWindows.BuildNumber >= 2600 Then
        bPingAvailable = True
    End If
Next


'was ping requested?
If WScript.Arguments.Named.Exists("ping") Then
    If bPingAvailable Then
        Verbose "will attempt to ping all connections to improve performance"
    Else
        WScript.Echo "*** /ping not supported prior to Windows XP"
    End If
End If
```

```
'either /list, /computer, or /container was specified:
Dim sName
If WScript.Arguments.Named("list") <> "" Then
    'specified list - read names from file
    Dim oFSO, oTS
    Verbose "Reading names from file " & WScript.Arguments.Named("list")
    Set oFSO = WScript.CreateObject("Scripting.FileSystemObject")
    On Error Resume Next
    Set oTS = oFSO.OpenTextFile(WScript.Arguments.Named("list"))
    If Err <> 0 Then
        WScript.Echo "Error opening " & WScript.Arguments.Named("list")
        WScript.Echo Err.Description
        WScript.Quit
    End If
    Do Until oTS.AtEndOfStream
        sName = oTS.ReadLine
        TakeAction sName
    Loop
    oTS.Close

Elseif WScript.Arguments.Named("container") <> "" Then
    'specified container - read names from AD
    Dim oObject, oRoot, oChild
    Verbose "Reading names from AD container " &
WScript.Arguments.Named("container")
    On Error Resume Next
    Set oRoot = GetObject("LDAP://rootDSE")
    If Err <> 0 Then
        WScript.Echo "Error connecting to default Active Directory domain"
        WScript.Echo Err.Description
        WScript.Quit
    End If
    Set oObject = GetObject("LDAP://ou=" & WScript.Arguments.Named("container") &
_
      "," & oRoot.Get("defaultNamingContext"))
    If Err <> 0 Then
        WScript.Echo "Error opening organizational unit " &
WScript.Arguments.Named("container")
        WScript.Echo Err.Description
        WScript.Quit
    End If
    WorkWithOU oObject

Elseif WScript.Arguments.Named("computer") <> "" Then
    'specified single computer
    Verbose "Running command against " & WScript.Arguments.Named("computer")
    TakeAction WScript.Arguments.Named("computer")

End If

'display output so user will know script finished
WScript.Echo "Command completed."
```

```
' ----------------------------------------------------------------------
' Sub WorkWithOU
'
' Iterates child objects in OU; calls itself to handle sub-OUs If
' /recurse argument supplied
' ----------------------------------------------------------------------
Sub WorkWithOU(oObject)
    For Each oChild In oObject
        Select Case oChild.Class
            Case "computer"
                TakeAction Right(oChild.Name,len(oChild.name)-3)
            Case "user"
            Case "organizationalUnit"
                If WScript.Arguments.Named.Exists("recurse") Then
                    'recursing sub-OU
                    Verbose "Working In " & oChild.Name
                    WorkWithOU oChild
                End If
        End Select
    Next
End Sub


' ----------------------------------------------------------------------
' Sub TakeAction
'
' Makes connection and performs command-specific code
' ----------------------------------------------------------------------
Sub TakeAction(sName)

    'verbose output?
    Verbose "Connecting to " & sName

    'ping before connecting?
    If WScript.Arguments.Named.Exists("ping") Then
        If Not TestPing(sName,bPingAvailable) Then
            LogBadConnect(sName)
            Exit Sub
        End If
    End If


    '###########################################
    '#          COMMAND CODE GOES HERE         #
    '#-----------------------------------------#
    '#                                         #


    '#                                         #
    '#-----------------------------------------#
    '#            END COMMAND CODE             #
    '###########################################

End Sub
```

```
' ----------------------------------------------------------------------
' Sub LogBadConnect
'
' Logs failed connections to a log file. Will append if file already exists.
' ----------------------------------------------------------------------
Sub LogBadConnect(sName)
    If WScript.arguments.Named.Exists("log") Then
        Dim oLogFSO, oLogFile
        Set oLogFSO = WScript.CreateObject("Scripting.FileSystemObject")
        On Error Resume Next
      Set oLogFile = oLogFSO.OpenTextFile(WScript.Arguments.Named("log"),8,True)
        If Err <> 0 Then
          WScript.Echo " *** Error opening log file to log an unreachable computer"
            WScript.Echo " " & Err.Description
        Else
            oLogFile.WriteLine sName
            oLogFile.Close
            Verbose " Logging " & sName & " as unreachable"
        End If
    End If
End Sub


' ----------------------------------------------------------------------
' Function TestPing
'
' Tests connectivity to a given name or address; returns true or False
' ----------------------------------------------------------------------
Function TestPing(sName,bPingAvailable)
    If Not bPingAvailable Then
        WScript.Echo " Ping functionality not available prior to Windows XP"
        Exit Function
    End If
    Dim cPingResults, oPingResult
    Verbose " Pinging " & sName
    Set cPingResults = GetObject("winmgmts://./root/cimv2").ExecQuery("SELECT *
FROM Win32_PingStatus WHERE Address = '" & sName & "'")
    For Each oPingResult In cPingResults
        If oPingResult.StatusCode = 0 Then
            TestPing = True
            Verbose "  Success"
        Else
            TestPing = False
            Verbose "  *** FAILED"
        End If
    Next
End Function

' ----------------------------------------------------------------------
' Sub Verbose
'
' Outputs status messages if /verbose argument supplied
' ----------------------------------------------------------------------
```

```
Sub Verbose(sMessage)
    If WScript.Arguments.Named.Exists("verbose") Then
        WScript.Echo sMessage
    End If
End Sub


' ------------------------------------------------------------------
' Sub LogFile
'
' Outputs specified text to specified logfile. Set Overwrite=True To
' overwrite existing file, otherwise file will be appended to.
' Each call to this sub is a fresh look at the file, so don't Set
' Overwrite=True except at the beginning of your script.
' ------------------------------------------------------------------
Sub LogFile(sFile,sText,bOverwrite)
    Dim oFSOOut,oTSOut,iFlag
    If bOverwrite Then
        iFlag = 2
    Else
        iFlag = 8
    End If
    Set oFSOOut = WScript.CreateObject("Scripting.FileSystemObject")
    On Error Resume Next
    Set oTSOut = oFSOOut.OpenTextFile(sFile,iFlag,True)
    If Err <> 0 Then
        WScript.Echo "*** Error logging to " & sFile
        WScript.Echo "    " & Err.Description
    Else
        oTSOut.WriteLine sText
        oTSOut.Close
    End If
End Sub


' ------------------------------------------------------------------
' Function QueryWMI
'
' Executes WMI query and returns results. User and Password may be
' passed as empty strings to use current credentials; pass just a blank
' username to prompt for the password
' ------------------------------------------------------------------
Function QueryWMI(sName,sNamespace,sQuery,sUser,sPassword)
    Dim oWMILocator, oWMIService, cInstances
    On Error Resume Next

    'create locator
    Set oWMILocator = CreateObject("wbemScripting.SwbemLocator")

    If sUser = "" Then

        'no user - connect w/current credentials
        Set oWMIService = oWMILocator.ConnectServer(sName,sNamespace)
        If Err <> 0 Then
            WScript.Echo "*** Error connecting to WMI on " & sName
            WScript.Echo "    " & Err.Description
```

```
                    Set QueryWMI = Nothing
                    Exit Function
              End If

       Else

              'user specified
              If sUser <> "" And sPassword = "" Then

                    'no password - need to prompt for password
                    If LCase(Right(WScript.FullName,11)) = "cscript.exe" Then

                        'cscript - attempt to use ScriptPW.Password object
                        Dim oPassword
                        Set oPassword = WScript.CreateObject("ScriptPW.Password")
                        If Err <> 0 Then
                        WScript.Echo " *** Cannot prompt for password prior to Windows XP"
                          WScript.Echo "       Either ScriptPW.Password object not present
on system, Or"
                            WScript.Echo "        " & Err.Description
                            WScript.Echo "        Will try to proceed with blank password"
                        Else
                            WScript.Echo "Enter password for user '" & sUser & "' on '" &
sName & "'."
                            sPassword = oPassword.GetPassword()
                        End If
                    Else

                        'wscript - prompt with InputBox()
                        sPassword = InputBox("Enter password for user '" & sUser & "' on
'" & sName & "'." & vbcrlf & vbcrlf & _
                        "WARNING: Password will echo to the screen. Run command with CScript
to avoid this.")
                    End if
              End If

              'try to connect using credentials provided
              Set oWMIService =
oWMILocator.ConnectServer(sName,sNamespace,sUser,sPassword)
              If Err <> 0 Then
                    WScript.Echo " *** Error connecting to WMI on " & sName
                    WScript.Echo "      " & Err.Description
                    Set QueryWMI = Nothing
                    Exit Function
              End If
       End If

       'execute query
       If sQuery <> "" Then
             Set cInstances = oWMIService.ExecQuery(sQuery,,48)
             If Err <> 0 Then
                   WScript.Echo "*** Error executing query "
                   WScript.Echo "      " & sQuery
                   WScript.Echo "      " & Err.Description
                   Set QueryWMI = Nothing
```

```
            Exit Function
        Else
            Set QueryWMI = cInstances
        End If
    Else
        Set QueryWMI = oWMIService
    End If

End Function

' ----------------------------------------------------------------------
' Function QueryADSI
'
' Executes ADSI query. Expects variable sQuery to include a COMPLETE
' query beginning with the provider LDAP:// or WinNT://. The query String
' may include a placeholder for the computer name, such as "%computer%".
' Include the placeholder in variable sPlaceholder to have it replaced
' with the current computer name. E.g.,
'   sQuery = "WinNT://%computer%/Administrator,user"
'   sPlaceholder = "%computer%
' Will query each computer targeted by the script and query their local
' Administrator user accounts.
' ----------------------------------------------------------------------
Function QueryADSI(sName,sQuery,sPlaceholder)

    Dim oObject
    sQuery = Replace(sQuery,sPlaceholder,sName)
    On Error Resume Next
    Verbose " Querying " & sQuery
    Set oObject = GetObject(sQuery)
    If Err <> 0 Then
        WScript.Echo " *** Error executing ADSI query"
        WScript.Echo "      " & sQuery
        WScript.Echo "      " & Err.Description
        Set QueryADSI = Nothing
    Else
        Set QueryADSI = oObject
    End If

End Function
```

# Capabilities

The wrapper script's /list:, /container:, /computer:, /recurse, /ping, and /log: functionality requires no coding on your part. Simply locate the following sections of the wrapper script:

```
'#############################################
'#            COMMAND CODE GOES HERE         #
'#-------------------------------------------#
'#                                           #


'#                                           #
'#-------------------------------------------#
'#                END COMMAND CODE           #
'#############################################
```

Then place your code in between these two sections. The variable *sName* is predefined and will contain the currently targeted computer. Your code will be called once for each targeted computer, and your code must use *sName* to connect to the targeted computer. If /ping is used, your code will not be called for unreachable computers.

Within your code, you can use any of the script's four built-in functions and subroutines to make your scripting job a bit easier.

## Querying WMI

You can quickly query WMI by using the *QueryWMI* function. Its basic syntax is this:

```
QueryWMI(sName,sNamespace,sQuery,sUser,sPassword)
```

The *sName* argument should be replaced by the variable *sName*, passing the name of the currently targeted computer. The argument *sNamespace* is the WMI namespace, such as *root\cimv2*. The argument *sQuery* stands for the WMI query you want to execute. Arguments *sUser* and *sPassword* can be passed as empty strings to use the current user's credentials; specify a user name in *sUser* and leave *sPassword* empty to have the script prompt for the user's password. Here is an example:

```
Set colProcesses = QueryWMI(sName, "root\cimv2", _
  "SELECT * FROM Win32_Process","DOMAIN\User","")
```

This code will query all instances of *Win32_Process* from the *root\cimv2* namespace, connecting to each targeted computer using the account *DOMAIN\User* and prompting for the password on each connection. You can then add code similar to the following:

```
WScript.Echo "Processes on " & sName
For Each oProcess in colProcesses
  WScript.Echo oProcess.Name
Next
```

This code will output the processes running on each targeted computer.

# Querying ADSI

The *QueryADSI* function works similarly to the *QueryWMI* function:

```
QueryADSI(sName,sQuery,sPlaceholder)
```

Use the variable *sName* in place of the *sName* argument to pass the current computer name. Your ADSI query goes in the *sQuery* argument. You might also pass a string in *sPlaceholder*; any occurrences of *sPlaceholder* in *sQuery* will be replaced with *sName*. For example, suppose you call the function as follows:

```
Set oADObject = QueryADSI(sName,"LDAP://
cn=%comp%,ou=Computers,dc=company,dc=com","%comp%")
```

Your query will be run for each targeted computer. If the first targeted computer is ServerA, your query will execute as `LDAP://cn=ServerA,ou=Computers,dc=company,dc=com`, with the *%comp%* placeholder replaced with the currently targeted computer's name.

# Writing a Log File

Your script can easily create output log files by using the *LogFile* subroutine:

```
LogFile sFile, sText, bOverwrite
```

Specify a complete path and file name for *sFile* as well as the log message for *sText*. If you specify True for *bOverwrite*, any existing file of the same name will be overwritten. If you specify False, the script will attempt to append the new entry to a file if one exists.

The wrapper script does not include an argument that enables the script user to specify a log file. If you would like an */output:* argument added, locate the following section of the script:

```
<named helpstring="Text file to pull computer names from" name="list"
required="false" type="string"/>
<named helpstring="OU to pull computer names from" name="container" required="false"
type="string"/>
<named helpstring="Run command against single specified computer" name="computer"
required="false" type="string"/>
<named helpstring="Display detailed messages" name="verbose" required="false"
type="simple"/>
<named helpstring="Use with /container to include sub-OUs" name="recurse"
required="false" type="simple"/>
<named helpstring="File to log names which can't be reached" name="log"
required="false" type="string"/>
<named helpstring="Reduce timeout wait by pinging before attempting" name="ping"
required="false" type="simple"/>
```

And add the following:

```
<named helpstring="File for output" name="output" required="false" type="string"/>
```

Then, call the *LogFile* subroutine as shown in this example:

```
LogFile WScript.Arguments.Named("output"), "Your log text", False
```

## Logging Bad Connections

Your script code should employ error-handling to detect bad connections and log
them. For example, if a WMI query fails, you might log the currently targeted
computer as a bad connection:

```
On Error Resume Next
Set oWMI = QueryWMI(sName,"root\cimv2","SELECT * FROM Win32_Process","","")
If Err <> 0 Or Not IsObject(oWMI) Then
 LogBadConnect sName
Else
 'connection was okay - your code goes here
End If
```

This code illustrates how to use the *LogBadConnect* subroutine: simply pass it the
*sName* variable to add the currently targeted computer to the bad connection log,
provided the script was run with the */log:* argument.

## Verbose Output

If the user running the script specifies the */verbose* argument, she will expect the
script to output detailed status and progress information. To add this capability to
your script, use the *Verbose* subroutine, as shown in this example:

```
Verbose "Connecting to WMI on " & sName
Set colProcesses = QueryWMI(sName, "root\cimv2", _
  "SELECT * FROM Win32_Process","DOMAIN\User","")
If Err <> 0 Or Not IsObject(oWMI) Then
 Verbose "Connection failed."
 LogBadConnect sName
Else
  WScript.Echo "Processes on " & sName
  For Each oProcess in colProcesses
    WScript.Echo oProcess.Name
  Next
End If
```

This code will provide notification that the script is attempting a connection. This
notification is displayed only if the */verbose* argument is supplied when the script
is run.

# Part VII
# Appendixes

## Appendix A
# URLs for Online Materials

This appendix contains URLs for additional scripting materials that you can find online. Note that Web URLs often change; in the event that any of the URLs listed in this appendix are inaccessible, try searching for the resources using a search engine such as Google or MSN®.

## Scripting-Related Resources

- *http://www.ScriptingAnswers.com*   My own Web site containing sample scripts, discussions related to scripting and automation, tutorials, training videos, and so forth

- *http://www.microsoft.com/technet/scriptcenter/default.mspx*   The Microsoft Script Center, which contains hundreds of sample scripts, tutorials, access to scripting-related webcasts, and other scripting resources

- *http://myitforum.techtarget.com*   An open forum with a number of scripting-related resources

- *http://cwashington.netreach.net/main/default.asp?topic=news*   A repository of sample scripts written in various scripting languages

- *http://desktopengineer.com*   Contains a variety of tools related to administration, including scripts and command-line tools

- *http://groups.msn.com/windowsscript/_homepage.msnw?pgmarket=en-us*   A discussion forum, on MSN Groups, focused on Microsoft® Windows® scripting topics

# Scripting-Related Downloads

- *http://www.microsoft.com/technet/scriptcenter/tools/wmimatic.mspx*   Scriptomatic, a tool that writes sample WMI scripts

- *http://www.microsoft.com/technet/scriptcenter/tools/admatic.mspx*   ADSI Scriptomatic, a tool that writes sample ADSI scripts

- *http://www.microsoft.com/technet/scriptcenter/tools/twkmatic.mspx*   Tweakomatic, a tool that writes scripts that tweak various operating system settings

- *http://www.microsoft.com/technet/scriptcenter/tools/logparser /default.mspx*   Log Parser, a tool that extracts information from various types of log files

- *http://msdn.microsoft.com/library/default.asp?url=/library/en-us/sdbug /Html/sdbug_1.asp*   The Microsoft Script Debugger

- *http://www.microsoft.com/downloads/details.aspx?FamilyId=C717D943- 7E4B-4622-86EB-95A22B832CAA&displaylang=en*   Windows Script Host version 5.6

- *http://www.microsoft.com/downloads/details.aspx?FamilyId=E7877F67- C447-4873-B1B0-21F0626A6329&displaylang=en*   The Windows Script Encoder

- *http://www.microsoft.com/downloads/details.aspx?FamilyId=408024ED- FAAD-4835-8E68-773CCC951A6B&displaylang=en*   The Windows Script Component Wizard

- *http://www.microsoft.com/downloads/details.aspx?FamilyId=01592C48- 207D-4BE1-8A76-1C4099D7BBB9&displaylang=en*   The Windows Script 5.6 Documentation

## Appendix B

# Troubleshooting Common Problems

Even though I've provided relevant troubleshooting information with each script or tool discussed in this book, I offer a few basic additional troubleshooting steps in this appendix that you can follow to help solve virtually any problem related to scripting or automation.

All the scripts in this book have been successfully tested in the target environment (usually a Microsoft® Windows Server™ 2003 environment with Microsoft Windows® XP Professional client computers), but variations in the configuration of your environment might result in problems running particular scripts.

## Checking the Basics

Begin by ensuring your system meets the basic requirements for scripting: Microsoft Windows 2000 or later, with the Windows Script Host (WSH) v5.6 installed. Some scripts are not designed to run on Windows 2000, and thus might require Windows XP or Windows Server 2003; carefully read the prerequisites accompanying each script for further details.

If you're receiving an error message of any kind, ensure that you can perform the exact same task manually, using the same computers and user credentials that the script was using. For example, if you're trying to run a script on your computer running Windows XP to add users to a Microsoft Active Directory® domain, attempt to perform the same task manually: open the necessary administrative tool on your computer running Windows XP and try to add a user to the same Active Directory domain. If you cannot perform the task manually, the script is also unlikely to succeed.

Avoid testing under circumstances different from those the script runs under. For example, if you are running a script that attempts to remotely change the local Administrator password on a specific computer, and that script is having problems, you cannot accurately test the situation by manually changing the Administrator password directly on the specified remote computer. The fact that you are not manually performing the task remotely, as the script is trying to do, changes the circumstances and will change your results.

## Modifying Remote Profile-Specific Information

None of the scripts in this book attempts to modify per-user information on a remote computer. Doing so is generally difficult; when you connect to a remote computer, your credentials are impersonated, and the per-user information you have ready access to (such as the HKEY_CURRENT_USER section of the registry or information stored in the user profile) is *your* per-user information, not the per-user information of the remote computer's currently logged-on user. Although it is possible to write scripts that modify the per-user information of the currently logged-on user, doing so is somewhat complex and beyond the scope of this book. Should you try to modify any of this book's scripts, keep this limitation in mind.

## Checking Permissions

Problems with permissions cause the most errors when running scripts. Remember that the user account used to run the script (which would be your logged-on user account or, if you use a tool like Runas to specify alternate credentials, the account represented by those credentials) must have permission to accomplish the task the script is trying to perform. Often, this means having local Administrator permissions on each computer targeted by the script. When in doubt, always attempt to *remotely* perform the task the script is trying to perform to ensure that you have sufficient permissions to do so.

## Getting Help

If you need additional help troubleshooting a particular script-related problem, consider posting a message in the Forums on *http://www.ScriptingAnswers.com*. The Forums are freely accessible (registration is required) and consist of a large community of users with varying levels of scripting experience. Generally, someone can help figure out the problem, offer a workaround, or offer a better solution.

# Index

# S

## X–Y–Z

# About the Author

**Don Jones** is an independent author, consultant, and trainer and is one of the industry's leading advocates for Microsoft Windows administrative scripting and automation. Don owns and operates ScriptingAnswers.com, a site dedicated to helping Windows administrators automate their environments. Don is the recipient of Microsoft's Most Valuable Professional (MVP) award and is a columnist for several industry publications

# Security resources and guidance
## —direct from Microsoft

### Microsoft® Windows® Security Resource Kit, Second Edition
ISBN: 0-7356-2174-8    Suggested Retail Price: $49.99 U.S., $72.99 Canada

Get the in-depth information and tools you need to help protect your Windows-based clients, servers, networks, and Internet services—with definitive technical guidance from the Microsoft Security team and two industry veterans. You'll learn how to plan and implement a comprehensive security strategy, assess security threats and vulnerabilities, configure system security settings, and more. You'll also find new coverage of service packs, Microsoft Office 2003 Editions, and Internet Information Services (IIS) 6.0. The CD provides must-have tools, scripts, templates, and other key resources.

### Assessing Network Security
ISBN: 0-7356-2033-4    Suggested Retail Price:  $49.99 U.S., $72.99 Canada

Don't wait for an attacker to find and exploit your security vulnerabilities—take the lead by assessing the state of your network's security. This book delivers advanced network testing strategies, including vulnerability scanning and penetration testing, from members of the Microsoft security teams. You'll find detailed information on how to perform security assessments, uncover security vulnerabilities, and apply appropriate countermeasures. The CD includes time-saving tools and scripts to reveal and help correct security vulnerabilities in your own network, plus a complete eBook.

### Microsoft Windows Server™ 2003 PKI and Certificate Security
ISBN: 0-7356-2021-0    Suggested Retail Price:  $59.99 U.S., $86.99 Canada

Capitalize on the built-in security services in Windows Server 2003—and deliver your own robust, public key infrastructure (PKI)-based solutions at a fraction of the cost and time. This in-depth reference cuts straight to the details of designing and implementing certificate-based security solutions for PKI-enabled applications. Get the inside information, real-world solutions, and best practices you need to avoid common design and implementation mistakes, help minimize risk, and optimize security administration. You'll find timesaving tools and scripts, plus an eBook, on the CD.

*To see more Microsoft Press® products for IT professionals, please visit:*

## microsoft.com/mspress

# For Windows Server 2003 administrators

Microsoft® Windows® Server 2003 Administrator's Companion
ISBN 0-7356-1367-2

**The comprehensive, daily operations guide to planning, deployment, and maintenance.**
Here's the ideal one-volume guide for anyone who administers Windows Server 2003. It offers up-to-date information on core system-administration topics for Windows, including Active Directory® services, security, disaster planning and recovery, interoperability with NetWare and UNIX, plus all-new sections about Microsoft Internet Security and Acceleration (ISA) Server and scripting. Featuring easy-to-use procedures and handy workarounds, it provides ready answers for on-the-job results.

Microsoft Windows Server 2003 Administrator's Pocket Consultant
ISBN 0-7356-1354-0

**The practical, portable guide to Windows Server 2003.** Here's the practical, pocket-sized reference for IT professionals who support Windows Server 2003. Designed for quick referencing, it covers all the essentials for performing everyday system-administration tasks. Topics covered include managing workstations and servers, using Active Directory services, creating and administering user and group accounts, managing files and directories, data security and auditing, data back-up and recovery, administration with TCP/IP, WINS, and DNS, and more.

Microsoft IIS 6.0 Administrator's Pocket Consultant
ISBN 0-7356-1560-8

**The practical, portable guide to IIS 6.0.** Here's the eminently practical, pocket-sized reference for IT and Web professionals who work with Internet Information Services (IIS) 6.0. Designed for quick referencing and compulsively readable, this portable guide covers all the basics needed for everyday tasks. Topics include Web administration fundamentals, Web server administration, essential services administration, and performance, optimization, and maintenance. It's the fast-answers guide that helps users consistently save time and energy as they administer IIS 6.0.

To learn more about the full line of Microsoft Press® products for IT professionals, please visit:

# microsoft.com/mspress/IT

# What do you think of this book?
# We want to hear from you!

Do you have a few minutes to participate in a brief online survey? Microsoft is interested in hearing your feedback about this publication so that we can continually improve our books and learning resources for you.

To participate in our survey, please visit:

**www.microsoft.com/learning/booksurvey**

And enter this book's ISBN, 0-7356-2166-7. As a thank-you to survey participants in the United States and Canada, each month we'll randomly select five respondents to win one of five $100 gift certificates from a leading online merchant.* At the conclusion of the survey, you can enter the drawing by providing your e-mail address, which will be used for prize notification *only*.

Thanks in advance for your input. Your opinion counts!

Sincerely,

Microsoft Learning

***Microsoft*** | Learning

*Learn More. Go Further.*

To see special offers on Microsoft Learning products for developers, IT professionals, and home and office users, visit: *www.microsoft.com/learning/booksurvey*

* No purchase necessary. Void where prohibited. Open only to residents of the 50 United States (includes District of Columbia) and Canada (void in Quebec). Sweepstakes ends 6/30/2005. For official rules, see: *www.microsoft.com/learning/booksurvey*